Implementing the Tokyo Round

Implementing the Tokyo Round

National Constitutions and International Economic Rules

John H. Jackson,
Jean-Victor Louis, and
Mitsuo Matsushita

Ann Arbor
The University of Michigan Press

Published in the United States of America by
The University of Michigan Press and simultaneously
in Rexdale, Canada, by John Wiley & Sons Canada, Limited
Manufactured in the United States of America

1987 1986 1985 1984 4 3 2 1

Library of Congress Cataloging in Publication Data

Jackson, John Howard, 1932–
Implementing the Tokyo Round.

Includes bibliographical references and index.
1. Tokyo Round (1973–1979) 2. Foreign trade regulation.
3. Tariff—Law and legislation. I. Louis, J.-V. (Jean-Victor) II. Matsushita, Mitsuo, 1933– . III. Title.
K4603 1973.J3 1984 341.7′54 83-19698
ISBN 0-472-10041-6

Acknowledgments

The authors would particularly like to thank the Dana Foundation, of Toledo, Ohio, for its support of some of the expenses of this project, as well as the Cook Foundation, of the University of Michigan Law School. In addition, Professor Jackson would like to acknowledge the assistance of the Rockefeller Foundation in his work during 1975–76 in Brussels, some of which led to the development of this project.

The authors would also like to acknowledge the able assistance of Ida Langermann (of Denmark) graduate student at the University of Michigan Law School, and William Ingram, student at this law school, who assisted greatly in the final editing and checking process for this volume. In addition, the authors would like to acknowledge the assistance of Mike Remington, Phillip Bohl, and Deborah Rose, research assistants to Professor Jackson at the University of Michigan Law School, for help during earlier as well as later phases of the work.

During the course of the research for this volume, each of the authors has both separately and jointly had the benefit of advice from a number of government officials, officials of international organizations, private attorneys, and other persons. It is impossible to acknowledge them all individually, and to do so might unfairly imply a degree of approval of this work which goes beyond their intent. This work is, of course, the responsibility of the respective authors alone. Nevertheless, the authors do express appreciation for the assistance and time which has been given to them by such persons.

Contents

CHAPTER 1
Law and World Economic Interdependence

John H. Jackson, Jean-Victor Louis, and Mitsuo Matsushita

Legal Constraints and International Economics

The world after World War II has effectively shrunk to the point where we watch foreign wars on our living room television sets, where more than $160 billion move across national borders every day,[1] where an economic depression in one country rapidly transmits its effects into other countries, where political violence in a Middle Eastern country causes farmers in Iowa to go bankrupt. The degree to which goods and services can flow across national boundaries in this interdependent world has helped create growing material prosperity in that world,[2] but it has also created extremely difficult problems of public and private management. The international governmental system, which includes the International Monetary Fund (IMF) and the General Agreement on Tariffs and Trade (GATT), was created mainly in the 1940s to assist in this management process,[3] but in recent years there has been legitimate concern about whether it can cope with changed circumstances for the last two decades of this century and thereafter.[4] A number of efforts have been undertaken to change the system, but national and international procedures and rules for such change are incredibly complex, and in some circumstances may be so rigid that change is prevented. The degree to which law, both national and international, either contributes to this rigidity or facilitates the processes of change is an issue of some importance. This book examines one part of that issue, focusing on national constitutional systems that affect the development of international agreements on economic matters. It does this by examining, for three key legal systems, the acceptance and implementation of the complex and extensive series of agreements resulting from the Tokyo Round of negotiations held under the aegis of the GATT.[5]

An example from an earlier period of history illustrates the focus of this inquiry. Immediately after World War II, several initiatives converged into a proposal to establish an International Trade Organization (ITO). After years of international negotiations, the 1948 draft Havana Charter was completed. This charter would have established an ITO to become the framework for international rules designed to prevent the kind of destructive national government "beggar-thy-neighbor" policies many thought had contributed to the causes of the war. Despite these elaborate preparations, the effort to create an ITO ultimately failed (although an earlier effort to create monetary rules and a monetary fund—the IMF—had succeeded). The ITO effort failed largely because of the domestic constitutional and political structure of the country then economically preeminent—the United States. It failed despite the fact that the major leadership for the effort to create it had come from the United States itself. But this leadership was that of the executive branch or presidency in the United States. Under the U.S. constitutional and legal requirements, for the government to formally accept the ITO charter, the executive branch had to get the approval of the U.S. Congress, and this the Congress refused to give. In 1950 it was clear that it would be futile to continue trying to obtain this approval, and the ITO was stillborn.[6]

At the same time as the efforts to create an ITO were occurring, another set of international economic rules was being drafted. These were embodied in an agreement entitled The General Agreement on Tariffs and Trade, commonly called the GATT. Unlike the ITO, the GATT did come into force, largely because particular laws at that time allowed the executive branch to commit the United States to the GATT obligations without further approval of Congress. In fact the GATT gradually had to fill the vacuum created by the ITO failure, and today it has come to play the central role in the international economic system as it relates to trade in goods. It plays this role uneasily, however, with a defective constitutional structure not designed to support it.[7]

This sequence of events amply demonstrates the importance of national constitutional and legal constraints on the process of formulating, implementing, or changing international rules. The compartmentalization of legal processes into international on one hand and national on the other can lead to serious misunderstandings of the world today. In fact, that world is a complex intertwining of national and international legal, economic, and other constraints and forces. The current expression *international interdependence,* so apt and yet so trite, often conjures up an image of economic forces and influences, but the legal systems of nations have also become interdependent, not only among themselves but also with the international legal systems that now are influencing daily events.

Over thirty years after the ITO's stillbirth, we can observe that this intertwining of national and international legal systems not only continues but has been made considerably more complex. No longer can one nation claim preeminent power, economically or otherwise. Hegemony has disappeared. An attempt to create new international rules or institutions or to change old ones now depends on the national legal and constitutional systems of a number of countries. Although it may be true in a realpolitik sense that such international endeavors do not depend on the legal constraints of all the 150 or more nations that now participate in international affairs, they do nevertheless depend greatly on a number of key countries. The number (and its composition) varies with the subject and with the type of international procedures followed in the endeavors. It is clear that the extent of a nation's trade will influence that nation's effective bargaining power in the procedures governing international trade.

As already mentioned, the purpose of this book and the studies in it is to examine the national legal systems of three key participants in international economic affairs, in order to evaluate the impact of those systems on international economic negotiations. This examination will focus on the legal and constitutional problems that channeled and affected the implementation of the results of the Tokyo Round negotiations in the context of the GATT. The authors feel that this focus will make it possible for them to use specific examples from the results of the Tokyo Round negotiations to illustrate concretely how the national legal systems affect the process of changing international legal rules.

We do not intend to examine the international rules themselves, nor to examine the *international* legal constraints on changing the rules.[8] This is not a study of the GATT legal system, nor of the legal systems of other international organizations as such. It is also not intended that this study be merely an account of a particular aspect of the Tokyo Round negotiations. Instead, we view the Tokyo Round as an ideal case study for pursuing our inquiry into the legal processes and constraints that influence international economic negotiations.

One of the purposes of this study, in addition to shedding light on the Tokyo Round negotiation process, is to search for possible legal factors, stemming from the national legal systems, that could affect future international negotiations on economic matters. For example, by examining the national constitutional and legal problems of negotiating, accepting, and implementing new international economic rules, we might discover that a certain configuration or juxtaposition of those national legal constraints effectively rules out the possibility of certain kinds of international economic rules. Thus, even though a particular international rule governing certain economic behavior might be advisable in economic and policy terms, it might be impossible to implement under the national legal systems of major participants. It might be that even if the national legal systems would not make a rule totally impossible, they could make it very difficult to negotiate and implement it. To put it another way: The authors of this book have been searching for international economic subjects that are nonnegotiable, or almost so, due to the national legal systems involved.

Questions about the operation, negotiation, acceptance, and implementation of international economic rules involve an extraordinarily complex mixture of several social sciences. Obviously, the subject of economics is involved, as is legal science, as suggested above. Finally, political science and other disciplines that examine a culture and its governing actors are also involved. A domestic legal rule, such as a constitutional rule that allocates power between the U.S. Congress and the President, may not in itself render it impossible to formulate, negotiate, and implement a new international reform. However, when the national constitutional principle is set in a context of a particular configuration of political forces, it is sometimes possible to see that the proposal is doomed. For example, if under the Constitution a particular proposal requires the approval of Congress, and if the political situation in Congress makes that approval virtually impossible, one can see that the combination of the legal rules and the political scene makes the reform impossible to obtain.

The studies in this book are designed to focus on legal constraints, but in doing so they cannot ignore the political context and the economic principles that are involved. Economic principles might call for freer or more liberal trade, but it might be found, for example, that the rules of a major participant country mandate a structure of decision making that tends to give increased power to farmers who have not been noticeably in favor of liberal trade. Consequently, analysis can show that the juxtaposition of legal rules and political and economic situations can effectively rule out certain types of reforms of the international economic rules of behavior, at least in the short run.

Perhaps some concrete examples would help to illustrate the more general propositions made. We have already examined the origins of the GATT and the failure of the ITO in order to illustrate the influence of national law on international negotiations. In reverse, one can show how the existence of international obligations resulting from the GATT has affected United States law. U.S. statutes, particularly several recent ones (enacted in 1974 and 1979), can only be understood in the context of the GATT.[9]

Other examples of the interconnection of national and international law, particularly as it has to do with economics, can be cited. For example, the GATT rules in Article XII relating to the use of restraints on imports for balance of payment reasons seem peculiar indeed. They authorize quantitative restrictions but not tariffs or a tariff surcharge, even though economists and policy makers would argue that a tariff surcharge is a preferred economic and policy response. One of the reasons for this anomaly may be that in major countries, tariffs generally have been considered to be within the authority and prerogative of the parliamentary branch of government. On the other hand, quantitative restrictions, particularly in circumstances such as a balance of payments crisis, have often been within the existing powers of the executive of national governments, and do not require further parliamentary action. It may be that this allocation of authorities in certain important national governments influenced the drafting of GATT Article XII in 1947. National *executive* officials, after all, negotiated the GATT, and structured Article XII to authorize a response to balance of payment problems within their own powers.[10]

Another important example of the interaction of national law and international rule change procedures occurred in 1967 at the end of the Kennedy Round of trade negotiations, in the context of the GATT. United States negotiators had different degrees of authority concerning certain of the agreements resulting from the Kennedy Round. Tariff reductions for the most part could be implemented directly by presidential action without further action from the Congress, but the Kennedy Round negotiators completed a separate adjunct package that included both tariff reductions and the elimination of certain nontariff barriers, recognizing that they did not have authority to accept that package and that it would need subsequent congressional approval. That never occurred, and consequently the adjunct package never came into force.[11]

A number of similar examples can be cited for the European Economic Community (EEC) and Japan. In the EEC, the rapidly evolving constitutional law of the EEC Treaty of Rome has been a source of difficult legal problems concerning external relations and the treaty-making power. Near the end of the Tokyo Round, as chapter 2 will relate, it was not clear whether some of the agreements resulting from the negotiations could be accepted by the EEC institutions as binding international law commitments, or whether the acceptance of each of the EEC Member States (in many cases requiring parliamentary action) was necessary also. The latter approach, obviously much more cumbersome and time consuming, would have had considerable impact on the result of the Tokyo Round. As it was, there probably were subjects that the negotiators decided to leave out of these agreements in order to reduce the risk of constitutional challenge.[12]

In Japan, the legal-constitutional structure probably had a different sort of influence. As a parliamentary system, the Japanese government structure appeared to impose fewer legal or constitutional restraints on the scope or content of the Tokyo Round subjects that could be accepted by the Japanese negotiators. The Japanese constitutional structure did, however, create some hurdles that were encountered during the process of implementing the agreements.[13]

These various legal difficulties—a majority of them, to be sure, turning on the question whether action by a legislature is needed before a government may negotiate, accept, or implement an international agreement—have led to the growing use in international economic affairs of informal agreements, sometimes called arrangements to avoid the connotation of the word *agreement.* For example, in the OECD (Organization for Economic Cooperation and Development) member countries have for many years annually entered into a trade pledge by which they promise not to use import restraints for balance of payments reasons related to oil price rises and certain others causes.[14] This agreement is admittedly not a binding international legal instrument, and since it is not, the governments concerned have considered it within their power to accept the pledge without referring it to their respective parliaments for action. Likewise, on the important matter of export credits, major OECD governments have negotiated for some years and have formulated a gentlemen's agreement, again without binding legal force.[15] Engaging in voluntary export restraint agreements, sometimes called orderly marketing agreements, as a means of protecting a market from too much penetration by imports has also become more common. One of the advantages of this form of activity is that it will usually not require legislative approval or authority from previous legislation.

Finally, there is the recent practice of developing a variety of codes of behavior addressed primarily to the multinational enterprise.[16] For example, the OECD adopted so-called voluntary guidelines in 1970. More recently, a Restrictive Business Practices "code" has been adopted by a consensus resolution of the United Nations General Assembly. Other similar activities are in progress. It is interesting and illustrative of some of the subject matter of this volume that so far the tendency in negotiating these codes is to insist that they be voluntary. One factor clearly leading to this approach is that it tends to avoid a series of legal and domestic constitutional problems in implementing these international guidelines or codes. These activities, however, give rise to another set of issues—namely, what will be the real effect of so-called voluntary principles or guidelines? Will they actually have an influence? Will they begin to lead to and be the basis for customary international rules of behavior? Will they be accepted by national governments in statutory law, or court decisions? These issues are for another study and are not directly analyzed in this book. Nevertheless, they do illustrate the significant role that national legal and constitutional constraints can have on the process of formulating and changing international rules relating to economic behavior (as well as other types of behavior).

It will be noted that in this book our focus in Europe is on the EEC, and that we have had to defer almost all analysis of EEC Member States law. Practicality requires this approach, but the legal and constitutional developments at the EEC level also present extraordinarily interesting examples for the central focus of this book. For the purpose of our analysis we have treated the EEC system as a sort of national one. Our use of the term *legal system* or *constitutional system* is designed to be broad enough to embrace law at the EEC level, without taking a position on whether EEC law should be considered national law or some species of international law.[17]

Analyzing Legal Constraints: Goal and Methodology of This Study

We would now like to indicate some of the specific areas of inquiry we each undertook in connection with our own national systems. We will also indicate some of the methodology we used in pursuing those inquiries.

Our main objective, as we have explained, was to examine the national legal and constitutional problems involved in the implementation of the results of international negotiations on trade. In that connection, we were interested in a series of subordinate questions. It was not possible to answer every one of them, but they provided the focus of our research. They included:.

1. What are the existing legal and constitutional constraints on the development of international trade policy, and to what degree are those constraints changeable?
2. Exactly how was each of the various Tokyo Round agreements implemented in the national legal system and administration of each of the entities examined? (Basically, ten major agreements and several understandings resulted from the MTN [Multilateral Trade Negotiations] otherwise known as the Tokyo Round.) These agreements will be discussed later in this chapter.

In connection with each of the agreements, each author tried to examine a series of factors, including:

1. The legal authority of the national negotiators to negotiate towards the agreement
2. The legal authority or procedure for the national negotiators to accept the international commitment of the agreement (as distinguished from implementation in domestic law)

3. The legal authority or procedure for implementing the international commitment of the agreement through changes in domestic law.

Additional questions helping focus the overall study included:

1. Given the existing legal and constitutional constraints (and understanding that there is at least some possibility for change), can the MTN agreements be made to work?
2. What further changes or adjustments may be needed in the three national governmental systems in order to accommodate potential nontariff measures and other trade agreements that could be negotiated in the future?
3. What will be the legal relationship between the international law of the MTN agreements and the laws in the national systems? Will the MTN agreements be self-executing? Will they have a direct effect? How will the courts and administrative procedures affect them?
4. To what degree will private litigants have an opportunity to challenge or interpret the MTN agreements?
5. What is the role of parliaments or the Congress in formulating, negotiating, and implementing international trade intitiatives? What public and citizen participation is necessary in each case?
6. What are the similarities or differences between the three national legal systems investigated, in connection with the domestic problems of implementation? For example, in the United States, will litigation and court procedures have a much greater influence than in Europe or Japan? Is the European legal and constitutional system, with the Luxembourg Court, moving in the direction of the United States in this regard?
7. Will the experiences of the Tokyo Round and its implementation likely lead national political leaders to be willing to embark on further international approaches to a number of emerging trade problems (such as the industrial potential of less developed countries)? For example, will the experience of the Tokyo Round implementation over the next several years bring political leaders to feel that in international negotiations they tend to lose political control over issues that influence their political fate?

In answering all these questions, we attempted to compare the three governmental legal systems examined in order to sharpen the understanding of the legal constraints, to suggest to other nations new approaches that might not otherwise have been thought of, and to examine whether there might exist in the differences between the three national structures certain potential dangers that could make further negotiations and implementation difficult or impossible.

The basic technique of investigation was for each author to examine his own legal system. As far as possible, this examination was empirical; that is, it relied on original documents, personal direct observations, and observations by other persons directly involved in the affairs of the MTN. When initial drafts were completed they were exchanged, and the three authors met for a detailed discussion of each draft and of the subject matter of each study. This process enabled each author to notice that his focus in his own study may have differed from that of his colleagues in theirs. This cross-cultural divergency was expected, and it was one of the reasons for making this study a comparative one. Discussing and noticing gaps in the analysis of one legal structure as compared to that of another prompted us to go back to the research and look more carefully at some of the information to see whether in fact some questions not previously thought of could be answered. The individual national studies that follow reflect this process of interchange. At certain points in our discussions we invited officials or practitioners from one or another of the national legal systems to join with us in extensive discussions of some of the subject matter, so as to draw on a wider group of judgments and information. In addition, we were able to draw on our own experiences in governmental affairs as well as in scholarly endeavors related to the subject of this book.

At the end of the process, after dealing with our own national legal systems, we formulated another chapter to try to draw some cross-cultural conclusions about those legal systems, as they affect international economic rules today. The differences between the three legal systems—the United States, the EEC, and Japan—are substantial. Each poses different problems. The United States is a large national entity, a common market with over two hundred years of history and experience, with extensive resources and a population of 230 million. The EEC is a newly formed legal entity, currently in the process of considerable constitutional evolution. Indeed, the procedures for implementing the Tokyo Round results have themselves become an important precedent in the constitutional evolution of the EEC in the allocation of jurisdiction between member states and the Community. Some of the problems of the EEC bear a striking resemblance to problems that arose early in the history of the United States. Others, however, are substantially different from any faced by the United States in the past or present.

Japan was an obvious choice to be among the three entities studied here, not only because of its astonishingly rapid economic growth and great economic importance today, but because of its potential for leadership in the near future, and because its economic system, as well as its constitutional and legal system, is different in some important ways from those of the other two entities studied.

The most problematic aspect of the focus of this book is the decision to omit other countries. One could profitably examine the comparable legal and constitutional problems and constraints in some of the major Member States of the European Economic Community, such as France, the United Kingdom, or Germany. Each of these national legal systems presents some important questions for policy makers. Likewise, omitting Canada and Australia tugs at our research heartstrings. We hope that other scholars will independently undertake similar comparative studies of these and other countries, including some major developing nations, and publish those studies in appropriate journals, bringing them to our attention. We felt, however, that to try at this stage to include more countries would have substantially delayed the completion and the publication of the results of our own studies. We do not justify concentrating this study on the three entities we have chosen by any a priori or indisputable scientific premises, but only by pragmatic considerations of time and resources.

GATT, the Bretton Woods System, and Trade Negotiation Rounds

Before turning to the particular studies of national legal systems in the next chapters, it may be useful to briefly set the stage of the discourse by outlining the history and status of the current international rules governing economic behavior for most of the world. The specialist who is familiar with this material can skip this section, but those who would like to learn or be reminded of the general structure of international trade rules today will find a brief overview of that subject here.

The international rules relating to economic activity today date principally from World War II. Before that time there were a number of different efforts to try to bring international trade and monetary affairs under some international discipline, but for the most part they failed.[18] International congresses convened to develop cooperation in the administration of customs as early as 1900, and other conferences occurred several times in the 1920s and 1930s. Among Woodrow Wilson's Fourteen Points in 1918 was one urging "the establishment of an equality of trade conditions among all the nations consenting to the peace," and the League of Nations covenant likewise mentioned the goal of equitable treatment for the commerce of all members. The 1919 peace treaties contain a Most Favored Nation (MFN) clause. The League of Nations undertook various studies of trade policy matters, focusing on MFN treatment and customs formalities. The failure to develop a systematic method of international discipline in trade and monetary practices, however, has been viewed as one of the causes of the Great Depression and of World War II.[19]

Sensitive to the economic causes of war, World War II leaders of many Allied nations began work to develop some postwar institutions that could fill the gap. Their statements seem to suggest two basic themes: (1) the relationship of economic forces to the causes of war and the need to develop institutions that could preserve the peace; and (2) the economic theory of comparative advantage that supported a policy of trade liberalization. Trade liberalization measures had been started in the 1930s. The United States, for example, in 1934 adopted the Reciprocal Trade Agreements Act, and pursuant to that act entered into a series of bilateral tariff reduction treaties.[20]

At the Bretton Woods conference in 1944, a charter was drafted for the International Monetary Fund and the International Bank for Reconstruction and Development. Although this conference focused on monetary and financial matters, the participants went on record to the effect that a counterpart international institution would be needed for trade.[21] As soon as the United Nations was organized, its subordinate unit, the Economic and Social Council, adopted a resolution calling for the convening of "a United Nations Conference on Trade and Employment" and in the fall of 1946 a committee was convened to prepare the way for such a conference. During 1947, preparatory conferences were held in New York and Geneva. These conferences began developing a draft charter for the ITO. At the same time, the GATT, designed to be a multilateral reciprocal tariff reduction agreement, was negotiated and completed at Geneva by the end of August 1947. In October, a Protocol of Provisional Application was signed by the conference participants. This protocol was designed to bring the GATT provisionally into force, pending a later adoption of the ITO charter and subsequent definitive application of the GATT. Unfortunately, as noted earlier, the ITO never came into force and the GATT was forced to play the role of the principal institution for discipline in international trade activity. It played this role uneasily, because it was not designed for it and did not include the institutional measures necessary to carry out such responsibility effectively. Indeed, the GATT, as such, has never come into force. It is only applied pursuant to the Protocol of Provisional Application, which specifies that Part II of the GATT (Articles III–XXIII) will be implemented insofar as it is "not inconsistent with existing legislation." This is the source of the so-called grandfather rights,[22] which except from some GATT rules national legislation that existed before the GATT was accepted.

Under the auspices of GATT, there have been seven major rounds of tariff and trade negotiation, as follows:[23]

1947—Geneva negotiation of the original GATT, including the tariff schedules

1949—Annecy, France

1950—Torquay, England

1955—Geneva (tenth GATT session)

1960–61—the Dillon Round

1962–67—the Kennedy Round

1973–79—the Tokyo Round, or Multilateral Trade Negotiation (MTN)

The first five rounds were characterized primarily by item-by-item negotiations for the reduction of tariffs, with very little attention given to nontariff barriers. Because of the growing complexity and difficulty of this technique, at the Kennedy Round it was decided to try a linear tariff reduction approach. The goal was a 50 percent across-the-board cut in all tariffs, with a variety of adjustments and exceptions. Tariff cuts actually averaged about 35 percent. In addition, the Kennedy Round attempted to address major nontariff barriers, but largely without success. The only significant result concerning nontariff barriers was the 1967 Antidumping Code.[24]

After 1967, there was a period of hiatus and confusion before an effort to launch a new round of negotiations developed. In the early 1970s the United States took the initiative in pushing for a seventh round of trade negotiations. This time it was decided to try to focus the negotiations on nontariff barriers. Because tariffs had been reduced over several decades, nontariff barriers had become significant restraints on international trade and major obstacles to further trade liberalization. The seventh trade round was launched in September 1973, in Tokyo, and thus the name Tokyo Round.

Although a significant portion of this negotiation concerned tariff reduction, a large part of its activity was focused on a variety of nontariff barriers. These proved the most difficult to negotiate, for a number of reasons. For one thing, it is very hard to quantify many nontariff barriers. In previous GATT negotiations nations had traditionally insisted on reciprocity. Each nation wanted to be able to report to its political groups that it had obtained at least as much as it had given up, and in negotiating tariffs there were various quantitative and statistical ways to support such claims. For example, the percentage reduction in a tariff would be multiplied by the value of the goods imported in recent periods, and that would be designated as the value of the tariff concession a nation had made. However, when it came to negotiating nontariff barriers, such as the rule governing how a country should apply its antidumping duties, it was hard to quantify gains and concessions.

Despite these difficulties, the Tokyo Round negotiations were surprisingly successful in formulating a series of agreements designed to reduce barriers to international trade, both tariff and nontariff. Ten major agreements and several understandings resulted from the negotiations.[25] Because it would have been difficult to amend the GATT,[26] none of the nontariff agreements or understandings were incorporated into the GATT system as a technical change in its text. Instead, most of the MTN agreements are stand-alone treaty instruments. The understandings of the Group Framework negotiations were adopted by the GATT Contracting Parties as decisions. The relationship of these agreements and decisions to the GATT itself is not a simple subject, and is not within the scope of this book. Some of the agreements purport to be interpretations of various GATT articles, and in a number of cases the agreements create problems of discriminatory treatment that could violate the MFN clause of the GATT (a matter touched on in chapter 4[27]). A few words about each of these MTN results may help the reader understand material that appears in later chapters.

Tariff reduction agreements. Little needs to be said about the Geneva (1979) Protocol and the Supplementary Protocol. In short, they are lists of items and the reduction in tariff on each that has been agreed to by each country. Each country has its own tariff schedule in the GATT, and the results of the Tokyo Round negotiations on tariffs have become incorporated as amendments to those schedules through the GATT processes. The negotiation was carried out on a linear basis, with a target of an overall reduction of 60 percent in tariffs (at least this was the target of the United States in authorizing legislation for its negotiators). Nevertheless, the results have generally been estimated as approximately a 35 percent reduction in the industrial tariffs of the major industrial participants of the negotiations.[28]

The Subsidies-Countervailing Duty Code. Officially entitled Agreement on Interpretation and Application of Articles VI, XVI, and XXIII of the General Agreement on Tariffs and Trade, the Subsidies-Countervailing Duty Code is perhaps the most important of the nontariff barrier codes negotiated in the Tokyo Round. It certainly was the most difficult to negotiate. It attempts to address a problem that is becoming increasingly difficult to manage in international trade, that of government subsidies to exports and other goods.

It is very difficult to define a *subsidy*. Myriad governmental practices could be called subsidies, including certain income tax exemptions as well as governmental support for research. Subsidies are usually divided into *export subsidies,* subsidies obtained only for goods that are exported, and *general subsidies* or *production subsidies,* subsidies received for all goods produced. The Subsidies-Countervailing Duty Code is divided into two subjects: (1) a number of rules that govern the application and the procedures by which a country is authorized to apply a countervailing duty to imports that have benefited from a subsidy; and (2) some rules directly applying to subsidies, along with a complaint procedure that operates through institutions established by the code and is supervised in the context of the GATT, by which one country can complain against the subsidy practices of another that seem to be harming economic competitors in the complaining importing country. The code is exceedingly complex, and represents a number of uneasy compromises between the contending international negotiators.

The Antidumping Code. The Antidumping Code is officially called Agreement on Implementation of Article VI of the General Agreement on Tariffs and Trade. In general, dumping occurs when a firm sells its goods for export at a price lower than it sells them for in its home market. For most of a century, there has been general international agreement that dumping is an unfair international trade practice, and that each importing country should have the right to impose antidumping duties on goods that are dumped on its market in order to protect its competing domestic industry. An Antidumping Code was negotiated in the Kennedy Round in 1967, but was not very successful. Indeed, U.S. constitutional problems and congressional antagonism prevented the United States from fully implementing it. Late in the Tokyo Round, it was decided to revise the Antidumping Code and enter into a new one that embodied many of the concepts that had already been negotiated in the Subsidies-Countervailing Duty Code. The definition of *injury* to a domestic competing industry in the Subsidies-Countervailing Duty Code was copied into the Antidumping Code. This may have been an unfortunate step, since although the two subjects are seemingly parallel their underlying policy foundations are substantially different. Dumping involves activity by particular firms, often private firms. Subsidy activity, on the other hand, is basically governmental, and can stem from legitimate internal social policies being pursued by a government. Nevertheless, the new code brings a series of new rules and concepts to antidumping activities, and must be considered one of the significant results of the Tokyo Round.

The Government Procurement Code. Another set of rules under the GATT is the Government Procurement Code, officially titled Agreement on Government Procurement. For many years, it has been increasingly obvious that "buy national" practices are a significant obstacle to further liberalization of international trade. The GATT explicitly excepts governmental purchases from some of its important trade obligations (the National Treatment Clause). Consequently, the enactment of government procurement rules requiring preference for domestically produced goods was a major loophole in the GATT system. For many years there have been discussions among nations, mostly in the context of the OECD, with a view to developing some sort of international discipline on these rules. This effort was moved into the Tokyo Round negotiation of the GATT and resulted in a new international agreement. At first reading the agreement appears to go very far in establishing a general nondiscriminatory national treatment rule of behavior for governments in their purchases of goods. However, there are important exceptions, and governments are bound to follow the code only for entities explicitly negotiated and placed on their entities lists. This practice significantly narrows the initial coverage of the Government Procurement Code, but it does provide a framework for future negotiations aimed at expanding the entities lists.

The Standards Code. The Standards Code, officially entitled Agreement on Technical Barriers to Trade, was created to deal with another set of trade barriers. A wide variety of product standards—for example, for the purpose of protecting human health, for the purpose of preventing pollution, for the purpose of making goods safer—has increasingly hindered the flow of international trade. Most standards have a legitimate policy basis, but standards can be written in such a way as to effectively limit imports, or to discriminate in favor of domestic goods as compared to imports. The Tokyo Round negotiators approached this problem primarily as a procedural one, establishing a new agreement that gives governments and other interested parties an opportunity to protest the development of standards that unnecessarily discriminate against imports.

The Customs Valuation Code. Officially entitled Agreement on Implementation of Article VII of the General Agreement on Tariffs and Trade, the Customs Valuation Code is aimed at the nontariff barriers created by the various methods used to value imported goods for customs purposes. The variety of complicated methods and the often arbitrary administration of valuation rules have been an impediment to trade. Before the code was implemented, U.S. law included nine different valuation methods, including the American Selling Price (ASP) method, which had been strongly criticized by trading partners of the United States since before the 1962–67 Kennedy Round of trade negotiations. The Customs Valuation Code is an attempt to bring some uniformity to national valuation procedures by providing a series of procedures for valuation, ranked according to preference; lower-ranked methods cannot be used unless a value cannot be determined under a higher-ranked method. Transaction value is the preferred method. The agreement will be administered through two committees. Dispute settlement will be the responsibility of a Committee on Customs Valuation under the auspices of the GATT, and technical issues will be submitted to a Technical Committee on Customs Valuation under the auspices of the Customs Cooperation Council. A protocol to the Customs Valuation Code was also negotiated; it was designed to attract more developing countries to the code.

Licensing Code. Officially entitled Agreement on Import Licensing Procedures, the Licensing Code expresses a concern that licensing procedures designed to implement a trade restriction may serve as additional restrictions in and of themselves. It calls for neutral rules that will be fairly and equitably applied and administered. Application forms and procedures for licensing should be as simple as possible. A concern for transparency of procedures is reflected in the code's requirement that rules governing import licensing procedures be published.

Civil Aircraft Agreement. One of the goals at the commencement of the Tokyo Round negotiations was to develop agreements relating to particular industrial sectors such as steel or chemicals. This goal was not achieved. The Civil Aircraft Agreement, officially entitled Agreement on Trade in Civil Aircraft, is the one agreement that embraces a range of trade barriers affecting a specific industrial sector. The agreement eliminates duties on civil aircraft, engines, and parts of civil aircraft and repairs on civil aircraft. The provisions of the agreements on technical barriers to trade and on subsidies as well as the GATT rules relating to quantitative restrictions are incorporated into the Civil Aircraft Agreement. The agreement also covers government procurement of civil aircraft.

Dairy Products Code. The Dairy Products code, officially entitled the International Dairy Arrangement, provides for a consultative arrangement. The International Dairy Products Council established by the agreement will serve as a forum for discussing and monitoring the international dairy market. In addition, protocols attached to the agreement set minimum export prices for various dairy products.

Arrangement Regarding Bovine Meat. Like the International Dairy Arrangement, the Bovine Meat Arrangement sets up a consultative group, in this case the International Meat Council. The arrangement basically establishes procedures for information exchange, market monitoring, and consultation through meetings of the council and otherwise.

Framework Arrangements. One of the negotiating committees of the MTN was called the Group Framework Committee, and was responsible for formulating four specific understandings. These concern differential treatment for developing countries; balance of payments measures; safeguard actions for development purposes; and an understanding regarding notification, consultation, and dispute settlement and surveillance. These arrangements or understandings were not established as separate treaty agreements, but were instead accepted by a decision (on November 28, 1979) of the Contracting

Parties of the GATT.[29] As such, they are not independent stand-alone treaties, but are part of the totality of GATT jurisprudence. For the most part, these arrangements do not have precise obligations; however, they do have significant impacts, at least in two respects: (1) the understanding concerning differential treatment for developing countries has been deemed to perpetuate the GATT 1971 waiver regarding the Generalized System of Preferences (GSP); (2) the understanding concerning dispute settlement procedures, with its annex (an Agreed Description of the Customary Practice of GATT in the Field of Dispute Settlement), established more precisely the framework of the various methods of dispute settlement under the GATT Article XXII and XXIII procedures.

In addition to these major codes and understandings, there were certain other multilateral agreements and a large number of bilateral agreements.

National Legal Systems and the MTN

With the stage now set, we turn to each of the three legal systems under examination in this book to explore the legal and constitutional problems posed in this chapter. Needless to say, it has not been possible to answer all the questions that motivated this study. The law in this area is very much in a state of transition, attempting to cope with the new and alarmingly difficult situations presented by ever-increasing international interdependence and rapidly changing economic conditions. We have, however, compared and contrasted three general subject areas, using the Tokyo Round experience as the principle basis for empirical evidence. These three subjects are: (1) the legal requirements in each legal system for approving and accepting the various MTN agreements (as international law obligations); (2) the question of direct effect—that is, the legal status of the MTN agreements within each legal system; and (3) the question of hierarchy of norms—that is, whether prior or later statutes or regulations, or each legal system's "constitution," will prevail among contradictory legal instruments such as the MTN agreements.

NOTES

1. N.Y. Times, Sept. 21, 1981, at D5, col. 1.
2. P. Samuelson, Economics 605, 626–27, 651 (11th ed. 1980).
3. International Monetary Fund, Articles of Agreement, *opened for signature* Dec. 27, 1945, 60 Stat. 1401, T.I.A.S. No. 1501, 2 U.N.T.S. 39, *as amended in* IMF Survey 97, April 3, 1978; The General Agreement on

Tariffs and Trade, *opened for signature* Oct. 30, 1947, 61 Stat. A3, T.I.A.S. No. 1700, 55 U.N.T.S. 187 [hereinafter cited as GATT]. The current version of the agreement is contained in 4 GENERAL AGREEMENTS ON TARIFFS AND TRADE, BASIC INSTRUMENTS AND SELECTED DOCUMENTS (1969) [herinafter cited as BISD]. *See generally* J. JACKSON, WORLD TRADE AND THE LAW OF GATT (1969) [hereinafter cited as WORLD TRADE]; G. CURZON, MULTILATERAL COMMERCIAL DIPLOMACY: THE GENERAL AGREEMENT ON TARIFFS AND TRADE AND ITS IMPACT ON NATIONAL COMMERCIAL POLICIES (1965); E. MCGOVERN, INTERNATIONAL TRADE REGULATION: GATT, THE UNITED STATES AND THE EUROPEAN COMMUNITY (1982); C. COOMBS, THE ARENA OF INTERNATIONAL FINANCE (1976); R. HUDEC, THE GATT LEGAL SYSTEM AND WORLD TRADE DIPLOMACY (1975); D. CARREAU, P. JUILLARD & T. FLORY, DROIT INTERNATIONAL ECONOMIQUE (2d ed. 1980); 1 F. HORSEFIELD, THE INTERNATONAL MONETARY FUND, 1945–1965: TWENTY YEARS OF INTERNATIONAL MONETARY COOPERATION, *Chronicle* (1969); J.M. KEYNES, THE COLLECTED WORKS OF J.M. KEYNES, SHAPING THE POSTWAR WORLD (D. Moggridge ed. 1980); D. CARREAU, T. FLORY & P. JUILLARD, *Chronique de Droit International Economique,* 1976, 1978 in ANNUAIRE FRANCAIS DE DROIT INTERNATIONAL (Centre National de la Récherche Scientifique); F. SOUTHARD, THE EVOLUTION OF THE INTERNATIONAL MONETARY FUND (Princeton Essays in Int'l Finance No. 135, 1979); A. LOWENFELD, THE INTERNATIONAL MONETARY SYSTEM (1977).

4. Address by Arthur Dunkel, Director-General of GATT, (Mar. 5, 1982) (printed in GATT Press Release No. 1312 (1982)); Jackson, *The Crumbling Institutions of the Liberal Trade System,* 12 J. WORLD TRADE L. 93 (1978).
5. *See generally The Tokyo Round of Multilateral Trade Negotiations,* Report by the Director-General of GATT (GATT/1979-3) Apr. 1979; *The Tokyo Round of Multilateral Trade Negotiations, Vol. II,* Report by the Director-General of GATT (GATT/1980-1) Jan. 1980.
6. WORLD TRADE, *supra* note 3, at § 2.5; Jackson, *The Birth of the GATT-MTN System: A Constitutional Appraisal,* 12 L. & POL'Y INT'L BUS. 21, 30 (1980); R. GARDNER, STERLING-DOLLAR DIPLOMACY 373–78 (1969); W. DIEBOLD, THE END OF THE ITO (Princeton Essays in Int'l Finance No. 16, 1952).
7. Jackson, *supra* note 6, at 30–36.
8. *See generally* works cited *supra* note 3; J. JACKSON, LEGAL PROBLEMS OF INTERNATIONAL ECONOMIC RELATIONS (1977) [hereinafter cited as INTERNATIONAL ECONOMIC RELATIONS]; R. HUDEC, ADJUDICATION OF INTERNATIONAL TRADE DISPUTES (1978); Jackson, *supra* note 6.
9. For example, see the following statutory sections: Trade Act of 1974, Pub. L. No. 93-618, 88 Stat. 1978 (1975) (codified at 19 U.S.C. §§ 2101–2487 (1976)), *as amended by* Trade Agreements Act of 1979, Pub. L. No. 96-39, 93 Stat. 295; Trade Agreements Act of 1979, Pub. L. No. 96-39, 93 Stat. 144 (1979) (codified at 19 U.S.C. §§ 2501–2582 (Supp. III 1979)), *adding* Title VII to the Tariff Act of 1930, Pub. L. No. 71-361, 46

Stat. 590 (1930). *See particularly* Trade Act of 1974, §§ 101, 102, 106, 121–23, 126, 201–03, 501–04; Trade Agreements Act of 1979, §§ 1–3, 201, 301–05, 402, 421–22, 441, 451, 501, 516A, 601, 701–05, 731–36, 772–73 (amending Tariff Act of 1930).

10. G. Curzon, *supra* note 3, at 128.
11. See Dep't of State, *U.S. Nontariff Barriers,* in 1 Williams Commission Papers 712 (1971), for a description of The American Selling Price (ASP) system and Congress's refusal to end it. *See also* S. Rep. No. 2059, 87th Cong., 2d Sess., 19 (1962); S. Con. Res. 38, 90th Cong., 1st Sess. (1967); Amendment to H.R. 17324, 90th Cong., 2d Sess., 114 Cong. Rec. 26,133 (1968); Pub. L. No. 90-634, Title II, § 201, 82 Stat. 1347 (codified at 19 U.S.C. § 160 (1976) for congressional reaction to the international Antidumping Code.
12. The line between constitutional challenge and strong political challenge is difficult to draw. Often the constitutional structure is what positions the potential political challenge (i.e., if the Constitution requires Congress to approve an agreement, then the politics of Congress become all-important). Some of the results of the Kennedy Round (in 1967) were strongly challenged in United States congressional and other procedures, and these challenges and criticisms were partly the impetus for developing a new U.S. procedure for negotiating in the Tokyo Round. Since this new procedure, as will be described in chapter 4, depended heavily on congressional approval of the results under a normal statutory but "fast-track" procedure, the potential for constitutional challenge in the courts was sharply reduced, and the true potential challenge in the Tokyo Round resulted from the politics of Congress. This clearly limited certain kinds of potential negotiations. For example, the 1974 act authorizing U.S. participation made it rather clear that certain kinds of subjects or industrial products would probably not be negotiable (such as textiles, or certain sensitive steel products). The situation in the EEC was more complex, and in general the EEC seemed reluctant to embark on major reformulations of international economic rules during the Kennedy Round. Even after exercising a certain amount of caution, the EEC negotiators ended the Tokyo Round with a large amount of ambiguity about the constitutional distribution of powers for approving its results. This is further explained in chapter 2.
13. *See* chapter 3.
14. Trade Pledge of 1974, 70 OECD Observer 41 (June 1974) (renewed annually through 1979). A recent shift in emphasis has occurred in the Declaration on Trade Policy, OECD Observer 3 (Special Supp. June 1980).
15. *See, e.g.,* N.Y. Times, July 7, 1982, at 30 (Midwest ed.).
16. *See, e.g.,* Centre on Transnational Corporations, Transnational Corporations: Material Relevant to the Formulations of a Code of Conduct, U.N. Doc. E/C. 10/18 (Dec. 1976); Centre on Transnational Corporations, Transnational Corporations: A Code of Conduct; Formulations of the

Chairman, U.N. Doc. E/C. 10/AC. 2/8 (1978), *reprinted in* 1 CTC REP. No. 6, at 5 (1979); The Set of Multilaterally Agreed Equitable Principles and Rules for the Control of Restrictive Business Practices, G.A. Res. 35/63, U.N. Doc. A/RES/35/63 (1980) adopting the draft report of Second Committee, U.N. Doc. A/C.2/35/6. *See generally* Rubin, *Harmonization of Rules: A Perspective on the U.N. Commission on Transnational Corporations,* 8 L. & POL'Y INT'L BUS. 875 (1976); LEGAL PROBLEMS OF CODES OF CONDUCT FOR MULTINATIONAL ENTERPRISES (N. Horn ed. 1980); Address by John H. Jackson, International Bar Association Meeting (Aug. 27, 1980) (printed in 25 L. QUADRANGLE NOTES 19 (Winter 1981)).

17. *See* Robertson, *Legal Problems of European Integration,* 91 RECUEIL DES COURS 105, 143–48 (1957).
18. WORLD TRADE, *supra* note 3, § 2.2, at 36–40; § 17.1, at 439–40.
19. *Id.* Sec. 2.2 at 37–39.
20. The 32 agreements are listed in *1945 Extension of Reciprocal Trade Agreements Act: Hearings on H.R. 3240 Before the House Comm. on Ways and Means,* 79th Cong., 1st Sess. 932 (1945); *See* WORLD TRADE, *supra* note 3, § 2.2, at 37; J. JACKSON, INTERNATIONAL ECONOMIC RELATIONS, *supra* note 8, at 396 (1977); Jackson, *The GATT in United States Domestic Law,* 66 MICH. L. REV. 249, 257–58 (1967).
21. United Nations International Monetary and Financial Conference (Bretton Woods, N.H., July 1-22, 1944), U.S. DEPT OF STATE PUB. No. 2866, PROC. & DOC. 941 (1948).
22. Protocol of Provisional Application of the GATT, Oct. 30, 1947, 61 Stat. A2051, T.I.A.S. No. 1700, 55, U.N.T.S. 308; WORLD TRADE, *supra* note 3, § 3.2 at 60–63; INTERNATIONAL ECONOMIC RELATIONS, *supra* note 8, at 401.
23. WORLD TRADE, *supra* note 3, §§ 10.4 and 10.5, at 218–29; Jackson, *supra* note 6, at 21.
24. Agreement on Implementation of Article VI of the GATT, GATT Doc. L/2812 (July 12, 1967), *reprinted in* BISD, *supra* note 3, 24 (15th Supp. 1968); *see generally* INTERNATIONAL ECONOMIC RELATIONS, *supra* note 8, at 481, 734–42; Long, *United States Law and the International Anti-Dumping Code,* 3 INT'L LAW. 464, 472–89 (1969).
25. See the Appendix for full listing and citations.
26. Jackson, *supra* note 6, at 32.
27. *See* the section in chapter 4 entitled Implementing the MTN Results in U.S. Law.
28. *Supra* note 22.
29. Action by the Contracting Parties on the Multilateral Trade Negotiations, GATT Doc. L/4905 (Nov. 28, 1979), *reprinted in* BISD 201 (26th Supp. 1979).

CHAPTER 2

The European Economic Community and the Implementation of the GATT Tokyo Round Results

Jean-Victor Louis

Introduction and Overview of EEC External Relations Law

In this chapter we will examine the legal problems of the European Economic Community (EEC) in connection with the negotiation and implementation of the agreements resulting from the Tokyo Round. After a short introduction on commercial policy and its importance in the EEC, we examine the negotiating process in the Tokyo Round from 1973 to its conclusion in 1979, and then consider the problems that appeared at the time of the conclusion of the agreements reached during the negotiations, and their potential effect in the legal order of the community. Finally, we will offer a few concluding remarks.

The most significant issues in the EEC context are the allocation of authority between the Community and its Member States, and the legal problems related to the opportunity for individuals to challenge the validity of a Community or national act that is alleged to be contrary to international agreements.

The EEC is a regional organization that was originally created by six nations of Western Europe by the Treaty of Rome of March 25, 1957.[1] Since the second enlargement on January 1, 1981, ten West European countries are members of the EEC.[2]

Like the European Coal and Steel Community (ECSC) and the European Atomic Energy Community (EURATOM), the EEC is one of the three European Communities, organizations whose aim is the economic integration of the countries concerned. As a customs union and a kind of economic union, the EEC develops comprehensive sets of rules, called common policies, in the fields of agriculture, transport, and external trade relations. The latter is, of course, the most important task of the Community as far as our study is concerned.

Article 113 of the Treaty of Rome provides:

> 1. After the transitional period has ended, the common commercial policy shall be based on uniform principles, particularly in regard to changes in tariff rates, the conclusion of tariff and trade agreements, the achievement of uniformity in measures of liberalisation, export policy and measures to protect trade such as those to be taken in case of dumping or subsidies.
> 2. The Commission shall submit proposals to the Council for implementing the common commerical policy.
> 3. Where agreements with third countries need to be negotiated, the Commission shall make recommendations to the Council, which shall authorize the Commission to open the necessary negotiations.
> The Commission shall conduct these negotiations in consultation with a special committee appointed by the Council to assist the Commission in this task and within the framework of such directives as the Council may issue to it.
> 4. In exercising the powers conferred upon it by this Article, the Council shall act by a qualified majority.

The Community has entered into various bi- and multilateral tariff and trade agreements. The most important multilateral trade negotiations before the Tokyo Round were those of the Kennedy Round, which were concluded in May 1967.

For the Community, the negotiations in the Kennedy Round were conducted by its Commission (an institution that represents only the global interest of the Community) acting on directives of the Council, an institution composed of members of the governments of the Member States.[3] The Kennedy Round was the first time that the Commission appeared as the sole negotiator for the Community in such a large multilateral negotiation (the Dillon Round (1960–61) was only a modest precedent) and that the Council was responsible for concluding such multilateral agreements for the EEC. The agreements resulting from the Kennedy Round (1962–67) were concluded as mixed agreements, signed by both the EEC institutions and by each of its Member States.[4]

The separation of the functions of the Commission and the Council is an important feature of the institutional structure of the Community. Generally, the Commission appears as the initiator of Community actions. It makes formal proposals to the Council, which has to use the proposals as the basis for its decisions. As far as external relations are concerned, and especially when there is a prospect of negotiating an international agreement that will be binding on the Community and its Member States, the Commission acts in its capacity as the Community's negotiator in close connection with the Council.[5]

The Committee of Permanent Representatives (COREPER), an internal organ of the Council, must be mentioned, because it plays an important role in the relations between the Commission and the Council.[6] The members of the COREPER are the Permanent Representatives themselves who are the ambassadors of the Members States of the European Communities (called COREPER II) or the Deputies (COREPER I). Due to their political character, the subjects related to external relations are treated by COREPER II. The COREPER prepares the deliberations of the Council and undertakes a close examination of every measure proposed by the Commission, especially in the field of external relations.

There is indeed a "constant tension between Council and Commission in the conduct of external relations,"[7] because the "foreign policy domain is notoriously the most jealously guarded area of national sovereignty. The Council has been reluctant to transfer powers of negotiation to the Commission and when it has done so, under the terms of the Treaty, it has been diligent in keeping the Commission on a tight rein."[8] The MTN (the Multilateral Trade Negotiations) at the Tokyo Round are a good example of those tensions.

The EEC Negotiating Process in the Tokyo Round

The ordinary negotiating process of a trade agreement—either bilateral or multilateral—concluded by the EEC generally includes different stages, which can be described as follows:

1. Preliminary talks between the Commission and the state(s) concerned
2. Report by the Commission to the Council, including a recommendation to open formal negotiations with the third state
3. The Commission's authorization by the Council to negotiate along the lines of the directives (mandate) approved by the Council on the recommendation formulated by the Commission and, as usual, carefully examined by the COREPER
4. Negotiation of the agreement by the Commission, with the assistance of a special committee composed of representatives of the Member States in charge of international economic relations (called the Committee of Article 113, or the 113 Committee)
5. Authentication of the formal result of the negotiations by way of an exchange of letters or the initialing (*paraphe*) of the agreement by the Commission[9]
6. Report by the Commission to the Council, which approves the result of the negotiations by a regulation or a decision[10] and decides to proceed to the final conclusion of the agreement
7. Formal conclusion through a complex procedure (approval plus conclusion) or by the signature on behalf of the Community, of the persons designated by the Council

If the agreement is deemed to be mixed, that is, if for reasons of the allocation of competence between the EEC and its Member States it (the Lomé Convention, for example) must be accepted not only by the EEC but also by the Member States, then the Member States must follow certain additional procedures. This procedure, which is dictated partly by the joint requirements of Articles 113 and 228 of the EEC Treaty[11] and partly by the practice followed by the Community, had to be adapted to multilateral negotiations like the MTN.

We will now examine the various stages of the Community's MTN negotiations, analyzing the role and influence of each Community institution and organ involved.

The Preliminary Stage of the MTN: From the EEC–United States Declaration of 1972 to the Tokyo Conference of 1973

Two important decisions made by the Community in 1972 influenced its future negotiations. The first was the joint declaration made by the United States and the Community on February 11, 1972[12] (pursuant to the Council's decision in December 1971) in favor of the opening of the MTN in 1973. The second was the endorsement of that declaration by the first Summit of Heads of State and Government of the enlarged Community[13] in Paris on October 19 and 20, 1972.[14] The Summit also invited the institutions of the Community to define, before July 1, 1973, a global conception for the negotiations, and expressed the hope that they would be concluded in 1975.

The Summit's declaration was particularly important not only because it represented a political green light for the Community but also because it accented some crucial points of the EEC's position: the principle of reciprocity in the concessions,[15] the link between commercial and monetary problems, respect for the "acquis communautaire," i.e., the common agricultural policy (CAP), and the will to seek a reduction of both tariff and nontariff barriers. It is in this context of a politically favorable global decision that the institutions of the enlarged Community began preparing the Community's position in the negotiations that were to open in Tokyo in September 1973.

At the beginning of April 1973, the Commission forwarded to the Council a communication on the "elaboration of a *global conception* in view of the next multilateral negotiation." The Council of General Affairs (foreign affairs ministers) examined the draft text on May 15. In spite of the fact that it had been well received by a majority of the members of the Council, the French Minister, Michel Jobert, reproached the Commission for having presented a tentative compromise between the positions of the future partners in the negotiation and not a proposal for the position of the Community. Supported by his Irish colleague and in some measure by the Italian Minister, Mr. Jobert asked for an "exposé des motifs" restating the fact that the results of the negotiations had to be balanced and that commercial negotiations would make no sense unless the convertibility of the U.S. dollar were considered.[16] As far as the text of the communication was concerned, Mr. Jobert insisted on the crucial importance of the common tariff and of respect for the CAP.

The Commission prepared the text of a preamble and made some important drafting changes in other parts of its communication. The then Director General of Foreign Affairs of the Commission, Edmund Wellenstein, presented the text to the COREPER on May 24.[17] Significantly, the French Permanent Representative, Etienne Burin des Rosiers, submitted an alternative preamble to his colleagues.[18]

As noted by an excellent observer of the Brussels scene, the staff of the Commission had taken Mr. Jobert's position into account in their new text;[19]— the Commission's and the French papers reflect the same preoccupations. As often in Gaullist and post-Gaullist diplomacy, the difference between the French and Commission positions is more one of emphasis than of substance. But on two points the more subtle wording of the Commission's text masked a divergence of opinions among the nine members, and in particular between France and the others. Those points were the monetary question (the link or parallelism with commerical negotiations) and the common agricultural policy.

On the first topic, France wished to confirm its preference for a return to fixed par value exchange rates and to reserve to the Community the possibility of subordinating the implementation of the MTN to the establishment of a new monetary order, stable and equitable, based on fixed but adjustable parities and on general convertibility of monies. The Commission, on the other hand, intended only to insist on the necessity of parallel efforts for the definition of an adequate monetary system.

The final text, adopted after a marathon session by the Council of General Affairs in Luxembourg on June 26, 1973,[20] constituted a compromise between the two positions. After recalling—in a footnote— the basic principles of a monetary reform as stated in the declaration of the 1972 Summit, the text continued with two important sentences proposed by the Belgian delegation:[21] "The Community shall evaluate the progress of those negotiations in the light of the progress which will be realized in the monetary field. When it considers the result of those negotiations, it will do so taking into account that progress."

As far as the CAP was concerned, the Commission's amended text started with the affirmation that the *principles* of the CAP could not be questioned. The final text, adopted by the Council after a night of discussion, declares more categorically that the CAP principles *and their mechanisms* could not be questioned and were not matters for negotiation. An allusion to the possibility of a declaration of the Community's intent to consider a more economically oriented structural policy disappeared. In the agricultural field, negotiating international agreements on specific products appeared as the Community's principal objective. The adoption of a code of conduct, or, as stated in the final text, of "concerted disciplines" is considered only as a residuary possibility for products that are not suited for such agreements.

The Council debates on the adoption of the "global conception" revealed the tension between the Commission's position and that of some of the Member States. i.e., between those who favored a liberalization of world trade and those who had a more rigid attitude and were particularly eager to prevent the proposed negotiations from damaging the cohesion of Community policies. It seems clear that without the weight of the political decision made by the Paris Summit of October 1972, and the deadline fixed for the adoption of the global conception, the compromise would have been much more difficult to achieve.

It is interesting to observe that during the preparation of the General Agreement on Tariffs and Trade (GATT) ministerial conference held in Tokyo on September 12–14, 1973, the question that most required special efforts at compromise was precisely that of parallelism between trade negotiations and monetary reform. The particular importance of these problems prompted the EEC Council of General Affairs to convene a special meeting. Normally, the formal meetings of the Council take place only in Brussels and Luxembourg, the two "working places" of the institution, and it is noteworthy that an exception to the rules was made in this case. The final text agreed to by the Council is closer to the initial wording of the preamble proposed by the Commission than to the text of the global conception.[22] The accent was put on "parallel efforts" for the adoption of a new monetary system and not on the necessary evaluation of the progress made in the realization of the reform. The Rambouillet compromise between the U.S. and French positions on the second amendment of the IMF Articles of Agreement and the decision adopted at Kingston, Jamaica, by the Interim Committee of the IMF on January 8, 1976,[23] deprived the debate of any political relevance. Recall that although the French authorities favored a return to fixed parities, the U.S. government was pleased with a system of floating currencies. The compromise consisted in the adoption of the new Article IV of the IMF Articles of Agreement, which left open the possibility—very remote indeed—of the adoption of a system of parities.

The Process of Negotiation from 1975 to 1979: The Actors on the Community Side

The Council's adoption of the global conception and approval of the conclusions of the 1973 GATT ministerial meeting at Tokyo served as authorization for the Commission to open formal negotiations. Unanimous conclusions adopted before and during the rounds of negotiations can be considered the directives the Council usually addresses to the Commission.[24]

The Commission played a prominent role during the negotiations, not only with respect to the Contracting Parties of the GATT, but also through initiatives directed to the Council and the Member States. For example, early in 1978 the Council convinced the Member States to adopt without exceptions the "Swiss formula" for the reduction of tariffs (i.e., greater reductions for higher tariffs) notwithstanding the objections of some Member States. The Commission did not have the same success in convincing some reluctant states, such as the United Kingdom and the Federal Republic of Germany, of the merits of selectivity in the application of the safeguard clause (one failure of the MTN negotiations).

During the negotiations, the Commission was assisted by a committee composed of representatives of the Member States, as provided for in the Treaty of Rome, the so-called Committee of Article 113. The Committee members sat at two levels: titulars and deputies. The titulars were director generals or directors, and the deputies were deputy directors or counsellors who were civil servants in charge of international economic relations. There were also ad hoc meetings of experts on specific questions.

It is generally agreed that the Committee's role in the MTN was unusually significant. In other trade negotiations, the Committee of Article 113 acts as the Commission's watchdog, due to the Member States' relative lack of confidence in the Commission as the Community's negotiator. The Committee can, for example, suggest to the Commission how Council directives may be interpreted, but it has no power to change the directives if they appear to be insufficient. That can be done only by the COREPER, which normally also exerts a kind of supervision over the whole process of negotiation.

The reasons for the greater role of the Committee in the MTN were:

1. The location of the negotiations in Geneva. That made it impossible for the COREPER seated in Brussels to exert political control of the Commission during the negotiations. It is the reason, for example, that the Council, in its session of November 20–21, 1978, charged the

Commission to pursue the negotiations "in narrow collaboration with the special committee of Article 113." It must be mentioned that the Member States considered it necessary to exert greater control after the experience of the Kennedy Round, in which the Commission representatives alone took some initiative to help the negotiation and referred afterwards to the Council for ratification.

2. The great technical complexity of the problems involved, especially those concerning nontariff barriers (for example, the Standards code, which requires the intervention of experts and not of generalists), and the inability of the Council to give specific directives for every point of the negotiations. For example, when adopting the orientations drafted by the Commission for the substantial phase of the negotiations, the Council in its session of January 17, 1978, referred also to the working hypothesis "élaborées ou esquissées au sein du GATT," and added: "Ceci ne signifie pas que tous les éléments de ces hypothèses de travail pour les négociations soient acceptés tels quels. Le Conseil charge la Commission de poursuivre, en liaison avec le Comité spécial de l'Article 113, la recherche de solutions précises et mutuellement acceptables dans les différents domaines."[25]
3. The necessity for the Commission to have, during a long process of negotiation, an ongoing source of information about the national administrations' point of view, especially when problems concerning one particular Member State were at stake. For example, we can read in the minutes of the Council of January 17, 1978, regarding the problem of government procurement: "The Commission recognizes the necessity to act with prudence when the question of drawing up precise agreements arises, and it pledges to the government of the Federal Republic of Germany that it will seek to avoid any difficulty of a constitutional nature regarding the 'Länder', *by a rigorous coordination with this country's delegation in the Committee of Article 113.*"
4. The guidance provided the Commission by the political directives framed in the global conception and the general conclusions adopted by the Council at crucial points of the negotiations, which allowed the Commission to pursue the negotiations without constantly referring to the political authorities

Thus, the COREPER's function was primarily that of preparing the sessions of the Council at the crucial stages of the negotiations. It was not the great conciliator it usually is in other matters. The compromises between the positions of the Member States were achieved through the action of the Commission in the Committee of Article 113. For example, the Committee had to solve the difficulities some Member States raised in the Council on April 3, 1979, at the very last moment before the decision was made to consider the global result of the negotiations satisfactory.[26] The COREPER recovered its leading role, however, when the political problems of allocating jurisdiction between the Community and the Member States in the conclusion and implementation processes were at stake in 1979.

Some Member States were not fully in favor of the minor role played by the COREPER during the negotiations. For example, France often raised questions on the subject in the COREPER. We must add that when it was impossible to reach an agreement at the level of the titular members of the Committee of Article 113, the question was brought before the Council.

The Council devoted many deliberations to the MTN. It examined problems related to the Tokyo Round on the following occasions:

1. On February 10, 1975, it adopted the directives for the negotiations of the MTN in the GATT following the adoption of the Trade Act of 1974 by the American Congress.
2. On January 17, 1978, before the beginning of the substantial part of the negotiations, it examined the working hypotheses elaborated by the negotiation groups or subgroups.
3. On April 4, 1978, it analyzed the tariff offers made by the main participants in the negotiations. It decided to authorize the Commission to present to its partners demands aimed at improving their offers, and to propose a list of possible retractions of concessions.
4. On June 27, 1978, it considered a schema of global agreement, with the hope of soon concluding the negotiations.
5. On September 19, 1978, it held deliberations after the Declaration of July 13 concerning the state of negotiations and the necessity to conclude before December 15. It expressed its deep concern over the situation that would be created by the expiration of the powers given to the US. government by the Trade Act of 1974 to waive the application of countervailing duties in the case of export subsidies, in the absence of an injury test. It stated that it would not be realistic to envisage the conclusion of the negotiations without an assurance that the waiver would continue. On this point, the Council fully endorsed the position of the Commission.
6. On October 17, 1978, after the decision of the U.S. Congress to adjourn its work till after January, 15, 1979 without having made a decision on the waiver problem, the Council affirmed that an unequivocal confirmation of the application of the waiver was necessary to conclude the negotiations, but in the meantime the Community declared that it was willing to pursue them.
7. On November 21, 1978, after bilateral contacts between the Commission and Robert Strauss (the chief U.S. negotiator) the Council confirmed its position of October 17.
8. On December 12 and 18, 1978, the Council met to examine the Commission's progress reports on the negotiations.
9. The Council held three sessions—on February 5 and 6, March 5 and 6, and April 2 and 3, 1979—to analyze the results of the negotiations. The Council took note of the Commission's intention to authenticate

the various texts and agreements that resulted from the negotiations, following a final examination by the Committee of Article 113.

10. On November 20, 1979, the Council decided to conclude the agreements resulting from the MTN.[27]

All those deliberations were based on reports of the Commission, which the Council considered and carefully discussed. It often succeeded in adopting its conclusions only after difficult negotiations between its delegations. This factor explains the formulation of some compromise solutions.

Consider, for example, the debate on the maximum percentage of tariff reductions held during the session of January 17, 1978. The Commission defended a formula of 40 percent maximum reductions, taking into account the compensations to be negotiated with the partners of the Community. The French delegation was against such a formula, for the following reasons: the uncertainty of the global context of the negotiations, particularly the necessity of some parallelism between tariff reduction and monetary evolution; the necessity to fight against protectionist tendencies; the need for guarantees concerning selectivity as far as compensatory duties and customs value were concerned; and the expansion of Community exports. So France proposed as an hypothesis a reduction of between 25 and 35 percent. The German delegation, on the other hand, expressed its preference for as substantial a tariff reduction as possible, for the sake of reciprocal promotion of commercial negotiations. It feared that offering a lower reduction would lead the Community to make more important concessions because of the pressures that could be exerted against it.

A compromise formula elaborated by the Presidency of the Council retained an initial offer "d'appliquer la formule d'origine suisse envisagée dans le document du GATT MIN/INF/11 du 23 décembre 1977 avec le coefficient 16."[28] This formula aimed at a reduction of 40 percent. At the same time, the Council adopted a declaration inscribed in its draft minutes that stated:

> Sans préjudice de l'Article 7 des conclusions ci-avant, le Conseil considère que la baisse moyenne finale applicable au TDC (tarif douanier commun) se situera dans une zone définie par les directives de négociation, arrêtées par le Conseil le 10 février 1975 avec un montant maximum de 35 pour cent, compte tenu de l'expérience passée, des exceptions probables et des ajustments à opérer au vu des résultats de la négociation non tarifaire.[29]

At first glance these statements seem contradictory, but the former referred to the initial offer and the latter to the final result of the negotiations. Thus, while satisfying France, the compromise was acceptable to the other delegations because the hypothesis was considered realistic. This can be considered typical of the conclusions of the Council discussions that occurred when the Member States' basic conceptions profoundly diverged. It can be necessary to adopt such peculiar positions in order to achieve a consensus in the Council. The alternative is for the Council to refer the orientations and observations formulated during its sessions—i.e., the sometimes divergent positions of the governments—to the Commission.

The Commission has been represented in the Council by its Vice-President in charge of external relations: Sir Christopher Soames when the Commission was presided over by Francois-Xavier Ortoli from 1973 to 1976 and Wilhelm Haferkamp during Roy Jenkins' presidency of the Commission. But as the Council of General Affairs often has many important topics on its agenda, various persons comprise the delegation of the Commission to a given meeting of the Council. For example, on October 16 and 17, 1978, the Commission was represented at the 540th session of the Council of General Affairs by its President (Mr. Jenkins), two Vice-Presidents (Mr. Haferkamp and Lorenzo Natali) and four members (Claude Cheysson, Guido Brunner, Richard Burke, and Étienne Davignon). The official press releases do not conclusively indicate which members of the Commission intervene in a particular debate. Sometimes one may read that the Council took note of the report presented by Vice-President Haferkamp, who normally introduced the debates on MTN, or that it heard a statement by Mr. Davignon, on industrial matters, or by Vice-President Finn Olav Gundelach, on agriculture—but this does not mean that there were no other speakers for the Commission.

The EEC Treaty does not impose upon the Council the duty to consult the European Parliament on commercial agreements under Article 113. It must only do so for Association Agreements under Article 238. On February 13, 1973, the Parliament adopted a resolution on procedures for its participation trade in agreements between the Community and third countries.[30]

The Parliament might want to become more involved in all stages of the agreement-making process for many reasons.[31] It wished to express its opinion on each proposal or recommendation formulated by the Commission at every stage of the procedure: before the opening of exploratory talks, before the authorization of formal negotiations, and before the recommendation to conclude the negotiated agreement. The Parliament had obtained some limited rights in this respect for the Association Agreements, and since trade agreements often have a similar context there are good reasons for extending the procedure provided for Association Agreements to trade agreements. A standard procedure of consultation should be followed for every type of agreement.

A second reason for greater Parliament involvement is that trade agreements contain provisions on tariff reductions that affect the Community's own resources, and the Parliament has been exercising powers in the budgetary field since 1971. Together with the Council it has become the budgetary authority of the Community.

A further reason is the fact that when trade agreements were concluded by states they were usually subject to national parliamentary approval, so that there is precedent for strengthening the role of the European Parliament in the negotiation and conclusion of trade agreements. But in the case of Association Agreements, where the Parliament *has* a formal right to be consulted by the Council, it was not happy with the modalities of its intervention. Since 1961, when the Association Agreement with Greece was concluded, the Parliament has considered that it should intervene when its opinion could influence the course of the negotiations. It is the reason that the Council, after many hesitations, adopted on February 25, 1964, a procedure known as Luns-I, which has the purpose of involving the Parliament in the negotiation phase of Association Agreements. The procedure provides for three phases:

1. Before the beginning of the negotiations for an Association Agreement, a debate can take place in the Parliament.
2. During the negotiations, close contacts are maintained between the Commission and the appropriate parliamentary committees.
3. At the end of the negotiations, but before the agreement is signed, the Council or its representative confidentially and unofficially informs the appropriate parliamentary committee of the substance of the agreement.

The Council's formal consultation of the Parliament pursuant to Article 238 takes place between the signing and the final approval of the agreement by the Council.

To try to meet some of the complaints the Parliament expressed in its resolution of February 13, 1973, on October 15 the Council adopted the rules of the so-called Luns II or Westerterp procedure for trade agreements.[32] Like Luns-I, the Westerterp or Luns-II procedure provides for three phases:

1. Before the beginning of the negotiations, the Parliament can organize a debate based on information given by the Council to the appropriate parliamentary committees.
2. At the end of the negotiations but before the signing, the President of the Council or its representative informs the appropriate committees, confidentially and unofficially, of the essence[33] of the agreement.
3. After the signing but before the conclusion, the Council informs the Parliament of the content[34] of the agreement.

In comparison with the Luns-I procedure the Luns-II procedure is remarkable in that at least in principle it does not provide for any intervention of the Parliament during the negotiations. This reflects a desire to avoid public debates at this stage, in order to preserve the position of the Community during the negotiations. It is evident that those rules do not prevent members of the Parliament from putting oral and written questions to the Council or the Commission or prevent the competent committees from asking for (confidential) information and organizing public debates.[35] The Commission dealt with this subject in its communication transmitted to the Parliament on June 8, 1973, on the role and influence of the Parliament, announcing that it would keep the appropriate committees informed of the progress of commercial negotiations.[36] The Parliament had to satisfy itself with those developments in spite of the fact that in its resolution of June 26, 1963, it had asked for the right of "ratification" (i.e., approval before signature) of every agreement to be concluded by the Community.[37]

One finds the same idea expressed some years later in the report of Sir Peter Kirk, appended to the report of Lord Ray on interinstitutional relations presented in the name of the Political Affairs Committee on May 5, 1978.[38]

Professor Joseph Weiler of the European University Institute has explained why the European Parliament has great difficulties in scrutinizing the foreign policy of the Community. The first factor he mentions is the strict interrelationship between external relations, which is under the jurisdiction of the Community, and foreign policy, which remains within the boundaries of Member State competence and is only subject to political cooperation. The second factor is the desire of the Parliament not to weaken the position of the Commission in its relations with the Council. A further constraint is the secrecy of the foreign negotiations, deriving both from international etiquette and from the fact that "public debate in the course of the negotiations might undermine the position of the Community negotiating organ."[39]

All these factors explain why the Parliament has made such modest use of the possibilities opened to it by the Luns-Westerterp procedure. From 1973 to 1978, three debates on the MTN were organized in the Parliament, at the initiative of the Committee on External Economic Relations (one of the twelve committees of the Parliament.) The first took place on July 4, 1973, before the opening of negotiations. The report of Christian de la Malène (UDE)[40] examined the position of the Community as reflected in the global conception drafted by the Commission on April 4, 1973. The second was organized on June 18, 1975. Gabriel Kastereit (UDE), President of the Committee on External Economic Relations, presented a report on the position of the Community in the GATT negotiations[41] four months after the Council had adopted the directives for the negotiations.[42] The third debate was initiated by a report of Pierre-Bernard Cousté (UDE) on the multilateral negotiations in the GATT[43] on June 16, 1978, some days before the Council adopted the scheme of a global agreement, but six months after the important session of the Council in January devoted to the adoption of the offer by the Community.

These debates do not seem to have made a substantial contribution to the negotiations. The resolution adopted by the Parliament expressed general support of the Community's position and a position in favor of reciprocity and progress in the monetary field and against protectionism. A preoccupation with disturbances in trade relations due to the world economic crisis appears clearly in the resolution of June 16, 1978.

The last debate the Parliament devoted to the Tokyo Round during the negotiation process opened with three oral questions,[44] with debate coming from the Committee on External Economic Relations,[45] the European Progress Democrats[46] and some members of the Parliament.[47] Those questions reflected a concern that the Tokyo Round might be concluded too quickly, without a guarantee from the U.S. Government on the waiver question, and expressed the fear of an unbalanced result of the negotiations.[48] Two days before, the same concern had been expressed in the oral question of a member of the Communist group, Gérard Bozolu (France).[49] Klaus von Dohnanyi, in the name of the Council's Presidency, restated the Community's intent to achieve a "substantial and balanced" final result. Individual, oral or written, questions to the Council or the Commission pursuant to Article 140 of the EEC Treaty were neither very numerous nor important during the negotiations process. There were informative questions related to the schedule of the negotiations,[50] the evolution of Japanese exports and the way to limit them,[51] and the importance of treating the real problems of international trade and preserving an effective tariff protection.[52]

The institutional limitations of its powers, the relative disinterest of the indirectly elected Parliament in international matters and the technical complexity of matters related to nontariff barriers in international trade explain the less important role played by this institution during the long negotiations.

The Termination of the Negotiations: March–April, 1979

The negotiations were concluded when the Contracting Parties initialed the minutes of the negotiations and the twelve annexed protocols, on April 12, 1979. The purpose of the initialing usually is to authenticate the result of the negotiations. It is considered the last act of this procedure. So it is the Commission, as the EEC institution responsible for the negotiations, which initials the international agreements. Formal authorization by the Council is not necessary. However, before officially ending the negotiations, the Commission usually addresses a report to the Council to enable it to discuss the merits of the negotiated agreement.

The Commission presented a report on the Tokyo Round to the session of the Council that took place on March 6, 1979. Although Germany, Denmark, and the Benelux countries were in favor of the Commission's conclusion that the agreement was satisfactory and balanced, the other members asked for supplementary negotiations, mainly in the field of tariff concessions.[53] Finally, the Council reached unanimity at its session of April 2–3, 1979. It was agreed that when adopting the minutes authenticating the results of the MTN on the tariff questions, the Commission should make a declaration in the following terms:[54] "A l'issue d'une première étape de réduction de cinq ans, la Communauté examinera si, compte tenu de la situation économique, sociale et monétaire, et de l'application par les partenaires des divers engagements souscrits dans le cadre des MTN, elle est en mesure de passer à la seconde étape." This decision should be made before the end of 1984 at the latest, by the Council acting unanimously.

The Council also decided to reexamine the Community's attitude toward the final approval of the result of the whole of the negotiations, in the light of the Commission's reports on the legislative measures for implementation adopted by the main developed countries. Furthermore, the Commission declared that the Community should implement the whole of its concessions only when all of its developed partners, having complied with their own parliamentary procedures, were in a position to enact their own concessions, which implies that their legislation should be satisfactory and that the results of the MTN should have been effectively and validly implemented.

As far as the procedure was concerned, the Council took note of the Commission's intention to proceed to the authentication of the texts and agreement that had resulted from the negotiations up to then,[55] after a final examination by the Committee of Article 113.

The Commission was asked to present to the Council, when convenient, and in light of reports on the measures taken by the partners of the Community, recommendations on the conclusion of the results of the MTN, in conformity with Community procedures. The Council would then decide whether it should give its approval to the conclusion.

When adopting these decisions, the Council included in its minutes a sentence that left open the question of the division of authority between the Community and its Member States for the conclusion of the agreements: "The fact that the Commission alone authenticates the results of the negotiations does not prejudge [ne préjuge en rien] the solution of the problem of the possible participation of the Member States in the legally binding acceptance of the various texts." It was this problem that caused the most significant difficulties in the Council during the months after the results of the negotiations were initialed.

The Preparation of the Conclusion in 1979: The Legal and Political Problems

On February 22, 1979, the COREPER instructed an ad hoc working group (composed of officials of the Permanent Representations of the Member States, plus, in the case of France and Germany, some representatives of the central administrations) to study various problems, notably legal ones, raised by the conclusion of the entire range of instruments resulting from the MTN. At the same time, the COREPER asked for the opinion of the legal service of the Council. (It should be noted that the COREPER's role in these institutional matters was much more important than it was during the course of the negotiations, where, as previously mentioned, the influence of the Committee of Article 113 was predominant.[56])

Three legal problems were significant:

1. The participation of the Member States in the signing (conclusion) of some agreements
2. The participation of representatives of the Member States in the management bodies created by the agreements
3. The number of Community votes in those bodies

The legal services of both the Commission and the Council offered their comments on these questions. The question on which there initially appeared to be some divergence in the positions of two legal services was that concerning the possibility of the Member States' concluding some agreements jointly with the Community.

The Commission's view was that the EEC had the authority to conclude the MTN agreements without the intervention of the Member States, on the basis of either Article 113 of the EEC Treaty or other provisions of the EEC and ECSC treaties, read in light of the jurisprudence of the Court of Justice, starting with the European Road Transport Agreement [ERTA] decision of March 31, 1971.[57] In the ERTA case, the Court decided in favor of the exclusive authority of the Community to enter into agreements with third states or international organizations when the Community institutions have previously adopted common rules of whatever kind in the matter concerned. As far as commercial policy is concerned, under the Treaty of Rome the authority of the Community in that field is exclusive of the authority of the Member States since the end of the transitional period (i.e., since December 31, 1969).[58]

The ad hoc group of the Council, on the other hand, following the opinion of the Council's legal service, took the position that some provisions of the MTN agreements to be concluded—in particular, the standards, government procurement, and civil aircraft codes—transcended the field of commercial policy under Article 113 of the EEC Treaty, and since common rules did not exist on the internal EEC level for all the matters covered by those codes, there was a possibility that Member States should conclude those particular agreements jointly with the Community.

The so-called Rubber Agreement opinion issued by the Court of Justice on October 4, 1979, seems to have brought the conceptions of both legal services closer together.[59] The Court held that insofar as the essential object of an agreement the Community plans to conclude is part of its commerical policy, Article 113 appears to be the only legal basis for it, despite the repercussions it can have for other Community policies.

In its communication of October 1, 1979,[60] the Commission concluded that the Community had the necessary powers to subscribe to the international commitments contained in the multilateral and bilateral agreements resulting from the MTN, without any need for the participation of the Member States:

> The powers derived from Article 113 of the EEC Treaty, combined, in the specific case of the tariff concessions relating to ECSC products, with Article 72 of the ECSC Treaty. Even though some of the instruments may have an effect in other areas, their actual purpose is to regulate various aspects of international trade, this being an area which undeniably falls within the sole powers of the Community, under the heading of trade policy.[61]

Although the legal aspects of the decisions to conclude may have been clarified, the political problems remained. Perhaps it would be correct to say that the main difficulty was saving face for those Member States which since the beginning had argued that it was necessary for the Member States to participate in the conclusion of at least some agreements resulting from the MTN.

The French presidency was anxious to find a compromise based on objective—if not legal—criteria. The solution proposed took into account the hard kernel of the positions of France and Great Britain. There was some legal justification for the Member States' conclusion of the ECSC Tariff Protocol,[62] and it was considered that lack of time made it impossible to thoroughly examine the foundation of the two countries' thesis as far as the standards and civil aircraft codes were concerned. It was suggested that the political consensus achieved in the Council should not affect the legal thesis advocated by the Commission and the Member States.

So it was finally decided, after much debate, that the Community alone should sign the bi- and multilateral agreements, but that the Member States (all the Member States and not merely some of them, as had been proposed during the discussions in the Council) could also sign and accept the Tariff Protocol (as far as ECSC products were concerned), the Standards Code, and the Civil Aircraft Agreement.

In spite of the Presidency's wish to avoid the appearance of arbitrariness in the Council's solution, it is difficult to understand this solution as anything but a purely diplomatic compromise. No objective reason seems to exist for adopting different solutions for the Standards Code and for the Government Procurement Code.

The Member States' participation in the conclusion of the Tariff Protocol needs some elaboration. Article 71 of the ECSC Treaty reserves to the Member States the authority for commercial policy as far as coal and steel products are concerned, except as otherwise provided by the treaty. As the Council notes in an answer to a written question: "such provisions are contained in particular in Articles 72 to 75."[63] This is why the Commission recommended concluding the tariff protocol for coal and steel products on the basis of Article 72 of the ECSC Treaty. Indeed, Article 72 provides a proper legal basis for measures fixing maximum tariffs, such as those included in the protocol. Nevertheless, the Council did not follow the Commission's recommendation. Nor did it accept its suggestion that the President of the Council should be authorized to designate the person who would have the power to bind the Member States. In this respect, it did not follow the precedent set by the approval of a list of concessions for coal and steel products in 1974.[64] Legally, the procedures are equivalent, but from a political point of view it is interesting to point to the insistence of the Member States that they themselves conclude the Tariff Protocol without interference of a Community institution.[65]

One can regret—as Jacques Steenbergen does[66]—that the Comission has never supported the idea that after the end of the transitional period the authority of the EEC in the field of commercial policy pursuant to Article 113 of the EEC Treaty absorbs the reservation of Article 71 of the ECSC Treaty, as has been recognized for social security or transport, for example. But, the Member States and the Council would most certainly have rejected that conception as far as tariff protocols are concerned, and it seems that the question of nontariff barriers had not been raised. Nobody seemed to believe that the codes based on Article 113 of the EEC Treaty should not cover ECSC products also.[67] One can agree with Steenbergen when he writes that "the lack of clarity in the relations between the EC Treaties (EEC, ECSC and EURATOM) requires a clear definition of the scope of the Community's signature."[68]

Surprisingly enough, due to the way the Tariff Protocols were prepared for the signatures by the GATT Secretariat "the 'European Community Schedule' made no distinction between EEC and ECSC products. The representatives of the Commission and the Member States all signed the document without qualification. Only the Danish government stipulated in the ratification document that the Danish signature only affected the Schedule in so far as it dealt with ECSC products."[69]

It is interesting to try to explain the insistence of Member States that they should conclude some of the MTN agreements jointly with the EEC. As far as the Civil Aircraft Agreement is concerned, the interest of Great Britain and France in a joint conclusion seems to be due to the great sensitivity of the industry concerned and the magnitude of the investments in it. For the Standards Code, one can mention the Member States' preoccupation with defending the interests of their own industries, taking into account the existence of thousands of national standards. As we shall explain later, however, those interests could be preserved without formally impairing the Community's capacity to conclude the agreement on its own.

In a statement included in the annexes to the Council's draft minutes of November 20, 1979, the Commission wished "to confirm that all the agreements at present submitted to the Council (with the exception of the ECSC aspect of the tariff protocol) are a matter for exclusive Community competence under Article 113 of the EEC Treaty."[70] It was agreed in the Council that the joint conclusion by the Community and the Member States—sometimes upon reservation of ratification—would not prevent the Community from concluding all the agreements negotiated in Geneva on the appropriate date before January 1, 1980.[71] The Council's decisions— formally dated December 10, 1979—approved both the multilateral and the bilateral agreements resulting from the negotiations and authorized the President of the Council to designate the person who would proceed with the formalities provided for in the agreements to bind the Community[72] or take whatever steps were required by the agreements to confirm the commitments entered into by the Community in the fields covered by bilateral agreements.[73]

The adoption of the rules of the GATT negotiated in the legal framework group[74] is not mentioned in the December 10 decisions and the rules have not been published in the *Official Journal.* In its report the Commission proposed that the EEC Council agree to those texts,[75] which became *decisions* of the Contracting Parties of the GATT acting collectively, and thus were not international agreements. The EEC Council formally agreed to the texts drawn up by the working party on the legal framework. The Permanent Representative of the Commission could then sign the bilateral and multilateral agreements at Geneva on December 17, 1979, and in this case the signature was sufficient to legally bind the Community.

Though not without precedent, the procedure does not correspond to the general practice followed by the Community in jointly concluding an international agreement. To avoid any legal uncertainty, the Council normally gives its formal approval of an agreement and concludes it in the name of the Community only after the completion of internal procedures in the Member States and ratification by them.[76] This solves the difficult problem of determining the precise legal consequences for the Member States of a joint agreement concluded by the Community but not definitely concluded by some Member States.

In the case of the MTN, the problem was tacitly considered as purely theoretical. It seemed clear to many delegations that if in the future the Court of Justice were to make a pronouncement on the Community's authority to conclude the MTN agreements[77] it would do so in light of its Rubber Agreement opinion in favor of the Community's exclusive jurisdiction. To that extent the ratification of the agreements by some Member States could not have any meaning in the Community's legal order, and was the result of purely political demands. But as far as relations with third states are concerned, it is difficult to deny legal effect to the Member States' intervention in the conclusion of the agreements. Both the Community and the Member State concerned are internationally liable for the violation of a mixed agreement, and a third country that claims to be a victim of a violation can choose to address the Community, the state, or both.[78]

Later, the Council seemed to try to minimize this problem. Questioned by a member of the Parliament on the importance of the legal uncertainties about the respective roles of the Community and the Member States in concluding the agreements, the Council answered that the problem did not reflect a fundamental conflict of authority. It stated that this was a tricky legal matter that should be resolved by relying on concrete cases of the Court of Justice as well as on the legislative practice of the Council. The solution adopted had been dictated by the necessity of having most of the agreements in force by January 1, 1980.[79] The Commission, asked the same question by the same member of the Parliament, answered that "questions related to Community competence are important and . . . this aspect has been discussed at length in the Council." The Commission added that different opinions on the nature and implication of authority in the field of external trade policy occur frequently, and that it always had defended the exclusiveness of the Community's authority.[80]

That some Member States' attitude toward this problem had a very political underpinning appears to be confirmed by the fact that they felt that their practical and political concerns about their role in the implementation of the agreements were met by the Council in its package deal of November 20, 1979.

The first problem dealt with, as indicated in the minutes concerning that package, was the participation of the Community and its Member States in the work of the administrative bodies provided for by the agreements—the so-called Committees of Signatories. The arrangement agreed on in the Council satisfied the Member States. Not only would they take part in the work of the Committees on a basis that would allow their presence to be identified within the Community delegation,[81] but they would be fully consulted and informed about both formal and informal contacts or discussions, and they would participate in all meetings where the degree of privacy is such that it is appropriate. Usual procedures would be followed to determine the Community's positions in the bodies. In a case where no common position could be achieved and it became urgent for a point of view to be put forward, and where the matter related specifically to the imports or exports of an individual Member State, the Community would as a general rule agree to a scenario whereby the Member State in question would be able to intervene.[82] The common position would be expressed within the bodies by the Commission, but Member States directly and specifically affected by the matter under discussion would be able to intervene within the framework of a previously agreed arrangement, and within the context of the common position.

The Member States' right to intervene in a field covered by the common commercial policy was at the borderline of what appears legitimate under Community law. The arrangement appeared to give the Member States some assurance that their individual interests would in any case be defended. On the other hand, it is worthwhile to note that the representation of the Community and its Member States has been organized in the same way for participation in the administrative bodies created by both the agreements concluded by the Community alone and those concluded also by its member states. Later, those same guidelines were adopted for the Community's participation in the work of the bodies created by the mixed agreements concluded in the framework of the UNCTAD program on commodities.

The usual procedures for determining the Community's position include the role of the Commission, as the Community's negotiator, with the assistance of the Committee of Article 113. When formal negotiations for concluding an agreement binding the Community are at stake, the Commission will ask for the Council's authorization. Such agreements are not negotiated in the various Committees of Signatories.

Another concern expressed by some Member States and particularly by France had to do with the allocation of authority between the Community and the Member States to adopt defensive measures against breaches of the agreements—in particular, the Standards Code—by the Community's trading partners. This concern has also been satisfied, as we will see later.

Therefore, it appears that there was no special reason for some Member States' desire for a mixed conclusion of some agreements. It was only a manifestation of the *combat de retardement* of some governments against the affirmation of the international legal capacity of the Community.

One question brought up in the Council remains unsolved. It has to do with the number of votes allocated to the Community's delegation within the administrative bodies created by the agreements. There is a tendency among Community officials to minimize the importance of the problem by arguing that consensus is a tacit rule in GATT matters, so that the question of available votes is not a crucial one and it should not be in the interest of the parties concerned to want more precision in this regard. This kind of political approach to the problem, however, leaves something to be desired from a legal point of view.

The Debate in the European Parliament, December 1979: For a Greater Involvement of the Assembly

The Parliament supported the opinion of the Commission on the exclusive authority of the Community to conclude the agreements.[83] But it expressed its position only on December 14, 1979, three weeks after the decisive November 20 session of the Council and three days before the conclusion of the agreements in Geneva on December 17. The appropriate committees of the Parliament had been kept informed of the results of the negotiations by a memorandum of the Council transmitted some days after the direct elections.[84]

The Parliament received the final report on the negotiations and the two proposed decisions of the Council mentioned above,[85] and the appropriate parliamentary committees organized a hearing with the President of the Council on November 21, the day after the crucial session of that body. Thus the debate that took place on December 13, 1979, in the plenary session of the Parliament was more or less improvised. This explains the first paragraph of the resolution adopted by the Parliament, which stated that the new members of the directly elected Parliament did not discuss in detail the results achieved in the negotiations.

As to the substance of the resolution, it must be noted that many interventions during the debates and also the final text of the resolution were more critical of the results of the MTN than the proposed resolution presented by Sir Fred Catherwood in the name of the parliamentary Committee on External Economic Relations.[86] The amendments adopted by the Parliament had a bearing on the situation of the less developed countries and on commerce with Japan—particularly the problem of European exports to that country.

The debates and the resolution also expressed the desire that the Parliament be more involved in the process of negotiating and concluding international agreements for the Community. Paragraph 21 of the resolution (Paragraph 17 of the proposal) reads as follows: "21. [The Parliament] charges its competent committees to elaborate and to submit to it proposals concerning, from one side, the participation of the E.P. in future trade negotiations, and from the other side, a procedure providing for the official ratification (sic) of future trade agreements by the E.P." As Sir Fred Catherwood, president of the Committee on External Economic Relations explained in his presentation of the draft resolution during the plenary session:

> This Parliament . . . needs to take the place of national parliaments, which do not have the competence to discuss these things directly with the Commission and the Council. We believe that this Parliament should comment and advise on these matters first before these things are done, and we are more anxious too to improve the Luns-Westerterp consultation procedure.

He added that the Parliament has "no intention of recommending a procedure which forces negotiators to show their hand in public, but we do not really believe that negotiators are so ignorant of each other's position that discussion with the parliament's committee is going to destroy their bargaining position."

Hans-Joachim Seeler, speaking for the Socialist group, supported the views expressed by the Committee on External Economic Relations. He considered that a first step would be to allow the Parliament to give its opinion after the information, in the framework of the Luns-Westerterp procedure. In this way, it could hope to influence the results of the negotiations. Later on, it would be desirable to have a provision for the approval (or at least a deliberation) of the Parliament before the agreement took effect.

The draft resolution was also supported by the European Peoples'

Party group (Christian Democrats), by the Liberal and Democratic groups, and by some other individual speakers. Carettoni Romagnoli, in the name of the Communist group, criticized the fact that the Parliament had been consulted neither before the initialing of the texts (the speaker said "signing") nor in October before the decision favoring the conclusion of agreements (the speaker said "ratification"). For these reasons, the Communist group did not understand the urgency of the debate "*quando le cose sono fatte.*"

The European Progress Democrats (the Gaullist group) opposed the position of the majority of their colleagues and tabled an amendment that would preclude the possibility for the Parliament to "ratify" trade agreements, as provided for in Paragraph 17 of the draft resolution. In their name, Nicole Chouraqui explained that ratification by the Parliament would be useless for the codes that would be approved by the national parliaments and that under the EEC treaty only the Council had the authority to conclude international agreements.

Mr. Haferkamp, the Commission's Vice-President for external relations, expressed the general support of that institution for a greater involvement of the Parliament and its committees in the process of international negotiations, but he did not give an opinion on the possible concrete solutions the Parliament should propose.

Finally, the amendment of the European Progress Democrats was rejected.

It is clear from this debate that in the future the directly elected Parliament will press its position in the Community's international policy. The circumstances, in particular the lack of time for a serious preparation, largely explain the deficiency of the debates and the Parliament's ready acceptance of the results of the MTN.

In a later answer to a written question by a member of the Parliament, the Council restated the official and legal view.[87] After confirming the correctness of the procedure followed up to that time, the Council noted that

> Article 228, § 1, al. 1, 2nd sentence of the EEC Treaty provides for the previous consultation of the Assembly in the cases in which the act bearing upon the conclusion of the agreement is based on an article of the Treaty conferring to the Council a "pouvoir d'action dont la mise en oeuvre suppose la consultation de l'Assemblée.[88]

This rather complicated formula refers to Association Agreements expressly provided for in Article 238 and agreements based on other articles of the Treaty from which, pursuant to the jurisprudence of the Court of Justice, a treaty-making power can be inferred (for example, in the field of CAP or transport policy). The Council added that the Parliament must in those cases be consulted before the Council adopts the act governing conclusion of an agreement, but that under the Treaty consultation did not mean approval. A modification of the Treaty would be necessary to increase the powers of the Parliament.

Nevertheless, in an internal document of the European Peoples' Party group in Parliament, entitled "Priorities in the institutional field," Sjouke Jonker, a Dutch member of the Parliament, mentioned as one of the "small steps" which he apparently considered it possible to take without modifying the Treaties "the establishment for the European Parliament, of a right of ratification of association, cooperation and trade agreements with third countries."[89]

In an important resolution of July 9, 1981, on relations between the European Parliament and the Council, the Parliament devoted some paragraphs to external relations. It only expressed a hopeful attitude and did not go as far as suggested by the document just quoted. It asked, in point 2(d), for a common declaration by Parliament, Council, and Commission to promote conciliation in external matters, announcing that a further report on its participation in external relations would be forthcoming. In Point 9 of the resolution, the Parliament asked to be consulted by the Council before any agreement pursuant to any of the treaties establishing the Communities was concluded. It also called for the confidential consultation of the parliamentary committees as provided by the interinstitutional agreements (Luns I and II procedures). The Parliament also expressed, in point 16(c), its desire to intervene at a reasonable time before the conclusion of agreements, and proposed that if it rejects an agreement, a consensus should be sought in the framework of a conciliation procedure. It charged its political committee to prepare a report on this problem.[90]

This later report was drafted by Erik Blumenfeld[91] and adopted by the Parliament on February 17, 1982. It proposed some improvements in the Luns-Westerterp procedures but refrained from asking, at the present stage, that the Parliament be given the right to approve (ratify) the international agreements. It only suggested that if the Parliament rejects an agreement by a majority vote, the Council and the Commission should start a conciliation procedure with the Parliament. The agreement would not enter into force until this procedure was completed.

All those suggestions would be realized without formal amendments of the treaties, through agreements between the institutions concerned.

One question must be asked: What can be achieved through an interinstitutional agreement? Such agreements have been concluded in recent years because it seemed difficult to revise the treaties and there was a general feeling that something had to be done to secure better collaboration between institutions or to solve a specific problem without embarking on the long procedure required for a formal revision. Good examples of such agreements are the March 4, 1975, joint declaration of the Parliament, the Council, and the Commission on conciliation[92] and the June 30, 1982, joint declaration by the Parliament, the Council, and the Commission on various measures aimed at improving budgetary procedures.

There is no unanimity on the legal value of those interinstitutional agreements.[93] Some have only political value. In any event, a case-by-case analysis seems to be required, and it is impossible generally to deny legal value to all those agreements. What can be said is that the institutions are free to organize the exercise of the authority conceded to them by the treaties, but they must act only within the range of that authority.[94]

An interinstitutional agreement may recognize the Parliament's right to approve international agreements, but there is no legal guarantee that the Council will not violate this right. Only a formal revision of the Treaty, or the development of a customary rule that the Court would sanction, would create such an obligation for the Council. Needless to say, it would not be easy to prove the existence of such a rule against the Council's will.

It must also be mentioned that the Economic and Social Committee (ESC)—a consultative organ of the Community representing the interest of socioeconomic groups—devoted four opinions to the Tokyo Round, adopted on its own initiative from 1973 to 1977. The first three dealt with the global conception,[95] agriculture,[96] and developing countries,[97] and the fourth with the problems of the MTN in 1977.[98] There was no debate on the results of the MTN in 1979, but the ESC decided to issue an opinion on the coherence of the external relations of the Communities.

Acceptance of the Mixed Agreements by the Member States

It may be profitable to give some details on the way the Member States themselves accepted the three mixed agreements discussed above, namely the Tariff Protocol of 1979 and the standards and civil aircraft codes.

With a reservation for one agreement, as will be explained later, all the Member States have accepted those three agreements. Belgium alone has accepted the additional tariff protocol that provided more concessions or concessions by some countries for which no list of concessions was annexed to the original protocol. The United Kingdom accepted some other agreements for the purpose of extending them to colonial territories.

Some Member States have signed the three agreements while reserving ratification or acceptance. Belgium and the Netherlands waited until April, May, and June, 1981, depending on the agreement concerned, for final ratification. In some cases the delay may have been due to the necessity to submit the agreements to the parliament in the country concerned. For Denmark there were only four days between signature and ratification. As of October 1982, Italy had signed but not yet ratified the Civil Aircraft Agreement. Other states, including France, have accepted all the agreements without reservation.

The Implementation of the MTN Results in the Community Legal Order

The implementation of the agreements resulting from the Tokyo Round raised two sets of questions that are common to every international treaty concluded by the Community.

> Does the agreement need to be complemented to be effectively applied? Or is it worded so completely and specifically that no further legislation is required?
>
> Does the agreement as such create obligations for and confer rights on the individuals concerned? Has the individual the right to invoke a provision of the agreement before a court of a Member State? May he ask such a court to decide about the compatibility of a Community or national measure with the rule of the agreement concerned? In other words, can a provision of the agreement have a direct effect in the legal order of the European Communities?

It is not possible to answer these questions completely. Obviously, the answers would depend on the content of every particular provision of very heterogeneous agreements. Some of them went into force on January 1, 1981, and not all of the enacting legislation has been passed yet. And the last word on direct effect will be for the Court of Justice of the European Communities, which has the comprehensive authority to interpret Community law.

Therefore, this part of our study contains only tentative answers to the questions raised by the implementation of the agreements. In any case, the subject requires further study.

The Problem of the Implementation of International Agreements in the Legal Order of the EEC, with Special Reference to the MTN Results

Under Article 228, Section 2 of the EEC Treaty, the bilateral and multilateral agreements resulting from the MTN are binding for the

Community and its Member States when the Community concludes those agreements. This does not mean that Member States become parties to the agreements concluded by the Community. Only the Community as such is engaged under international law vis-à-vis the other parties to the agreement; the agreement is binding on the Member States as an act of the institutions forming part of the Community's legal order.[99]

Thus it is not only unlawful but legally impossible for a Member State to denounce a treaty concluded by the Community alone.[100] As far as a mixed agreement is concerned, the denunciation would only affect the part of the agreement that exceeded the authority of the Community. In the case of the MTN results, since the mixed conclusion of some agreements occurred only because of political considerations, it can be argued that a Member State's denunciation of mixed agreements would not have any legal effect in Community law. As Jacques Bourgeois, a member of the Commission's Legal Service, mentions, the mixed conclusion of an agreement does not give any supplementary guarantee to third countries that the agreement will be satisfactorily implemented. "If pursuant to the division of powers in the internal Community sphere implementing measures are to be taken not by the Community but by the Member States, they are legally bound to do so by virtue of the Treaty itself (Article 228)."[101]

The Council approved the MTN agreements through an unqualified decision (*Beschluss,* not *Entscheidung* in the sense of the Article 189, paragraph 4 of the EEC Treaty).[102] No other act than those decisions and the signature is required to give the agreements the force of legally binding instruments vis-à-vis third states and in the Community legal order; this results from the *International Fruit Co.* and *Bresciani* cases decided by the Court of Justice.[103] As we will see later, approval of the agreement by means of a decision is not an obstacle to its direct effect.

Based on the jurisprudence of the Court since the *International Fruit Co.* case, it is the general opinion that the international agreements concluded by the Community are subordinate to the EEC Treaty but superior to the acts of the Community institutions.[104]

To be concretely applied, the international agreements often need specific measures of implementation. This is the case with some of the multilateral agreements resulting from the MTN, and we will examine them in some detail. Others do not need significant complements in Community law either because they correspond to the actual state of the Community norms or because they are rules of conduct for the Member States or the Community and do not need implementing measures.

Thus there was no need for measures implementing the Licensing

Code, because the Community rules already met its requirements. The list of references the Commission transmitted to the GATT concerning the basic legislative texts adopted at the Community level on the implementation of the agreement contains regulations and decisions adopted from 1970 to 1979 (before the agreement went into force).[105] The basic text was Reg. (EEC) No. 193/75,[106] as last amended by Reg. (EEC) No. 1576/80,[107] which contained detailed rules for applying the system of import and export licenses and advance certificates for agricultural products. But later on, this regulation was replaced by Reg. (EEC) No. 3183/80;[108] its text consolidates the previously existing texts and introduces no change in substance.[109]

Other measures have also been taken for the sake of legal certainty and uniformity of the legal sources in the sectors where a common policy or common rules exist in the legal order of the Community.

It should be noted that American authorities took a great interest in the Commission's implementation of the agreements. Officials of the Office of the Trade Representative visited the Commission repeatedly. Their main preoccupation was that the legal texts be drafted in such a way as to allow judicial remedies in case of violations of the rules deriving from the Agreements. Professor Jackson has mentioned a parallel interest of the Community during the drafting of the U.S. legislation.[110]

In the field of CAP, regulations have been adopted to comply with the obligations entered into for those products—for instance, amendments to sluice-gate price coefficients and to levies on turkey parts, the introduction of import or export certificates, and so on.[111]

Tariff concessions required (as usual) the adoption of regulations reducing the tariffs fixed by the external common tariff.[112]

The same preoccupation with effectiveness appears in the way the Community has implemented the codes concerning nontariff barriers.

For example, the Antidumping Code and the Subsidies-Countervailing Duty Code have been transposed into Reg. (EEC) No. 3017/79 "on protection against dumped or subsidized imports from countries not members of the European Economic Community" that went into force on January 1, 1980.[113] That regulation took the place of Reg. (EEC) No. 459/68, as last amended by Reg. (EEC) No. 1681/79, adopted in accordance with Article VI of the GATT and the 1967 Antidumping Code.[114] So there is a strict parallelism between the situation at the international level (abrogation of the 1967 code by the new agreement) and the situation in Community law. These subjects are now treated by a single instrument in which everyone concerned can find the applicable rules. The new elements contained in Reg. (EEC) No. 3017/79 are rather limited, so there is no revolution in the Community legislation. Those new elements include material on subsidies

(Article 3), new rules for the determination of injury (Article 4),[115] more publicity in the investigation process (Article 7), more precise rules on confidential treatment (Article 8), the obligation to publish in the *Official Journal* the reason for the undertakings under which a subsidy is eliminated or limited or its injurious effects are suppressed and under which prices are revised or exports halted (Articles 9 and 10). All those rules could have been inserted in the existing regulation, and most of them were complete in themselves, needing no further elaboration except for an indication of the authority concerned or where its decisions would be published. But the EEC institutions considered it "appropriate to take advantage of this occasion to proceed to a general streamlining, linguistic simplification and consolidation of the rules in question."[116]

One must also mention that for ECSC products, the Commission adopted Recommendation (an act that has the the same legal effect under the ECSC Treaty as a directive in the EEC field) No. 3018/79/ECSC, of December 21, 1979,[117] on protection against dumped or subsidized imports from countries not members of the ECSC. This recommendation is based on Articles 74 (dumping provision) and 86 (general obligation of the Member States to further the Community's endeavors of the ECSC Treaty). It is analogous, for ECSC products, to the principles and definitions laid down by Reg. (EEC) No. 3017/79.

The procedures surrounding the Agreement of Implementation of Article VII of the GATT (the Customs Valuation Code) were similar. The EEC and the United States had to put the agreement into effect by July 1, 1980. In this field also the Commission has proposed a Council regulation to implement the agreement and replace Reg. (EEC) No. 803/68.[118] The Council adopted Reg. (EEC) No. 1224/80,[119] which was amended by Regulation No. 3193/80 of December 8, 1980.[120]

Those are matters directly related to the Customs Union, and for which the Community has exclusive authority. Furthermore, the agreements are precisely drafted, so the Community's implementation is essentially of an editorial and administrative nature.[121]

The situation is very different in the case of the Standards Code and the Government Procurement Code. The Community has adopted directives on those matters, but does not have exclusive authority. The Community rules cover only some of the standards applied in the Community, but there are also numerous national rules and statutes concerning these. This partly explains not only some Member States' insistence on taking part in the conclusion of the Standards Code,[122] but also the sensitivity of the problem of allocating authority between the Community and its Member States for implementing the rules on standards.

The two levels of obligation provided for in the agreement are as follows:

i. central and federal governments are directly responsible for the technical regulations and standards that they bring into force
ii. central and federal governments are responsible for significant disturbances of international trade caused by new technical regulations or standards issued by decentralized standards institutes and non-governmental bodies.[123]

It appears that the United States and the EEC agreed that the United States would accept a "best endeavours" clause concerning the parties' obligation to make sure that their local and nongovernmental bodies comply with the provisions of the code in exchange for the EEC's agreeing to provisions on access to certification systems for suppliers of like products originating in the territories of other parties.[124] The Community's main concerns about the implementation of the code appear in the text adopted by the Council (the decision of the Council of January 15, 1980).[125] The decision refers to a general principle inscribed in the GATT preamble and relating to the desire expressed by the Contracting Parties to enter into "reciprocal and mutually advantageous arrangements," and provides for a procedure to ensure that reciprocity exists and to allow the Community to take the measures suitable for the situation. Title III of the decision (Articles 3 to 7) is entirely devoted to the measures to be taken in case of nonreciprocity.

The decision distinguishes between a situation in which a Community directive exists in the field concerned and one in which there are only national standards. In the first case, the Commission can decide on appropriate measures after consulting a Committee composed of representatives of the Member States. The Council can then confirm, modify, or repeal the decision of the Commission (Article 5, Section 2). It is remarkable that even though there are Community directives on the matter concerned, a Member State can take provisional measures until the decision of the Commission (Article 5, Section 3). Those provisional measures remain applicable and the decision is suspended if the Member State concerned brings it up before the Council within ten days after the Commission adopts the decision. The Council decides by a qualified majority.

If there are no Community directives in the matter concerned, Member States can, again, take appropriate measures. They must inform the Commission and the other Member States; and if the Community or a Member State so requires, consultations can take place in the committee the decision provides for (Articles 6 and 8). Appropriate measures normally consist of suspending the obligation to certify products originating in another Contracting Party. Those measures are, of course, provisional. It is only the Committee on Technical Barriers to Trade created by the code (Article 13) that may authorize one or more parties to suspend, in respect to any other party, the application of obligations under the code (Article 14.21). But because working parties or technical experts groups may intervene and because consultation procedures must be undertaken before the Committee intervenes, provisional measures can last for a considerable time.

The other problem to be treated in a directive was that of access to certification, as provided for in Article 7 of the Code. This question has long been an obstacle to the adoption of directives on the elimination of technical hindrances to commerce among EEC Member States. Some Member States fear that their markets may be invaded by products admitted into the common market as a result of a relaxed procedure in another Member State. Therefore they insist on the right of all Member States to check the procedure of EEC certification. It must be clear not only to the Member State where certification is asked, but also to all its partners and the Commission, that the supplier is "able and willing to fulfill the requirements of the system" (Article 7.2 of the code) and that the other conditions provided for in the code are fulfilled. A committee for EEC certification has to be created; it is to provide for an appeal to the Council, at the initiative of any Member State, of the Commission's decisions in the matter.

By the guarantees it provides, the directive should make it easier for some Member States to consent to the adoption of new directives on Community standards. They would no longer have any reason to fear the easy importation by their partners of products too competitive with their own.

At present, it is not possible to foretell when or even whether that directive will be adopted. Some Member States believe they have sufficient guarantees against undesired imports from third states through the safeguard mechanism laid down by the January 15, 1980, decision and the general clause of Article 115 of the EEC Treaty. Others want to retain as many ways as possible of blocking the importation of products from third countries as an argument for negotiating in the difficult context of the economic crisis.

The problems raised by the Government Procurement Code were somewhat different, because Community legislation was more extensive. There was no doubt that, as Article 228, Section 2 of the EEC Treaty provides, the Member States were bound by the code through the Community obligation, and so the rights of the third states and their enterprises and suppliers were protected. In that respect, the necessity of a Community act was doubtful.[126] Some experts felt that insofar as the Code contained rules more favorable to the suppliers than the Community rules, it was automatically binding on the Member States in their relations with firms originating in the Community, under principle of Community preference.

In spite of those considerations, the Commission proposed the adoption of a new directive. Its argument was that Directive No. 77/62/EEC, coordinating procedures for awarding public supply contracts,[127] only governs "access to public contracts at intra-Community level, and does not apply to products originating in non-member countries supplied from those countries."[128] So "the implementation of this Agreement is not therefore in itself enough to change existing Community law."[129] The Commission thought that "the Directive cannot continue to apply, as it stands, to the purchasing entities covered both by it and by the Agreement without creating the possibility of their becoming subject to two sets of irreconcilable arrangements."[130] So the Commission prepared a proposal for a Council directive amending Directive No. 77/62/EEC,[131] and the Council asked the opinion of the Parliament on this proposal, based on Article 100 of the EEC treaty.[132] The Commission proposed inserting the rules of the code in the directive in order to create a single instrument, as had been done with antidumping and customs valuation legislation. Unlike the directive, however, the code deals only with contracts concluded by central (national or federal) authorities, and not with public supply contracts under all public authorities. It does not apply to services, but only to products and, in some cases, services directly linked to the supply of products. It deals only with purchases made by civil authorities or by military organizations for civil purposes. But the threshold of application to the contracts concerned is lower than in the directive (150,000 SDR [Special Drawing Rights], i.e., 140,000 EUA [European Units of Account][133] in lieu of 200,000 EUA), and the code provides for more openness and publicity surrounding procedure.

The Commission indicated the purposes of the proposed directive in an (unpublished) explanatory memorandum.

> In seeking a suitable solution to the problem [raised by a situation in which the contracting authorities to which both the Directive and the Agreement apply would be required to apply both sets of arrangements] the Commission's first concern has been not to relinquish, even in part, what has been achieved in this field under Community legislation and, secondly, to retain the directive as the sole instrument for extending access to contracts within the Community. The Commission has decided, therefore in accordance with the orientation set out in its report of 8 October 1979 on the Geneva GATT MTN COM (79) 514 final, in favour of aligning the provisions of Directive 77/62/EEC to those of the MTN Agreement insofar as the latter are more favourable to suppliers in the area covered by the two instruments.[134]

In the Council, the approach proposed by the Commission yielded to adoption of a more limited directive 80/767/EEC[135] that would serve the unique purpose of implementing the agreement. So the text only deals with the obligations of central authorities, the lowering of the threshold for the contracts concerned, the augmentation of the time limits, and the openness of the procedure. Two advantages of a separate directive have been cited. The first is purely political; the German government would not need to consult the Länder in the Bundesrat, a consultation that would have been imposed if Directive 77/62/EEC was to be modified. The other advantage is that a more limited directive would be easier to modify after the revision had been made within three years.

So Directive 77/62/EEC remains as a separate text. It is only changed by Directive 80/767/EEC as far as it is necessary to comply with the code.

The Commission tried to resolve drafting problems when elaborating its initial proposal; the language of GATT agreements is often more flexible or ambiguous than the Community language, and the Commission had to decide either to use the looser drafting of the code or to precisely define every concept used in it. In its report, the Parliament pointed to one example of "a very imprecise formulation which can be the source of legal contestations" in the original draft proposal. Artice V, Section 7 of the Government Procurement Code allows additional suppliers to bid under certain conditions. The paragraph adds: "The number of additional suppliers permitted to participate shall be limited only by the efficient operation of the procurement system." Those words were translated—too loosely for the Parliament—in Article 9 of the proposal, as follows: "The number of such suppliers shall be limited only by the need to ensure the effective operation of the procedure for awarding contracts." This version was somewhat less obscure, but the authorities concerned retained a great deal of discretion.

The Commission had also proposed more adequate drafting on other points. It will be sufficient to quote Article V, Section 13, paragraph c of the code and compare it with the text of Article 7 of the initally proposed directive. The code provides that: Entities shall reply *promptly* to any *reasonable* request for *relevant information* submitted by a supplier participating in the tendering procedure . . ." (emphasis added). The proposed directive read as follows on that point: "The *contract documents* and *supporting documents* shall be sent to candidates who request them . . . within *four working days* of receiving such request" (emphasis added). So the rule appeared to have gained legal precision. Nevertheless, in its definitive version the directive does not intend to concretize the provisions of Articles V and VI of the Government Procurement Code. Instead, Article 7 of the directive points out a guiding principle for the Member States:

> For the purposes of the award of public contracts by the contracting authorities referred to in Article 1(1), Member States shall apply in their relations conditions as favourable as those which they grant to third countries in implementation of the Agreement, in particular those in Articles V and VI on the selective procedure, information and review.[136]

The Member States are given more autonomy in adopting measures compatible with the code, in consultation with the Advisory Committee for Public Contracts.

Member States were required to adapt their legislation to the directive and the code no later than January 1, 1981, but not all the states were able to do so. A GATT document gives the precise status of this question.[137]

It is worthwhile to observe that the directive analyzed above was the only text of implementation submitted by the Council to the Parliament for consultation.[138] It was indeed a case where consultation was compulsory under Article 100 of the EEC Treaty. Theoretically a consultation for the other texts was also possible on an optional basis, but there were many measures that had to be adopted before January 1, 1980. The only possibility would have been to consult the Parliament on the results of the Tokyo Round and on the measures of implementation at the same time. It is also fair to remember that the great majority of the Community acts deal with transposing the provisions of the agreements and that the Parliament did consider the Commission's final report expressing in general terms intentions concerning the implementation of the agreements.

The Problem of the Direct Effect of the Agreements

The problem of the possible direct effect of international agreements concluded by the Community was treated by the Court of Justice in some well-known decisions—*International Fruit Co.*,[139] others in the same vein, like *Schlüter*,[140] and *Bresciani*.[141]

International Fruit Co. (also called the GATT decision) is particularly interesting for our subject because it deals with the problem of the GATT's effect on internal Community law. The Court decided that international law was superior to Community law, but denied that the GATT had any direct effect on the legal order of the Community in that case. The structure of the GATT appeared to the Court of Justice as an obstacle to a direct effect. The Court mentioned in particular that:

> cet accord, fondé aux termes de son préambule, sur le principe de négociations entreprises sur "une base de réciprocité et d'avantages mutuels", est caractérisé par la grande souplesse de ses dispositions, notamment de celles qui concernent les possibilités de dérogation, les mesures pouvant être prises en présence de difficultés exceptionnelles et le règlement des différends entre les parties contractantes.[142]

In this respect the Court mentions:

1. The obligation of the Contracting Parties to enter into consultations either bilateral (Article XXII, Section 1) or multilateral (Article XXV, Section 1)
2. The provisions for the resolution of disputes (Article XXIII), including the possibility for the Contracting Parties to authorize a Contracting Party to suspend the application of some concession or obligation resulting from the GATT, and the right to terminate membership
3. The unilateral suspension of an obligation[143] in case of serious injury—either after consultation, or, in case of emergency and as a provisional measure, without prior consultation (Article XIX)

The Court concluded from its analysis of the GATT that Article XI (quantitative restrictions), Article II (irreversibility of tariff concession),[144] and bilateral agreements on customs duties, pursuant to Article XXVIII (2) "ne sont pas de nature à engendrer, pour les justiciables de la Communauté, le droit de s'en prévaloir en justice.[145]

Since the *International Fruit Co.* and *Schlüter* decisions, there had not been till very recently[146] another opportunity for the Court to confirm or modify its jurisprudence on the effect of the GATT in the Community legal order, which has been heavily criticized by an number of writers. Professor Waelbroeck particularly objected to the Court's accent on the possibility of derogations and the nonlegal process of dispute resolutions in the GATT, and he supported an interpretation of direct effect based on the exact wording of the GATT's provisions.[147]

We must also mention in this context the *Nederlandse Spoorwegen* decision,[148] in which the Court stressed the importance, for the application of international agreements in the field of commercial policy, of the principle of substitution of the Community in its Member States' international obligations. The Court held:

> de même, la Communauté étant substituée aux Etats membres, en ce qui concerne l'exécution des engagements prévus par le GATT, l'effet juridique contraignant de ces engagements doit être apprécié par rapport aux dispositions afférentes dans l'ordre juridique communautaire et non par rapport à celles qui leur donnaient précédemment effet dans les ordres juridiques nationaux.[149]

That pronouncement means that when engaged in a problem of applying the GATT or a related agreement to which the Community is a party, a national tribunal is not allowed to decide pursuant to the criteria that normally apply to international agreements. It must abide by the rules that apply in the legal order of the Community as a result of the jurisprudence of the Court of Justice, with due reference to the Court pursuant to the procedure of preliminary rulings if there is no such jurisprudence or if the jurisdiction considers that a change in the Court's jurisprudence is possible and desirable. Thus the unpublished decision of a tribunal of Milan—of April 2, 1980—giving effect to Article XX, Section 1 of the GATT without reference to the Court under Article 177 of the EEC Treaty is contrary to the EEC Treaty as well as to the GATT system itself.

The Court's denial of the direct effect of GATT provisions was also noteworthy because there is a divergence between German and Italian decisions on that point. The Italian Supreme Court has decided that an act of its parliament that was adopted after Italy has adhered to the GATT and was contrary to the GATT rules was inapplicable to that extent. The German courts, on the other hand, refused the direct applicability of the GATT.[150]

The *Bresciani* decision of February 5, 1976, though not dealing with the GATT or obligations deriving from negotiations pursuant to it, is a very important step in the development of the direct effect of international agreements concluded by the Community.[151] The decision concerns the effect of Article 2, Paragraph 1 of the Yaoundé Convention of 1963. It is the same as Article 13, Section 2 of the EEC Treaty, a provision bearing on elimination of quantitative restrictions, which the Court recognized has direct effect. But in deciding in favor of the same effect for the Yaoundé Convention, the Court did not consider the wording of the provision decisive. It analyzed "l'esprit, l'économie et les termes de la Convention et de la disposition visée" and concluded that the absence of reciprocity in the obligations contracted by the Community and the African states and Madagascar was not an obstacle to direct effect because it was in the very nature of such an agreement to favor the development of the associated partners. The Court decided that "ce déséquilibre dans les obligations assumées par la Communauté vis-à-vis des Etats associés qui est dans la logique même du caractère spécifique de la Convention, n'est pas un obstacle à la reconnaissance par la Communauté de l'effet direct de certaines de ses dispositions.[152]

The Court's insistence that the absence of reciprocity was not an obstacle to the direct effect of the obligations contracted by the Community and its Member States must be understood in the context of its statements in the *International Fruit Co.* decision about the structure of the GATT, which was based on the principle of reciprocity and mutually advantageous arrangements. Is it possible to conclude that the agreements that result from the Tokyo Round would not have direct effect in the Community legal order, since the same principle is also essential in those agreements? Must they remain at the level of international obligations, the situation of the enterprises or individuals concerned being regulated in internal law only by the Community and national legislation?

In a 1982 case—referred to as the *Polydor* case—concerning the interpretation of the Free-Trade Agreement between the EEC and Portugal, the Commission defended the argument that

> the concept of direct effect, as developed in Community law, must not as such be transposed to the field of the Community's international relations, for two reasons. The first is based on the different nature and aims of international agreements. The second reason is that it is necessary to maintain in the context of these free-trade agreements a balance of the advantages and disadvantages which may exist between the parties to an international treaty.[153]

The Commission noted, among other things, that the balance is substantially different if private parties can enforce an international agreement within the Community but cannot do so in other contracting states. The Commission proposed that "the Court should recognize direct effect only where the provisions are drafted in an entirely clear way for all the parties or where provisions which leave room for interpretation have been clarified by the contracting parties."[154]

The Court did not decide on direct effect in its *Polydor* decision. It avoided answering the question put by the Court of Appeal of England and Wales and extensively treated before the Court by Polydor, the Commission, and the agents of the governments of Denmark, France, Germany, the Netherlands, and the United Kingdom. It did this by limiting itself to analyzing the difference between the interpretation of restrictions on trade in goods pursuant on the one hand to the Treaty of Rome and on the other to the Free-Trade Agreement. The Court justified the distinction by considering that the two treaties did not have the same purpose. The purpose of the Free-Trade Agreement is to consolidate and extend the economic relations between the Community and Portugal; the Treaty of Rome seeks to unite national markets into a single market with the characteristics of a domestic market.

In a decision of October 26, 1982, not yet published, *Kupferberg,* the court has ruled in favor of the direct effect of Article 21, Paragraph 1 of the same agreement between the EEC and Portugal. The decision prohibits fiscal discrimination against the products imported from the other party to the agreement. The Court stated that the contracting parties to an agreement could limit the internal effect of its dispositions. But in the absence of the expression of such a common will, and especially of any indication in the agreement about the way it should be implemented, it is up to each party to determine appropriate ways to achieve the ends of the agreement. So the fact that courts of one party might make some dispositions of an agreement directly applicable and courts of another might not does not by itself warrant finding an absence of reciprocity in the implementation of the agreement. The Court also mentioned that the existence of an institutional framework for consultations and negotiations on the application of the agreement does not prevent the courts from directly applying the agreement. Furthermore, the existence of specific escape clauses does not by itself affect the direct applicability of some provisions of the agreement. So the Court concluded that neither the nature nor the policy of the agreement prevents a private party from involving a disposition of the agreement before a national tribunal.

This conclusion has important implications. It suggests that there is no theoretical obstacle against the direct effect of an agreement resulting from the MTN. The unconditionality and the preciseness of the provision, which must be examined within the framework of each agreement, is the test that the Court will likely apply.

It also appears that the nature of the Council's act approving an international agreement—decision or regulation—is irrelevant to the problem of direct effect. We have mentioned that the Council has approved the Yaoundé Convention by a decision, and that the same form was used to approve the MTN agreements.[155]

The jurisprudence of the Court demonstrates that it is the very nature of a particular provision of Community law—of which international law is a part—that determines its direct effect. Is the provision clear, precise, and unconditional? To what extent are any of its elements discretionary? The simple fact that the rule needs implementation measures does not deprive it of direct effect. The existence of a margin of discretion is the determining criterion. The judge cannot rely on loose standards or best efforts clauses that are only rules of conduct for the authorities concerned. If there is no room for discretion and if the implementation measure does not conform to the result pursued by the international or Community obligation, the judge may check the implementation measure against the international or Community rule. A well-established jurisprudence exists now on the direct effect of EEC directives. The judge can disregard a national measure incompatible with an EEC directive that the state has not implemented if the obligation concerned is precise and unconditional.[156] He can also compare the implementation measure and the result prescribed by the directive.[157]

In the case of the MTN agreements, the problem is somewhat more complex. One hypothesis would be that a citizen of a non-EEC state would be allowed to contest a national measure (of a Member State) before a Court of a Member State, alleging that this measure is not applicable to him in spite of its conformity to a Community regulation or directive, because the latter is not compatible with a provision of an international agreement concluded by the Community. This was clearly the problem raised before the Court in the *International Fruit Co.* case, where national measures preventing imports were based on regulations of the Commission that were allegedly inconsistent with the GATT.

The fact that the Community act is a regulation or a directive does not in itself make a difference from the point of view of Community law. There may be a problem in both cases if the national measure is a statute and if the national jurisdiction does not admit the supremacy of Community law on legislative measures.[158]

We do not think that the existence of a system of solution of disputes that includes the possibility that the obligations contracted by the agreement will be suspended is an obstacle to the recognition of direct effect of provisions of an MTN agreement. It can be said that if the Contracting Party concerned has not decided to seek recourse in consultation and in the Managing Committee of the agreement, there is no reason to deprive an individual enterprise of the rights deriving from the agreement. A possible violation in a tendering procedure for government purchases might be mentioned in this respect.

Producers in a GATT Contracting Party can invoke the invalidity of an antidumping regulation of the EEC before a national tribunal of a Member State, just as they can require the annulment of this regulation before the Court of Justice if their action is considered admissible—that is, if they have a direct and individual interest in the annulment of the act concerned.[159] The action before the national tribunal in this respect may be directed against the—purely automatic—national acts of execution of the Community regulation.

As the Court has expressed in its *Kupferberg* decision, the absence of reciprocity, that is, the inability to call directly on a provision of the agreement (and not just on national legislation of implementation) before the tribunals of another Contracting Party, does not bind a judge of a Member State to deny direct effect to a provision of the agreement in the Community legal order. The other Contracting Parties' application of the agreement does not derive only from the attitude of their judicial authorities. It is a broader question, the appraisal of which is not just for the judiciaries of the Member States of the Communities.

On the other hand, before a national tribunal it is not possible for an enterprise to complain directly of a violation by a foreign country of an international rule like the Antidumping Code in respect to products originating in other Contracting Parties that are not members of the EEC. The Community regulation, in conformity with the GATT code, provides a special procedure normally initiated by a request by or on behalf of the industry affected (see Article 5 of the Antidumping Code and of Reg. [EEC] No. 3017/79). The national judge cannot interfere with this procedure and substitute his own judgment for that of the Commission on the existence of dumping or of subsidy, the existence and extent of injury, the causal link between the dumped or subsidized imports and injury, the measures that are appropriate to prevent or remedy the injury caused by dumping or the subsidy, and means of putting such measures into effect (Reg. [EEC] No. 3017/79, Article 6). Those decisions require a thorough examination of a very complex economic situation from a unified Community view. The authority to impose antidumping or countervailing duties by way of regulations (Article 13) is within the exclusive jurisdiction of the Community because it is a measure of common commercial policy under Article 113. In the antidumping field, the Community has not been satisfied just to adopt common principles; it has unified the rules and the procedure of application in such a way that the intervention of a Member state is, as we have pointed out in discussing the jurisprudence of the Court, purely automatic.

For those reasons, the action of the tribunal of Milan,[160] based on Article XX, Paragraph 1 of the GATT, in halting by an emergency decision the importing to Italy of some fibers originating in the United States because American producers were benefiting from the "artificial advantages" of abnormal prices of oil and natural gas seems objectionable.

General Appraisal

We can now formulate some conclusions from the analysis we have presented.

Professor Jackson has stressed the important differences between the EEC legal system of negotiating international trade agreements and that of the United States.[161] The original feature of this EEC system consists of the close collaboration between the Council, the organ of conclusion, and the Commission, the organ of negotiation.

The Council's great influence on the process of negotiation has often been described. There is a sort of balance between the Council's right to give the Commission directives for negotiation (which are often very precise) and the Commission's right to ask for modifications of those directives during the course of a negotiation. The preciseness of the directives handicaps the bargaining power of the Commission but there is some flexibility in the fact that they can be modified.

In the case of the MTN, impressions derived from a first overview of the global process are that the Commission generally received the directives it asked for. Typical examples were the adoption of the Swiss formula for tariff reductions or the tactical approach for the presentation of tariff concessions. The difficulties between the two institutions, if one excepts some minor problems,[162] appeared when the Community had to solve highly sensitive political questions such as the attitude toward the position of the United States on the waiver problem at the end of 1978, or the authority of the Community and the Member States to conclude the agreements.

The absence of major difficulties between the two institutions during the negotiations is due to the close collaboration of the Commission with the Committee of Article 113, as we have described. This collaboration was effective for the preparation of the Community positions of negotiation as well as for the conduct of the negotiations themselves. For example, during the aborted attempt to reach a global agreement in July 1978, simultaneous negotiations were conducted with the titular members of Committee 113 under the chairmanship of an official of the Commission, and by the Commission with the other Contracting Parties.

The highly technical features of the negotiations augmented the role of experts. The Commission's officials proceeded to the current negotiations with the collaboration of an ad hoc committee of national experts. Those experts were well informed about the requisites of the national industries concerned, with which, of course, they had a very close relationship. The role of those experts explains why it is very difficult to identify interventions of industrial or other pressure groups during the negotiation. They usually act at the national level.

On the other hand, the central position of the Commission and its role in the negotiations explain why the other Contracting Parties prefer to address themselves to that institution and not to the Council or to each Member State of the Community. It was very difficult for such third states to enter into bilateral contacts in order to influence the position of the Community when it had six members. With ten members or more it is—and will be—almost impossible. The mediation capacity of the Commission is thus incrementally increased.

If the process of negotiation is effective, it is not democratic. In two or three Member States, national parliaments have been asked to approve some agreements resulting from the MTN. But with the development of the commercial policy of the Community it is possible that their intervention will not be required in the future. If the jurisprudence of the Court is respected, mixed agreements will become exceptional in the case of treaties that are essentially concerned with commercial policy. The national parliaments' loss of power is not balanced by the assumption of like powers by the European Parliament. Under the Treaty of Rome the Parliament need not be consulted on trade agreements. The Parliament will probably ask for a more effective role in external affairs, particularly in trade agreements that traditionally are subject to parliamentary approval under the constitutional law of the Member States. It is also likely that the Parliament will introduce more political considerations in the examination of trade agreements.

If the European Parliament has little influence in negotiating and concluding trade agreements, implementing them is also a responsibility of the other EEC institutions unless the necessary measures are to be based on another provision of the treaty that should require a previous consultation of the Parliament, such as Article 100. But in principle, Article 113 is the correct legal basis for both the conclusion and the implementation of agreements that do not exceed the field broadly considered commercial policy. The Parliament is not consulted on unilateral measures adopted by the Community to implement the agreements, and one can almost say that the entire process of implementation escapes its attention. That is why Sir John Steward-Clark, member of the European Parliament, asked the Commission to ensure that "regular annual reports are made available to us in the Parliament on the success of the implementation of the GATT Agreements."[163]

The implementation of the MTN agreements raises another set of questions. We have noticed the Community's practice of transposing the provisions of the agreements into Community law through the adoption of directives or regulations. There is a risk that the international origin of the rules will disappear, particularly where national law and regulations have to complete Community acts. The Community's implementation of the MTN agreements raises the problem of the effectiveness of their provisions in the Community legal order. It is clear from the jurisprudence of the Court of Justice that international law has primacy over Community secondary legislation, both prior and subsequent, but if the judge denies that the agreements have direct effect he cannot give an international agreement priority. So the problem of direct effect is crucial. In the absence of jurisprudence on the question, as far as the MTN results are concerned this author concludes that to the extent that they are part of Community law and superior to secondary legislation the national judge should be allowed to take them into consideration and give them priority if there is a real conflict between a provision of an agreement and a provision of Community law.

But the problem of implementation of the MTN results is not

merely legal. It is also a problem of political will and of practical means. Problems raised by dumped or subsidized imports, government procurement, and access to certification are charged with great political connotations. The pressures coming from political, national, or regional authorities and the industries concerned will be great. The difficulties faced by the Commission in implementing parallel rules in intra-Community relations show that there is no guarantee that the effect of the MTN codes will be miraculous. The Commission does not possess all the necessary means to effectively control the application of the agreements in the Member States. No matter how precise the international and Community rules are (and they are not always very precise) there are possibilities for cheating and the resurgence of protectionism. Facing national administrations implementing complex national regulations, the Commission cannot—as in other sectors of Community law—fully exercise its role as watchdog of the Community. It is also clear that its zeal will be proportional to the goodwill of the partners of the Community.

NOTES

1. Belgium, the Federal Republic of Germany, France, Italy, Luxembourg, and the Netherlands were the original six nations.
2. In 1973, Denmark, Ireland, and the United Kingdom joined the European Communities (EEC, EURATOM, and ECSC), and on January 1, 1981, Greece became the tenth member of the Communities. Portugal and Spain are also expected to join.
3. Technically, there are three European Communities, based on three separate treaties: the ECSC, based on the treaty signed in Paris on April 18, 1951; EURATOM, based on the treaty signed in Rome on March 25, 1957, and the European Economic Community, established by another Treaty signed at Rome on the same day. The four basic institutions of the three European Communities are the Commission, the Council, the Court of Justice and the Assembly (the European Parliament). A convention annexed to the two Rome treaties provided for a single Court of Justice and a single European Parliament to apply the three Community treaties, but it was not until 1965 that a single Council and a single Commission were established. Since this merger a particular institution has played a role for all three communities, although that role may differ according to which community is being represented. The Commission has fourteen members (one from each Member State, plus an additional member from each of the four major states). It is analogous to the executive arm of government and administers the largest bureaucracy (about 9,000 permanent officials). The Council is composed of a representative from each Member State (a minister) and is designed primarily

to decide on policy and pass legislative initiatives presented to it by the Commission.

The third institution is the Court of Justice, which sits in Luxembourg and has eleven judges and five advocate generals. The Court has fairly ample jurisdiction to decide questions of interpretation involving the basic treaties, regulations, directives, and other EEC acts, and international agreements and other legal matters of the EEC. Finally, there is the European Parliament, which since 1979 has been chosen by direct elections in the Member States, but has limited powers, except in financial matters.

The EEC can act by adopting various formal instruments, termed regulations, directives, decisions, and so on. These are normally adopted by the Council upon a proposal from the Commission. A regulation has immediate and direct applicability in the Community. Directives were designed to provide a means by which the EEC could direct Member States to take action to carry out an objective either general or particular laid down in the instrument. However, this has not prevented the Court of Justice from ruling that portions of a directive could have direct effect for individuals or enterprises. A decision is an act that applies to particular cases and particular persons.

The Council, or Council of Ministers, meets with different members of the governments of the Member States depending on the matter concerned. For example, when the ministers of foreign affairs of the Members States meet, the Council is called the Council (of Ministers) of Foreign or General Affairs. The Council also has a secretariat, including a legal service, and has a number of subordinate committees or bodies, such as the COREPER (Committee of Permanent Representatives), or the Committee of Article 113 (explained in the text).

In recent years there has also developed a European Council, i.e., meetings of the Council at the level of the heads of government from the Member States. Although there is no written constitutional status for the European Council, nevertheless its decisions generally have great force within the Community, since the prime ministers or presidents can subsequently instruct their representatives in the regular EEC Council to act in accordance with the decisions of the European Council.

Parallel to the procedures established by the treaties is, of course, the very important process of political cooperation in the field of foreign policy. Heads of government in the European Council and ministers of foreign affairs meet to coordinate the foreign policies of the Member States and to achieve common positions.

4. *See* C.O. KIM, LA COMMUNAUTÉ ÉCONOMIQUE EUROPÉENNE DANS LES RELATIONS COMMERCIALES INTERNATIONALES 103–05 (1971).

5. Article 228, Section 1 of the Treaty of Rome states:

> Where this Treaty provides for the conclusion of agreements between the Community and one or more states or an international organization, such agreements shall be negotiated by the Commission. Subject to the powers vested in the Commission in this field, such agreements

shall be concluded by the Council, after consulting the Assembly where required by this Treaty.
The Council, the Commission or a Member State may obtain beforehand the opinion of the Court of Justice as to whether an agreement envisaged is compatible with the provisions of this Treaty. Where the opinion of the Court of Justice is adverse, the agreement may enter into force only in accordance with Article 236.

6. *See* Article 4 of the treaty signed on April 8, 1965, merging the institutions of the three communities.
7. *See* Weiler, *The European Parliament and Foreign Affairs: External Relations of the European Economic Community,* in PARLIAMENTARY CONTROL OVER FOREIGN POLICY 151, 156. (A. Cassese ed. 1980).
8. *Id.* and the authors quoted in that article. It might more accurately be said that the Council is reluctant to authorize the Commission to open and conduct negotiations, because the Commission has the capacity to negotiate under the terms of the treaty, as the author mentions.
9. An informal intervention of the European Parliament usually takes place before the conclusion of negotiations, as we shall see later on.
10. *See supra* note 3.
11. Article 113 of the EEC Treaty is quoted in the text under the section entitled Overview of EEC External Relations Law, and Article 228, Section 1, is quoted *supra* note 5.
12. BULL. EUR. COM. (No. 3) 58–60 (1972).
13. The participants in such meetings are the President of France and the heads of government (prime ministers, chancellors, presidents of the council of ministers, and so on) of the other Member States. The previous meeting took place in The Hague on December 1 and 2, 1969. Since 1975 those meetings have been replaced by those of the European Council. *See supra* note 3.
14. See the final declaration of the Summit. BULL. EUR. COMM. (No. 10) 15–25 (1972).
15. This principle had also been stressed in the declaration of December 12, 1971 and in the joint declaration of February 11, 1972.
16. Le Monde, May 16, 1973, at 38, col. 2; La Libre Belgique, May 16, 1973; THE ECONOMIST, June 9, 1973, at 11–12.
17. Le Monde, May 26 and 27–28, 1973. See the text of the Commission of April 9, as amended on May 22, 1973 in BULL. EUR. COMM. (No. 2) (Supp. 1973).
18. Le Monde, May 27–28, 1973, at 23, col. 3.
19. Lemaitre, *Pour une Réciprocité Effective,* Le Monde, May 27–28, 1973, at 23, col. 3.
20. The text was adopted after an unconcluded debate on June 4. *See* Doc. I/135/73 (COMER 42). See *supra* note 3 for explanation of the Council of Ministers of Foreign Affairs.
21. Le Monde, June 27, 1973.
22. *See* BULL. EUR. COMM. (No. 9) 8–9 (1973).
23. For a general view of the second amendment, see J. GOLD, THE SECOND

AMENDMENT OF THE FUND'S ARTICLES OF AGREEMENTS (IMF Pamphlet No. 25, 1978).

24. The Council adopted directives for the MTN during its session on February 10, 1975, often referred to as the "*basic directives* given to the Commission" (emphasis added), for example, in an answer to written question No. 821/78 by Vincent Ansquer, member of the European Parliament. 22 O.J. EUR. COMM. (No. C 92) 4 (1979). But it did not formally modify those directives in its further meetings during the active negotiation phase.
25. Informal translations are: "elaborated or outlined in the context of GATT," and "This does not signify that all of the elements of this working hypothesis for the negotiations are accepted as such. The Council charges the Commission to pursue, in contact with the Special committee of Article 113, study of solutions that are precise and mutually acceptable in the different domains."
26. *See* EUROPE: DAILY BULL. (No. 2653) at 4 (Apr. 4, 1979).
27. Problems related to the Tokyo Round were also raised at other sessions of the Council: on December 3 and 4, 1973; January 20 and 21, 1974; April 5 and October 18, 1977; March 7, May 2, and June 6, 1978; May 8, June 12, July 24, and October 22 and 29, 1979.
28. See point 7 of the conclusions of the Council of January 17, 1978.
29. An informal translation is: "Without prejudice to Article 7 of the conclusions above, the Council considers that the average final reduction applicable to the community tariff will be in a zone defined by the directives of negotiation established by the Council on February 1975, with a maximum amount of 35 percent, taking account of the past experience, probable exceptions, and adjustments in the light of results of non-tariff negotiations."
30. 16 O.J. EUR. COMM. (No. C 14) 16, (1973). *See also* 1963–1964 EUR. PARL. DOC. (No. 31) (1963), and resolution of June 27, 1963.
31. *See generally* Weiler, *supra* note 7, at 163; Quintin, *Participation de l'Assemblée parlementaire européenne au déroulement de la procédure de négociation des accords commerciaux,* 11 REV. TRIM. DR. EUR. 221 (1975); H.W. RENGELING, ZU DEN BEFUGNISSEN DES EUROPÄISCHEN PARLAMENTS BEIM ABSCHLUSS VÖLKERRECHTLICHER VERTRÄGE IM RAHMEN DER GEMEINSCHAFTSVERFASSUNG: FESTSCHRIFT FÜR H.J. SCHLOCHAUER 877–98 (Ingo von Münch, ed. 1981).
32. Formally adopted on October 15, 1973, the procedure had been suggested and already applied at the end of 1972. The first case of application was the conclusion of the first commercial agreement in Egypt, in 1972. *See* E. GRABITZ & TH. LAUFER, DAS EUROPAISCHE PARLAMENT 165 (1980).
33. In French: "substance."
34. In French: "teneur."
35. Weiler, *supra* note 7, at 171, gives an example of the effectiveness of the procedure in the case of the preferential trade agreements with Egypt in 1972:

The relevant parliamentary committees were informed confidentially prior to the signature on 18 December 1972. An amendment by way of protocol was inserted as a result of comments made by the Committee of External Economic Relations. It was then debated in Parliament, on 10 May, which once again called for a better consultation procedure and implementation of all suggestions in the Giraudo report (which led to resolution of 17 February 1973). The agreement was finally concluded in October 1973.

36. BULL. EUR. COMM. (No. 6) 10 (1973).
37. *See* Rengeling, *supra* note 31, at 885.
38. *Id.* at 885–86.
39. Weiler, *supra* note 7, at 154–57. *See also* Quintin, *supra* note 31.
40. 1973–1974 EUR. PARL. DOC. (No. 118) (1973). The UDE (European Democratic Union, now the Union of European Progress Democrats) is the Gaullist group in the Parliament.
41. 1975–1976 EUR. PARL. DOC. (No. 106) (1975).
42. There was a debate in the Parliament on this topic on March 12, 1975, but it is worthwhile to note that it was triggered by an oral question put by Mr. Cousté in the name of the European Progress Democrats and not by an initiative of the competent committee. *See* 1974–1975 EUR. PARL. DOC. (No. 521) (1975).
43. 1978–1979 EUR. PARL. DEB. (No. 231) Annex at 297 (June 16, 1978). 1978–1979 EUR. PARL. DOC. (No. 86) (1978), resolution of June 16, 1978.
44. Following Parliament regulations, there are three sorts of oral questions: oral questions without debate, oral questions with debate (Article 47) and oral questions put during the question time.
45. 1978–1979 EUR. PARL. DOC. (No. 454) (1978).
46. 1978–1979 EUR. PARL. DOC. (No. 483) (1978). The European Progress Democrats were represented by Mr. de la Malène.
47. 1978–1979 EUR. PARL. DOC. (No. 485) (1978). The Parliament members were Jochen Van Aerssen and others.
48. *See supra* note 45.
49. 1979–1980 EUR. PARL. DEB. (No. 237) 158 (Dec. 13, 1978). *See also* written question No. 821/78 by Mr. Ansquer to the Council, 22 O.J. EUR. COMM. (No. C 92) 4 (1979).
50. *See, e.g.,* written question No. 1256/77 by Mr. Cousté, 21 O.J. EUR. COMM. (No. C 124) 42 (1978), or oral question by Lothar Krall, 1977–1978 EUR. PARL. DEB. (No. 216) 246 (Apr. 22, 1977).
51. *See* question by William Hamilton, 1977–1978 EUR. PARL. DOC. (No. 197) (1977); question No. 20 by John Osborn 1978–1979 EUR. PARL. DEB. (No. 207) 99 (Oct. 13, 1976); and question No. 296/77 by Gérard Bordu, 20 O.J. EUR. COMM. (No. C 233) 13 (1977).
52. *See* written questions No. 821/78 and No. 107/79 by Mr. Ansquer (Communist group) 22 O.J. EUR. COMM. (No. C 92) 4 (1979); 22 O.J. EUR. COMM. (No. C 205) 6 (1979).
53. *See* EUROPE: DAILY BULL. (No. 2654) (April 5–6, 1979); Fin. Econ. Tijd, March 7, 1979.

54. Italy removed its ultimate objections some days after the meeting of the Council. An informal translation would be, "At the end of a five-year-long stage of reduction, the Community will examine whether, taking into account the economic, social, and monetary situation, and the application by the partners of the various engagements undertaken during the MTN, it is in a position to pass to a second stage."
55. Some negotiations took place until July 1979, and the Community did not officially drop the possibility of an agreement on selective escape clauses until then.
56. On the procedure within the Council, see Bourgeois, *The Tokyo Round Agreements on Technical Barriers and on Government Procurement in International and EEC Perspective,* 19 COMMON MKT. L. REV. 5, 21–22 (1982).
57. Commission of the European Communities v. Council of the European Communities, 1971 E. Comm. Ct. J. Rep. 264, 275.
58. *See, inter alia,* Opinion of the Court Given Pursuant to Act. 228 of the EEC Treaty of 11 November 1975, 1975 E. Comm. Ct. J. Rep. 1355.
59. This fact is important because it had been argued among the delegations that on the points where an agreement existed between the two legal services, the decision of the Council should be in favor of a conclusion by the Community alone; in the absence of such agreement, there should be a joint conclusion by the Community and its Member States, at least for some agreements.
60. *GATT Multilateral Trade Negotiations-Final Report on the GATT Multilateral Trade Negotiations in Geneva (Tokyo Round)* [hereinafter cited as *Report*] and proposal for Council decision, COM (79) 514 final.
61. *Report, supra* note 60, at 35.
62. This will be discussed later in this chapter.
63. Written question No. 1697/79 by Hanna Walz to the Council (Feb. 11, 1980) 23 O.J. EUR. COMM. (No. C 156) 41 (1980).
64. Unpublished Decision of the Representatives of the Governments of the Member States of the ECSC convened in the Council of July 22, 1974.
65. *See* Decision of the Representatives of the Governments of the Member States of the ECSC convened in the Council of December 10, 1979. 23 O.J. EUR. COMM. (No. L 71) 179 (1980).
66. Steenbergen, *The Tokyo Round,* 28 SOCIAAL ECONOMISCHE WETGEVING 752, 762–63 n.51 (1980). *Compare* Bourgeois, *supra* note 56, at 22–23.
67. On this question, see Steenbergen, *supra* note 66, at 763, and Bourgeois, *supra* note 56, at 22–23.
68. Steenbergen, *The Status of GATT in Community Law,* 15 J. WORLD TRADE L. 337, 344 (1981).
69. Steenbergen, *supra* note 68, at 339 n.8. *See also* GATT Doc. L/4914/Rev. 5 at 1 (Nov. 13, 1981).
70. *See also* the answer of the Commission to written question No. 2444/79 by Karel Van Miert, 23 O.J. EUR. COMM. (No. C 105) 31 (1980).
71. *See* BULL. EUR. COMM. (No. 12) 74 (1979).
72. Decision of December 10, 1979, Article 2 (Multilateral Agreements). 23 O.J. EUR. COMM. (No. L 71) 2 (1980).

73. Decision of December 10, 1979, Article 2 (Bilateral Agreements). 23 O.J. Eur. Comm. (No. L. 71) 130 (1980).
74. MTN/FR/6.
75. *Report, supra* note 60, Part III, at 129.
76. On this problem, see Maresceau, *The Effect of Community Agreements in the U.K.*, 28 Int'l & Comp. L.Q. 241, 246 (1979). This author mentions an exception: the decision of March 22, 1972, of the Council approving the Fourth International Tin Agreement, 15 O.J. Eur. Comm. (No. L 90) 1 (1972). This decision was taken and published before all the Member States had ratified this multilateral convention.
77. This might occur, for example, in a preliminary ruling requested by a national tribunal under Article 177 of the EEC Treaty.
78. See Steenbergen, *supra* note 68, at 343–44 and Bourgeois, *supra* note 56, at 29, on the impossibility of stating clearly—and the interest in *not* stating clearly—where the dividing line between the respective powers of the EEC and its Member States lies.
79. Written question No. 1697/99 from Mrs. Walz on Feb. 11, 1980. 23 Eur. Comm. (No. C 156) 42 (1980). U.S. legislation authorizing and implementing the MTN agreements was adopted by the Congress and President in July 1979. This statute imposed certain conditions for U.S. approval of the MTN agreements; among them were certain timing requirements that made it important for the EEC to approve and implement the agreements by January 1980. *See* chapter 4, the text accompanying note 128.
80. 23 O.J. Eur. Comm. (No. C 137) 36 (1980).
81. The insistence of (some) Member States on participating in the groups is understandable in light of their responsibility to manage some codes like the Code on Standards. Although there are indeed some two hundred directives in that field, the national standards are very numerous, as we will discuss later, in the text accompanying note 122. It is perhaps true that Commission officials are not in the best position to defend purely individual national points of view.
82. It seems that the Commission was not very happy with the possibility of unilateral intervention by a Member State and insisted on the necessity of a prior arrangement.
83. *See* 1979–1980 Eur. Parl. Doc. (No. 1-561) (1979); 23 O.J. Eur. Comm. (No. C 4) 55 (1980).
84. *See* memorandum of June 16, 1979 (EP 59.337) restricted.
85. *See* COM (79) 514 final, *supra* note 60.
86. Proposed resolution unanimously adopted by the members present less a vote and three abstentions, on November 29, 1979. *See* 1979–1980 Eur. Parl. Doc. (No. 1-561) (1979). The resolution itself has been published in 23 O.J. Eur. Comm. (No. C. 4) 55 (1980).
87. Written question No. 28/80 by Mr. Jonker, March 17, 1980. 23 O.J. Eur. Comm. (No. C. 156) 80 (1980).
88. An informal English translation of the French quoted: "authority that presupposes consultation with the assembly as a prerequisite to implementation."

89. *See* 1981–1982 EUR. PARL. DOC. (No. 1153) 6 (1981). See also the working paper prepared by Dr. van Aerssen for the Committee on External Economic Relations on April 4, 1980, quoted by Rengeling, *supra* note 31, at 887.
90. 24 O.J. EUR. COMM. (No. C 234) 52 (1981).
91. 1981–1982 EUR. PARL. DOC. (No. 1-685) (1981). In its communication of May 12, 1982 (COM (82) 177 final) on the role of the Parliament in the elaboration and conclusion of international agreements and acts of accession, the Commission did not follow all the suggestions contained in the Blumenfeld resolution, published in 25 O.J. EUR. COMM. (No. C 66) 68 (1982).
92. This procedure provides for a conciliation between Parliament and Council when the latter wishes to depart from an opinion issued by the Parliament on a proposal from the Commission that has financial implications for several years.
93. *See* Rengeling, *supra* note 31, at 894 et seq.
94. *Id.* at 895.
95. 17 O.J. EUR. COMM. (No. C 115) (1974).
96. *Id.*
97. 18 O.J. EUR. COMM. (No. C 62) (1975).
98. 20 O.J. EUR. COMM. (No. C 126) (1977).
99. On this, see 12 J.-V. LOUIS & P. BRÜCKNER, LE DROIT DE LA COMMUNAUTÉ ÉCONOMIQUE EUROPÉENNE, RELATIONS EXTÉRIEURES 62 (1981), and Bourgeois, *supra* note 56, at 24. Some authors defend the view that the Member States can be held internationally responsible for Community treaty violations. They take their argument from the draft articles on treaties concluded between states and international organizations or between international organizations, prepared by the International Law Commission ([1979] 1 Y.B. Int'l. L. Comm'n 137).

    Article 36 of this draft provides:

    > Third States which are members of an international organization shall observe the obligations, and may exercise the rights, which arise for them from the provisions of a treaty to which that organization is a party if:
    >
    > (a) the relevant rules of the organization applicable at the moment of the conclusion of the treaty provide that the States' members of the organization are bound by the treaties concluded by it; or (b) the States and organization participating in the negotiation of a treaty as well as the States' members of the organization acknowledged that the application of the treaty necessarily entails such effects.

    See Hans van Houtte, International Law and Community Treaty-Making Power, 3 NORTHWESTERN JOURNAL OF INT'L LAW & BUSINESS 633 (1981).
100. *Compare* Barav, *Oral Intervention,* in DIVISION OF POWERS BETWEEN THE E.C. AND THEIR MEMBER STATES IN THE FIELD OF EXTERNAL RELATIONS 90 (C.W.A. Timmermans and E.L.M. Völker, eds. 1981).

101. *See* Bourgeois, *Some Comments on the Practice,* in DIVISION OF POWERS BETWEEN THE E.C. AND THEIR MEMBER STATES IN THE FIELD OF EXTERNAL RELATIONS 107 (C.W.A. Timmermans and E.L.M. Völker, eds 1981).
102. Decisions of December 10, 1979. 23 O.J. EUR. COMM. (No. L. 71) (1980).
103. *See infra* notes 139, 141.
104. *See* 12 J.-V. LOUIS & P. BRÜCKNER, *supra* note 99, at 182 and references quoted there; Boulouis, *La jurisprudence de la Cour de justice des Communautés européennes relative aux relations extérieures des Communautés,* RECUEIL DES COURS: ACADEMIE DE DROIT INTERNATIONAL 343, 385–86 (1978); Tizzano, *Recenti sviluppi in tema de accordi internazionali della CEE,* DIRITTO COMUNITARIO E DEGLI SCAMBI INTERNAZIONALI 19, 34 (1981).
105. *See* GATT Doc. LIC/1/Add. 3 (July 31, 1980).
106. 18 O.J. EUR. COMM. (No. L 25) 10 (1975).
107. 23 O.J. EUR. COMM. (No. L 161) 15 (1980).
108. 23 O.J. EUR. COMM. (No. L 338) (1980).
109. *See* GATT Doc. LIC/1/Add. 8 (Mar. 11, 1981).
110. *See* chapter 4, text following note 142.
111. *Report, supra* note 60, COM (79) 514 final, at 81.
112. *See* Reg. (EEC) No. 3000/79, 22 O.J. EUR. COMM. (No. L 342) (1979).
113. Reg. (EEC) No. 3017/79, 22 O.J. EUR. COMM. (No. L 339) (1979).
114. *See* 11 O.J. EUR. COMM. (No. L 93) 1 (1968); 22 O.J. EUR. COMM. (No. L 196) 1 (1979). On this regulation, see Bellis, *La réglementation anti-dumping de la Communauté économique européenne,* CAHIERS DE DROIT EUROPÉEN [hereafter CAH. DR. EUR.] (No. 5–6) 495–539 (1979).
115. *See* Bellis, *New Community Protection against Dumping and Subsidies,* 5 EUR. L. REV. 145–47 (1980). "Whilst Regulation 459/68 based on the 1967 Code required the Community to prove that dumping was the principal cause of injury, Article 4(1) of Regulation 3017/79 only requires a showing that the dumped or subsidised imports are causing injury . . ." *Id.* at 146. The author gives a summary but very good comparison of the two texts. *See also* de Bus, *La C.E.E. et le code sur les subventions et les droits compensateurs,* 17 REV. TRIM. DR. EUR. 33 et seq., particularly 52 et seq. (1981); Didier, *Deux années d'application du nouveau règlement anti-dumping de la CEE,* CAH. DR. EUR. 21, n. 2 and references cited therein (1982).
116. Preamble to Reg. (EEC) No. 3017/79.
117. 22 O.J. EUR. COMM. (No. L 339) 15 (1979).
118. 11 O.J. EUR. COMM. (No. L 148) (1968). See proposal for a Council regulation on the valuation of goods for customs purposes, COM (79) 604 final.
119. 23 O.J. EUR. L. COMM. (No. L 134) 1 (1980).
120. 23 O.J. EUR. L. COMM. (No. L 333) 1 (1980). There are also many Commission regulations on this subject.

    a basic regulation implementing certain provisions of Articles 1, 3, and 8 of Reg. (EEC) No. 1224/80; Reg. (EEC) No. 1495/80; 23 O.J. EUR. COMM. (No. L 154) 13 (1980) a regulation on the interpretive notes and generally accepted accounting principles: Reg. (EEC) No. 1494/80; 23 O.J. Eur. Comm. (No. L 154) 3 (1980)

a regulation concerning the declaration of particulars relating to customs value and documents to be furnished: Reg. (EEC) No. 1496/80; 23 O.J. Eur. Comm. (No. L 154) 16 (1980)

a regulation extending, as a transitional measure, the validity of certain regulations based on the Brussels Definition of Value (BDV), Reg. (EEC) No. 1493/80; 23 O.J. Eur. Comm. (No. L 154) 1 (1980)

a number of regulations concerning costs of transport, the place of entry, and postal charges, i.e., measures implementing Reg. (EEC) No. 1224/80: Reg. (EEC) Nos. 3177–3180; 23 O.J. Eur. Comm. (No. L 335) 1, 3, 62, 64 (1980)

a regulation extending as a transitional measure the validity of certain regulations adopted pursuant to Reg. (EEC) No. 803/68 until no later than June 30, 1981: Reg. (EEC) No. 3295/80; 23 O.J. Eur. Comm. (No. L 334) 12 (1980)

121. It must be noted that the new system of valuation of goods for customs purposes replaces the BDV, introduced by the Convention on the Valuation of Goods for Customs Purposes, which was concluded in Brussels in 1950. The Member States of the Community dropped the BDV on July 1, 1980. *See* van Raan, *The Valuation of Goods for Customs Purposes,* Intertax 126, 127, 129 n.7 (1981).

122. *See supra* note 81.

123. *See Report, supra* note 60, at 99–100.

124. *See* Arts. 14.24, 7.2 of the Standards Code.

125. 23 O.J. Eur. Comm. (No. L 14) 36 (1980).

126. See a different view in Steenbergen, *supra* note 66, at 771. He considers that the agreement concluded by the Community has become, through the directive, directly binding for the Member States vis-à-vis third countries. According to Fischer, a member of the Commission's legal service, "[t]he Community accepted that the code would fully apply to government procurement by its Member States, whereas for example the U.S. accepted only 'best endeavour' obligations for government procurement by their Member States." The Community's concession "was rather dictated by the fact that inside the Community government procurement is essentially operated by national and rarely by Community authorities." General discussion in Division . . . , *supra* note 100, at 92.

127. 20 O.J. Eur. Comm. (No. L 13) 1 (1977). For the problems raised by the application of this directive, in force since July 1, 1978, see the Commission's answer on March 28, 1980 to a question of Lord Bethell. 23 O.J. Eur. Comm. (No. C 110) 15 (1980).

128. *Report, supra* note 60, at 104.

129. *Id.*

130. *Id.*

131. *See* COM (79) 621 final; 22 O.J. EUR. COMM. (No. C 287) 9 (1979).
132. *See* report by Kai Nyborg, 1979–1980 EUR. PARL. DOC. (No. 1-814) (1980).
133. An SDR normally is approximately (plus or minus 20 percent) the value of one U.S. dollar.
134. COM (79) 621 final.
135. Directive of the Council of July 22, 1980. 23 O.J. EUR. COMM. (No. L. 215) 1 (1980). *See also* the Council resolution of the same date concerning access to public supply contracts for products originating in third countries, *id.*, and a statement by the Council and the Commission on Article V (14) (h) of the code.
136. 23 O.J. EUR. COMM. (No. L 215) 1, 3 (1980).
137. GATT Doc. GPR/3/Add. 10 (July 2, 1981).
138. Another one would have been the proposed and not yet adopted directive on standards.
139. International Fruit Co. v. Produktschap voor Groenten en Fruit, 1972 E. Comm. Ct. J. Rep. 1219.
140. Schlüter v. Hauptzollamt Lörrach 1973 E. Comm. Ct. J. Rep. 1135.
141. Bresciani v. Administrazione Italiana delle Finanze 1976 E. Comm. Ct. J. Rep. 129.
142. *International Fruit Co.*, 1972 E. Comm. Ct. J. Rep. at 1228, Ground 21. An informal English translation is: "this agreement, according to terms of its preamble based on the principle of reciprocal and mutual advantageous negotiations, is characterized by a great flexibility of its provisions, notably those concerning exceptions, measures that can be taken in the event of exceptional difficulties, and the resolution of disputes between contracting parties."
143. Or the withdrawal or modification of a concession.
144. *Schlüter,* 1973 E. Comm. Ct. J. Rep. at 1157–58.
145. *See, e.g., International Fruit Co.,* 1972 E. Comm. Ct. J. Rep., at 1228, Ground 27. An informal translation is: "are not of the nature to create, for litigants in the Community, the right to invoke them in judicial proceedings."
146. The Court of Justice has confirmed its refusal to give direct effect to provisions of the GATT in recent, unpublished decisions (not yet published in English) of March 16, 1983.

    In its decision *Società Italiana per l'Oleodotto Transalpino [SIOT]* and *Ministère italien des finances, le Ministère de la marine marchande, la Circonscription douanière de Trieste et le Port autonome de Trieste* 1983 C.J. Comm. E. Rec., the Court has ruled that article V of the GATT could not have direct effect for the reasons given in its decision *International Fruit Co.*

    In its decisions of the same date, *Administration des finances de l'Etat, Società Petrolifera Italiana S.p.A [SPI]* et *S.p.A Michelin Italiana [SAMI]* 1983 C.J. Comm. E. Rec., the Court also refers to its previous decisions (*International Fruit Co.* and *Schlüter*) and denies direct effect to the tariff protocols concluded in the framework of the GATT.

It holds that, due to the system of the GATT as well as to their own system, tariff protocols can only have effect through the customs tariff of the Contracting Parties.

The author does not believe that these decisions justify a fundamental change in the ideas expressed in the text. The question of the possible direct effect of a provision of a MTN Code or of another Agreement will be answered by the Court on a case-by-case basis.

147. Waelbroeck, *L'effet direct de l'accord relatif aux échanges commerciaux du 22 juillet 1972 entre la CEE et la Confédération suisse,* 29 Annuaire suisse de droit international 113 (1973).

148. Nederlandse Spoorwegen v. Inspecteur der Invoerrechten en Accijnzen 1975 E. Comm. Ct. J. Rep. 1439.

149. *Id.* at 1450, Ground 16. An informal translation is:

> likewise, the Community having been substituted for Member States, with regard to carrying out obligations of the GATT, the legal constraints of these obligations must be understood in relation to particular characteristics of the juridical order of the Community, and not by reference to those dispositions of the national legal systems which in the past gave effect to the GATT.

150. *See* Waelbroeck, *Effect of GATT within the Legal Order of the EEC,* 8 J. World Trade L. 614, 619–20 (1974).

151. *Bresciani,* 1976 E. Comm. Ct. J. Rep. 129, at 140–43.

152. *Id.* at 142, Ground 23. Informal translations of the two passages are as follows: "the spirit, the economic situation, and the terms of the Convention and of the disposition envisaged" and "This asymmetry in the obligations assumed by the Community vis-a-vis the Associated States, which is under the logic of the specific character of the Convention, is not an obstacle to the recognition by the Community of a direct effect of some provisions of this Convention."

153. Oral submissions by the Commission at the sitting of the Court. Polydor Ltd. v. Harlequin Record Shops Ltd. 1982 C.J. Comm. E. Rec. 329.

154. These arguments have been elaborated by Bourgeois, *supra* note 56, at 25–26.

155. *See id.* at 26.

156. Publico Ministero v. Ratti, 1979 E. Comm. Ct. J. Rep. 1629, 1642, Ground 23.

157. Nederlandse Ondernemingen, 1977 E. Comm. Ct. J. Rep. 126.

158. See the case law of the French Conseil d'Etat; among others, Conseil d'Etat 1979 Lebon 384, and *Actualité juridique—Droit administratif* (Jan. 20, 1980) at 39–40.

159. Art. 173, Sec. 1.2, EEC Treaty. *See,* for annulment actions by producers and importers against antidumping regulations, NTN Toyo Bearing Co. and Others v. Council of the European Communities, 1979 E. Comm. Ct. J. Rep. 1185.

160. Europe: Daily Bull. (No. 2885) at 6 (Apr. 9, 1980) and (No. 2886) at 7 (Apr. 10, 1980).

161. *See* Jackson, *United States–EEC Trade Relations: Constitutional Prob-*

lems of Economic Interdependence, 16 COMMON MKT. L. REV. 453, 475 (1979).

162. *See, e.g.*, the reservations made by some Member States that induced the Council in the night of March 5–6, 1979 to ask the Commission to improve the results of the negotiations on some points. EUROPE: DAILY BULL. (No. 2633) at 8–9 (Mar. 7, 1979); Le Monde, March 7, 1979.

163. 1979–1980 EUR. PARL. DEB. (NO. 249) (Dec. 13, 1979).

CHAPTER 3

Japan and the Implementation of the Tokyo Round Results

Mitsuo Matsushita

Since Japan is a country poor in natural resources, her traditional trade policy has been to import raw materials, process them into manufactured or semimanufactured products, and export those products abroad. Therefore, the international trade environment has had a tremendous impact on the welfare of the country. Indeed, it is not too much to say that the great economic growth of Japan in the 1960s and the 1970s was made possible by the relatively free world trade system. In this sense Japan benefited a great deal from the Kennedy Round of negotiations in the late 1960s, and it is perhaps correct to say that Japan is one of the countries in the world that benefited most from the Tokyo Round and its results.

The Japanese government has been actively implementing the results of the Tokyo Round agreements, and, as explained later, the National Diet has enacted laws for this purpose. As will also be discussed later, some trade barriers have been removed or lessened by the implementation of the Tokyo Round. In due course, it is expected that other Japanese trade barriers and restrictions against foreign imports will be substantially lessened by the implementation of the various agreements.

However, questions about trade barriers and measures limiting Japanese exports to other countries (especially industrialized countries like the United States and the Member States of the European Common Market), and foreign exports to Japan, remain unanswered after the Tokyo Round. A number of Japanese practices, such as customs inspection processes, various safety standards, industrial policy, and so on have been alleged by the U.S. government to be trade barriers. Also, orderly marketing arrangements between Japan and the United States and European countries have had a strong impact on restraining exports from Japan to those countries. These aspects have not been sufficiently covered by the Tokyo Round and the resulting agreements. Those problems need some attention, as do the MTN (Multilateral Trade Negotiations) agreements and their implementation. In the following pages, both of these aspects will be discussed.

In the section entitled Constitutional and Legal Framework of Japanese Government Actions in International Economic Relations, some basic legal problems concerning the MTN codes will be taken up, including the basic constitutional framework of the government and the policy-making process in Japan, the constitutional requirement that treaties be approved by the National Diet, and the constitutionality of the MTN codes. The legal effect of the MTN codes and the relationship between the codes and conflicting domestic laws and regulations will also be examined.

In the section entitled An Overview of the Basic Japanese Public Laws Regulating International Trade, a description of the regulatory framework for international trade controls in Japan is given, and some of the more important domestic laws and regulations are briefly described.

The section entitled Implementation of the Tokyo Round Agreements in Japan describes the implementation of the MTN codes. The National Diet, the legislative branch of the Japanese government, has enacted some laws and the enforcement agencies have issued some implementing regulations to bring Japanese law into harmony with the codes.

In the section entitled Legal Remedies for Government Agencies' Violations of the MTN Codes, the topics investigated include legal techniques for recourse against the government on the basis of the MTN codes. The legal remedies available to citizens and private foreign enterprises when the domestic laws and regulations do not conform to an MTN code will be examined.

Finally, in the section entitled Conclusions, some important trade issues that have not been covered by the MTN codes will be discussed. These include orderly marketing arrangements, import quotas on some agricultural products, restrictive business practices, the distribution system, some authorized cartels, customs inspection processes, safety standards, and industrial policy.

Constitutional and Legal Framework of Japanese Government Actions in International Economic Relations

The Constitutional Framework of the Government

The Basic Constitution

Under the Japanese Constitution,[1] there are three basic organs of the state: the National Diet, the Cabinet, and the Judiciary.

Under Article 42 of the Constitution, the National Diet consists of the House of Representatives and the House of Councillors; the former is the lower house and the latter the upper. The National Diet is the highest organ exercising state power (Article 41), and the members of both houses are elected by the people. The National Diet is the legislature, and a legislative proposal becomes law when it has been approved by both houses. A legislative proposal may be introduced in the National Diet either by the Cabinet or by an individual member of the National Diet. Proposals can be introduced in either house, except that the budget must be submitted to the House of Representatives first. Whenever the House of Councillors' decision on a treaty is different from that of the House of Representatives, the decision of the House of Representatives is regarded as the decision of the National Diet if unanimity cannot be obtained in a joint conference of both houses, or the House of Councillors has not acted on the proposal for a treaty within thirty days after it received a decision of the House of Representatives approving it.

Administrative power is vested in the Cabinet, which is composed of the Prime Minister and other ministers. The Prime Minister is appointed from among the members of the National Diet by a resolution of the National Diet (Article 67), all political parties participating. In practice, the controlling party selects its leader, and then this person is elected as Prime Minister when the National Diet meets for this purpose.

The Cabinet is jointly responsible to the National Diet where the exercise of the administrative power is concerned. The Prime Minister appoints the ministers, and the majority of them must be appointed from among the members of the National Diet. The Cabinet must resign when the House of Representatives passes a resolution of nonconfidence or rejects a confidence resolution, unless the House is dissolved within ten days. The Cabinet is charged to execute general administrative duties, including (1) executing laws; (2) establishing and maintaining diplomatic relationships; (3) concluding treaties; (4) preparing the budget and introducing it in the National Diet; (5) issuing Cabinet orders; and (6) granting clemency.

The third branch of the government is the Judiciary, which consists of the Supreme Court and lower courts. Courts have the power of judicial review. Article 98(1) declares that the Constitution is the supreme law of the land, and laws, orders, imperial decrees, and other regulations contrary to its provisions are null and void. Article 98(2) declares that treaties to which Japan is a party and the established international law shall be faithfully observed.[2]

The Japanese governmental system is that of a parliamentary-cabinet system, as opposed to a presidential system. There is a fusion of the legislative and the executive authorities. However, the Judiciary is independent, and it can exercise judicial review of both legislative and administrative actions.

The Policy-Making Process in the Japanese Government

Extraparliamentary processes are vitally important in the policy-making process in Japan. Policies, including economic policies, often take the form of legislation. Even though, as explained above, a law is passed by the National Diet, in reality the process preceding the parliamentary process is vitally important. Often ideas for policies are conceived in various ministries and in the Liberal Democratic Party (LDP), which is the party currently in control. Sometimes the LDP formulates policies. The process involved is very complex, and a brief sketch must suffice.[3]

When an idea for a policy is formulated in a ministry, officials in charge discuss the matter with key LDP persons, and after obtaining their informal approval, draft a legislative proposal that is sent to the Legislation Bureau of the Cabinet. After the Legislation Bureau amends it, the proposal is sent to the LDP again for a more formal examination. Then it is examined in a Cabinet meeting. When the Cabinet has given its approval it is introduced in the National Diet.[4] As long as the LDP holds the majority in both houses, a legislative proposal made by the Cabinet after extraparliamentary consent by the LDP is likely to pass, unless there is an unusual situation—unless, for example, the opposition party offers a very strong obstruction of the debate, or the National Diet runs out of time to examine the proposal because other bills have taken up too much time. Normally, however, the Cabinet bill would pass without amendment.[5]

The extraparliamentary process therefore, is as important, or perhaps more important, than the parliamentary process in formulating economic policies. Most of the bills are formulated through this process by the government and introduced in the Diet.

If the matter is very controversial, the opposing parties may offer a strong resistance in the National Diet. However, the most they can do is to engage in delaying tactics, and if the LDP is determined to pass a proposal it is usually enacted into law despite the opposition.

In the area of foreign and international economic policies, the opposition parties have raised relatively few opposing arguments to proposed bills, possibly because they were too complex and technical and not very interesting to the opposition. Most of the international controversies in the Diet center on political issues like the Security Treaty between the United States and Japan. Thus there was not much opposition to the signing and implementation of the Tokyo Round agreements.

The Cabinet can enter into an international agreement with other nations without the Diet's approval, and such an agreement is binding on the Japanese government as a matter of international law. However, as long as the Diet has not given its approval, the agreement cannot be legally enforced in Japan if there is a conflicting domestic statute or if the agreement contains provisions that restrict the rights of citizens.

Interministerial Rivalries in Formulating and Executing Foreign Economic Policies

Although there is relatively little legislative opposition in the area of foreign or international economic policies, one cannot say that there is no conflict and struggle in making and executing policies having to do with the foreign economic relations of Japan. Quite often there are tensions and conflict concerning foreign economic policies among the various agencies and ministries in charge of formulating and executing them. The major government agencies in charge of economic policies include the Ministry of International Trade and Industry (MITI), the Ministry of Agriculture, Forestry and Fisheries (MAFF), the Ministry of Finance (MOF), the Economic Planning Agency (EPA), the Ministry of Health and Welfare (MHW), and the Ministry of Foreign Affairs (MFA). Except for MFA, which is in charge of foreign diplomacy, and EPA, which oversees a global economic policy, each of the ministries supervises and promotes some industrial sectors, and it is the ministry in charge of a particular industry that is usually responsible for formulating the industrial or agricultural policy concerning it.

Sometimes the policies of various ministries collide. For example, MFA may have a policy of maintaining a friendly relationship with foreign nations and may wish to abolish import quotas for some agricultural products imported from overseas. However, MAFF, as the advocate and promoter of the Japanese agriculture, may have a different policy and wish to restrict imports from abroad. MITI is in charge of supervising and promoting mostly industrial goods, and may have a restrictive policy for industrial products that are not internationally competitive and a liberal trade policy for products that are. Even though the Cabinet is the forum in which such conflicts are to be reconciled, and, therefore, the Cabinet's deciding on a measure concerning foreign economic policy usually means that the conflict has been resolved, sometimes such conflicts persist and are difficult to solve. In these cases the LDP may act as a moderator in the conflicts and may try to reconcile the different attitudes by suggesting a compromise.[6]

In any event, the bureaucracy plays a vital role in Japanese politics and also in economic policy. It is in the key ministries where the best human resources and information about industries are pooled together. It is natural, then, that the real power struggle takes place there, in the very heart of the Japanese power structure. In this sense, something comparable to the conflict and tension between the Congress and the executive branch in the United States might be seen in the relationship among the key ministries.[7]

These ministerial conflicts and rivalries are not openly reported, however, even though they may be common knowledge among those who know something about the Japanese government. No official report or comments are made. Therefore, we must be satisfied with some reports that have trickled out through newspaper accounts. Some examples of such ministerial conflicts on trade may be useful at this point.

During the late 1970s there were increased European imports into Japan of adjusted butter (an ingredient used in confectionery). In 1975 imports of this item were about 3,000 tons; in 1980 they climbed to a high of 17,000 tons. MAFF, fearing that this would have some impact on domestic farmers, planned an import restriction. However, MFA and MITI objected very strongly, fearing that such a measure would touch off a trade conflict between Japan and the European exporting countries. Discussions were held among those ministries, and finally a compromise was reached: MAFF would withdraw its plan to restrict imports of adjusted butter from Europe, and the Japanese government would instead request the European producers or their governments to adopt some voluntary measure to restrain exports from those countries to Japan.[8] In this instance, MAFF basically represented the interests of domestic producers and other ministries emphasized the importance of a good relationship among trading partners.

In the United States–Japan negotiations on textiles and autos, there were conflicts of policies between MITI and MFA. In the 1974 textile negotiations, MITI emphasized the importance of protecting domestic producers of the products and opposed Japanese concessions to the United States. MFA emphasized the importance of friendly relations and took a more flexible attitude toward such concessions.[9]

In the auto negotiations,[10] MITI took the position that it should have charge of the negotiations with the United States, since whatever agreement might be made would have to be implemented domestically through administrative guidance or legal measures—and MITI has some control and influence over the auto industry in Japan and MFA does not. MFA, on the other hand, maintained that it should be commissioned to negotiate with the United States, since such negotiations are part of diplomacy, over which it has exclusive control and authority. The minister of MITI, when asked his view regarding the negotiating authority in the Committee on Commerce and Industry of the House of Representatives in the National Diet, answered, "Properly MITI should be in charge of this negotiation."[11] Actually, MFA conducted the negotiations, but MITI was extensively involved—a sort of compromise between the two positions.

The Relationship between the Constitution, Treaties, and Domestic Laws

The Constitution and Treaties

Article 73(3) of the Japanese Constitution provides that the Cabinet is empowered to enter into treaties with other nations. However, a proviso states that the Cabinet must obtain prior, or, depending on the circumstances, subsequent approval of the National Diet. This requirement is designed to guarantee that the National Diet will have some control over the treaty-making power of the Cabinet, since treaties sometimes involve provisions that restrict the rights of private individuals.

As already indicated, the treaty-making power is vested in the Cabinet. In important agreements, the Cabinet decides whether the government will participate. Administrative practice, however, has established that various branches of ministries have the authority to enter into minor agreements with foreign agencies when the agreements merely confirm existing treaties or constitute minor procedures for enforcing them.

There are various terms for international agreements between Japan and foreign governments. Some well-known ones are: *joyaku* (treaty), *kyoyaku* (convention), *kyotei* (agreement), *torikime* (arrangement), *sengen* (declaration), *giteisho* (protocol), *ketteisho* (act), *kokanbunsho* (exchange of notes), *kokanshokan* (exchange of letters), and *oboegaki* (memorandum). Whether an agreement between Japan and a foreign government falls under the category of treaty (*joyaku*) provided for in Article 73(3) of the Constitution is determined, however, by its substance rather than its name. Whether an agreement is considered a treaty is significant, because only treaties, and not every international agreement entered into by the Cabinet, require Diet approval.

It is generally held that whether an agreement is a treaty in the sense of Article 73(3) depends on whether it affects the rights of individuals—that is, whether it contains provisions binding or prohibiting the conduct of private individuals. If it does, it is regarded as a treaty and must be approved by the National Diet.[12]

Some examples of international agreements for which no approval of the National Diet is necessary are: (1) an international agreement pertaining to technical details of diplomacy; (2) an international agreement providing for detailed rules for implementing a treaty that has already been approved by the National Diet; and (3) an international executive agreement within the framework of the powers delegated to the Cabinet by legislation.[13]

In practice, the requirement that the National Diet approve a treaty is not strictly observed. Often the government takes the view that agreements are within the framework of authority that has previously been delegated by legislation, and therefore need not to be submitted to the Diet. The 1974 United States–Japan Textile Agreement is such an example. There are also a number of commercial agreements between various nations and Japan providing for rights and obligations of the governments involved which seem to affect the rights of individuals and yet were dealt with as executive agreements and not as treaties. A few examples are: (1) the trade agreement between Japan and Malta,[14] (2) the trade agreement between Japan and the Ivory Coast,[15] and (3) the trade agreement between Japan and the Central African Republic.[16]

A view often expressed by Japanese government officials is that if an international economic agreement is not self-executing but requires domestic legislation in order to implement it, the Cabinet need not submit the agreement to the National Diet for approval. Rather, implementation will take place either through domestic legislation already enacted by the Diet, or, if such legislation is lacking, the government will introduce the necessary legislation for Diet approval. When the United States and Japan made their textile agreement, the opposition parties asked the Japanese government why it had entered into such an agreement, which would have a serious impact on the freedom of trade in Japan, without submitting it to the National Diet. The Director General of the Cabinet Legislation Bureau answered as follows:

> If . . . an international agreement is enforced not as such but through a domestic law, then restrictions of the rights of individuals are governed by that domestic law. In this situation, we believe that such an agreement need not be submitted to the National Diet. When our government and a foreign government have agreed on a matter under the Constitution, it is not necessary to put such agreement under the democratic control of the National Diet as long as such agreement is not enforced directly (that is, such agreement does not impose obligations and restrictions upon the conduct of citizens in Japan) and is not in conflict with a treaty which has

been approved by the National Diet. It is to be understood as an executive agreement of which no such approval is necessary.[17]

The General Agreement on Tariffs and Trade (GATT) was submitted to and approved by the National Diet. Accordingly, it is a treaty in the sense of Article 73(3), and it is therefore probably correct to say that the Cabinet already had broad power to enter into executive agreements in order to implement provisions of the GATT. However, some MTN codes have been submitted to the National Diet and have already been approved. Also, as will be explained later, some amendments to the domestic legislation were made in order to incorporate those MTN agreements into Japanese domestic laws on tariffs and trade. The Cabinet could have chosen not to submit those agreements to the National Diet for its approval on the theory that they are implementations of the GATT and the Cabinet has already been given the power to enter into executive agreements for its implementation. Even though the reason the Japanese government submitted them to the National Diet for approval was not made clear, we can guess that it did so because, although the provisions of the GATT were general, much of the language of the codes was more specific. Consequently, the government felt it necessary to submit them to the National Diet to make sure that it had no objection to their contents.

On July 27, 1979, the Japanese government signed the Geneva Protocol incorporating the results of the tariff negotiations in the Tokyo Round. The Japanese government signed most of the other codes on December 17, 1979, on the condition that they would be accepted when the National Diet gave its approval. The agreements were formally and officially accepted on April 25, 1980, after the approval of the National Diet. In Japan, the MTN codes (except for those concerning dairy and meat products, which will be discussed later) are thus treaties in the sense of the Japanese Constitution. In addition, some implementing domestic laws incorporating the terms agreed on in the MTN codes have been enacted.

Constitutionality of the MTN Codes in Japan

As explained in the preceding paragraphs, the GATT and various MTN codes are treaties in the sense of the Japanese Constitution. What is the legal situation when a treaty is in conflict with a provision of the Constitution? For example, if a provision of one of the MTN codes or the domestic laws implementing them conflicts with a constitutional provision, which is given priority? This problem may occur, for example (if it occurs at all) when an enterprise or individual subject to a regulation imposed by the domestic statute incorporating an MTN code objects and brings an action against the agency enforcing such a rule, alleging that the code or the law violates a provision in the Japanese Constitution. Another possible situation is one in which the question of constitutionality is raised in the National Diet. For example, one of the MTN codes or one of the laws implementing a code might adversely affect the interests of small business in Japan, and some members or political parties supported by small business might raise the question of its constitutionality. As a matter of domestic legal priority, it is not settled whether a constitutional provision or a treaty prevails when the two are in conflict. There are two conflicting schools of thought,[18] one maintaining that the Constitution prevails and the other asserting that a treaty prevails. The first bases its rationale on, among other things, the amendment procedure of the Constitution. In order to amend the Constitution a referendum is required, but the conclusion of a treaty needs only the approval of the National Diet. This theory maintains that should a treaty be given priority over the Constitution, it would mean that the Constitution, which must otherwise be amended by means of a national referendum, can be amended in substance by the conclusion of a treaty that conflicts with it. This would be contrary to the basic principle of the sovereignty of the people, which is regarded as one of the fundamental principles of the Constitution.[19]

On the other hand, the theory that maintains that a treaty prevails over the Constitution holds that the Constitution is based on the principle of internationalism, and thus, since it is the expression of the national will of only one nation, it must yield to a treaty, which is the expression of the will of the international community.[20]

Without going into detail, it must be stated that the former theory is more persuasive than the latter, since to hold that a treaty prevails over the Constitution would mean that the most fundamental rights provided for in the Constitution (such as the Bill of Rights) could be overridden if the Cabinet decided to enter into a treaty repudiating them. This seems an absurd proposition.

In the *Sunakawa* case,[21] the Supreme Court in an indirect way took the position that the Constitution prevails over a treaty. The case concerned the effect of the Status of Forces Agreement between the United States and Japan, which was based on the Security Treaty between those two countries.[22] The Supreme Court stated that the Security Treaty had great political importance, and was not subject to judicial review of the courts *unless some of its provisions were clearly and obviously unconstitutional.* In this particular case the Court adopted the doctrine of political question and thereby avoided a judicial review of the constitutionality of the treaty. It is, however, noteworthy that in dicta the Court recognized the possibility of judicial review of a treaty, depending on the nature of the treaty, when some of its provisions seem clearly and obviously unconstitutional.

One constitutional provision relevant to the MTN codes is Article 22, which guarantees the freedom of occupation. This is interpreted to include the freedom of trade or business, which, however, can be restricted if that is necessary for the public welfare.[23] Since the freedom to engage in export, import, or other types of international economic transactions is regarded as part of the freedom of occupation, such activities are covered by Article 22.[24] Under the MTN Government Procurement Code, for example, the Japanese government is in principle obligated to maintain open tendering procedures in government procurement contracting, and, as will be explained later, some changes have been made in the domestic regulations concerning government procurement. Under the new rules, the government agencies and some government corporations must use open tendering or selective tendering rather than individually negotiated contracts in purchasing instruments from suppliers. A supplier who under the individually negotiated contract procedure has supplied some instruments to the government corporation operating telecommunications might be defeated in bidding under the new open tendering system, because his price is higher. This supplier might bring an action against the government alleging that the new domestic bidding system is contrary to the freedom of contract that is a part of the constitutional guarantee of freedom of occupation, since freedom of contract should include a government corporation's freedom to select a supplier as it sees fit. Moreover, he might argue that this contract system deprives the corporation of the right to choose suppliers and deprives him of the right to be chosen as the supplier. Or the government corporation might raise a claim alleging that it enjoys the right to select a supplier, and cannot be deprived of that right by the MTN code. What is the constitutional implication of such allegations?

There is a line of cases[25] that has interpreted Article 22. The issue was whether domestic legislation restricting the rights of individuals was justified under the Constitution because it was designed to achieve some socioeconomic goal. The Supreme Court has held that a judgment on whether a restriction is in fact necessary to achieve such a goal is best made by the legislative branch of the government and should in principle be left to the discretion of the National Diet.[26] Under this reasoning, if a law that restricts the rights of individuals is designed to achieve some social or economic policy (for example, the protection of small enterprises), the Court will refrain from making a judgment on the wisdom of such restriction. It is easy to see that under this rule any legislation that is designed to achieve an economic policy (including international economic policy) and that restricts freedom of trade will be considered justified unless it is flagrantly unreasonable. Domestic regulations on government procurement based on the MTN code are most likely to be regarded as regulations enacted for the purpose of embodying an international economic policy. Thus it is almost certain that any regulation implementing the MTN Government Procurement Code will be held constitutional.

Most of the MTN codes and implementing domestic laws are designed to achieve some economic policy goals. For example, the Antidumping Code and the Countervailing Duty Code and implementing laws in Japan may be regarded as measures aimed at maintaining a fair trade rule in international trade, and should be justified under the Constitution.

Therefore, on the whole, there should be little problem with the constitutionality in Japan of the MTN codes and of domestic laws that implement them.

The Legal Effect of the MTN Codes in Japan, and Conflicting Domestic Laws and Regulations

Under the prevailing Japanese doctrine on the Constitution and international law, there is no question that a treaty that has been duly approved by the National Diet and that contains matters regulating activities of individuals in Japan is self-executing.[27] Accordingly, the MTN codes that have been approved by the National Diet have the effect of domestic laws. Nevertheless, the Japanese government usually enacts domestic laws with the same contents as the treaties to make certain that the treaties have that effect. As will be noted later, the Japanese government has enacted domestic laws that are designed to implement the MTN codes, and therefore generally have the same contents as the Codes.

What about the relationship between the MTN codes or the implementing laws and those laws and regulations that may come in conflict with them? To state the conclusion first, whenever there is a conflict between a treaty and a domestic law or regulation, the treaty overrides the domestic law or regulation regardless of whether the National Diet approves the treaty before or after it approves the conflicting domestic law or regulation. There is no court decision on this precise point yet. However, the commentaries[28] agree that a treaty should be given higher priority than a domestic law or regulation regardless of when it was approved by the Diet. Accordingly, we can conclude that if there is a conflict between a domestic law or regulation and a provision in the MTN codes or implementing laws, the latter will prevail.

The writings maintaining that a treaty overrides a conflicting domestic law are based on Article 98(2) of the Constitution, which declares that a treaty and the established international law shall be faithfully observed. To admit that there can exist a law that conflicts with a treaty would be contrary to this constitutional command.[29] It is also maintained that the effectiveness of Article 98(2) is guaranteed only by maintaining the supremacy of a treaty over a conflicting domestic law, and that the constitutional provision restrains the National Diet from enacting a law that would deny the effect of a treaty the Diet has already approved.[30]

As already indicated, we can predict with reasonable certainty that courts will go along with this theory when a problem comes up. There can be a conflict between a treaty and domestic legislation or between a treaty and an administrative action based on legislation, but whatever the case, it appears certain that the treaty will prevail.

Government inaction can also be a violation of the MTN codes. For example, if the government has not taken a measure required under one of the codes, its inaction can be regarded as a violation. Legal remedies in such cases will be discussed later.

It must be noted that only a treaty that has been approved by the National Diet is covered by Article 98(2) and is given a higher priority than a domestic law. An international agreement that has been entered into between the Japanese government and a foreign government but not approved by the National Diet has no such legal effect.[31] This conclusion can be easily derived from the doctrine that the National Diet's approval of a treaty is required to guarantee that the legislative power of the Diet is not infringed on by Cabinet treaty making.

Of course, in practice, a court will always try to reconcile an international agreement with domestic legislation, and will not lightly find a conflict.

An Overview of the Basic Japanese Public Laws Regulating International Trade

Various Japanese public laws regulate and control international transactions—i.e., exports, imports, investments, and related matters. In addition, many administrative regulations implement those basic laws. One salient feature of the laws and their enforcement is that the enforcement agencies (the various ministries) are given wide powers to enact rules and regulations. Unless one is familiar with those administrative regulations, it is difficult to understand the realities of the enforcement. Moreover, some laws that regulate domestic affairs (for example, various safety standard laws for appliances, foods, cars, and so forth) also have a great impact on international trade. There may also be de facto barriers to trade, such as the distribution system, business customs and practices, the language, and so on. Also it has been claimed that industrial policy exercised by the Japanese government has constituted barriers to entry into the Japanese market vis-à-vis foreign commodities and enterprises. It is impossible to describe all of the relevant laws, regulations, and customs. We must be satisfied with a description of the most basic laws on trade.

The basic public laws in Japan regulating international trade are: (1) the Foreign Exchange and Foreign Trade Control Law[32] (the Control Law), (2) the Export and Import Transactions Law[33] (the Transactions Law), (3) the Customs Tariff Law,[34] and (4) the Tariff Law.[35] In addition, a number of other laws affect foreign trade, including the Anti-Monopoly Law,[36] the Export Insurance Law,[37] the Export Inspection Law[38] and various other laws providing for inspection and approval of products (such as the Food Sanitation Law, the Pharmaceutical Affairs Law, the Industrial Standardization Law, and others[39]). Some explanation of export and import controls exercised under these laws follows.

Export Control

The major laws controlling exports from Japan are the Control Law and the Transactions Law. The former authorizes MITI to enforce an export approval system for some designated commodities, and the latter permits private exporters to enter into export agreements between themselves with some governmental supervision.

The Control Law

Article 47 of the Control Law provides: "Export of goods from Japan shall be permitted with the minimum restrictions thereon consistent with the purpose of this Law." As this language makes clear, the basic principle is the freedom of export, and restrictions should be kept to the minimum. It is also clear that export controls must be consistent with the purpose of the law. The purpose of the law is enunciated in Article 1: "This Law has as its objective the healthy development of the national economy together with international balance of payments equilibrium and currency stabilization." (This means, in short, economic objectives.) Accordingly, any restriction of exports imposed for any other purpose would be held outside the scope of the law and therefore *ultra vires*.

Under Article 48 of the Control Law, MITI is authorized to enforce an export approval system through a cabinet order. Article 48 provides: "Any person desiring to export goods from Japan may be required to obtain the approval of the Minister of International Trade and Industry for particular types of goods and/or for particular destinations and/or for methods used for transactions or payments, as provided for by Cabinet Order." In 1949 the Cabinet issued the Export Trade Control Order[40] (the Export Order) authorizing MITI to institute an export approval system. The language of Article I of this order is almost identical to that of Article 48 of the Control Law. However, Article 48(2) reiterates the purpose of the Control Law, stating that restrictions by the Export Order must be "within the limit of necessity for the maintenance of the balance of international payments and the sound development of international trade or national economy."

This export control has been used for a variety of purposes: for example, to prevent rare materials (such as tungsten) from being drained from the domestic market, to observe international commitments (such as the embargo against Rhodesia, Co-ordinating Committee for Multilateral Export Controls [COCOM] countries, Iran, and others), to maintain public order (i.e., to prohibit the export of narcotics, weapons, obscene literature, and so on), and, above all, to carry out orderly marketing agreements (which will be discussed later). To achieve those purposes various means of control are used, including: (1) embargo, in extreme situations; (2) price controls (usually a minimum price or check price); (3) quantity control (usually maximum quantity for export); and (4) sometimes restrictions on distribution channels.

The constitutionality of export controls under the Export Order has been challenged at least twice. In the COCOM case,[41] the plaintiffs had planned to exhibit some products in a trade show in mainland China, but their request for export approval had been denied by MITI for the reason that those products were contraband under the COCOM agreement. The plaintiffs maintained that MITI could only establish export controls if they were necessary to achieve the objective of the law, namely, "the maintenance of the balance of international payments and the sound development of international trade or national economy." The export control in question, it was argued, was exercised for international political or strategic goals and thus fell outside the scope of the law.

The Tokyo District Court held that since the right of individuals to export was a constitutional right that could only be restricted if that was necessary for the purpose of public welfare, and since the public welfare in this particular case was expressed in the purpose of the Control Law (Article 1),[42] the controls exerted by MITI were for the purpose of international politics or strategy, which was outside the scope of the Control Law. In particular, the court held that the exercise of controls infringed on the constitutional guarantee of freedom of occupation and was unconstitutional. But the plaintiffs were denied money damages indemnity for the reason that the government officials showed no malicious intent or negligence in making the decision on this contraband.

In the *Textile* case, MITI's export control was challenged again.[43] This time the issue was an export control designed to enforce the 1974 United States–Japan Textile Agreement, in which the Japanese government had agreed to restrain the export of textile products from Japan to the United States. The Federation of Textile Industries of Japan, which represented the Japanese textile producers, brought a suit against the government alleging that the contemplated control would be unconstitutional and illegal because: (1) it would be contrary to the principle of freedom of occupation embodied in Article 22 of the Constitution; and (2) it would be contrary to provisions of the GATT, which in principle prohibits restrictions of export. This suit was withdrawn during its progress due to the fact that the Multifiber Agreement was completed in 1974 within the framework of the GATT, and the Federation was satisfied with the treatment of Japanese exports of textile products under that agreement.

MITI often uses administrative guidance[44] as a means of control in conjunction with the Export Order. Such guidance (an informal request) may ask exporters to keep up an export price, or hold down the quantity of exports to a certain country. If this guidance is not complied with, then MITI usually invokes an order. A prominent example of this was the 1981 auto export restraint.[45] Because the United States Congress threatened to pass a law setting up quota limitations on the imports of autos from foreign countries, MITI decided that it would be a better policy to implement voluntary export restraints. Accordingly, MITI requested that each auto exporter keep the number of autos exported to the United States within the maximum indicated by MITI. If this maximum number would likely be exceeded, then MITI would invoke the compulsory export approval system under the Export Order. As this example shows, administrative guidance is often a preliminary stage before export controls are invoked.

The Transactions Law

The Transactions Law permits exporters to enter into export agreements, under which they fix export prices, set a quantity to be exported, or determine other terms of business.[46] Basically, the function of the Transactions Law is to authorize private exporters to enter into export agreements and to exempt such agreements from the Anti-Monopoly Law.[47] If an agreement only contains terms of export trade (i.e., export price, quantity, and so on), it must be filed with MITI, and if it contains terms restricting domestic trade (i.e., purchase terms of merchandise to be exported[48]), MITI's approval must be obtained.

Formally, the Transactions Law provides only for private export agreements and does not involve government export control except for an order issued under Article 28. (This will be explained later.) However, the government is actually heavily involved. Usually MITI advises exporters to enter into export agreements whenever it foresees some possible trade conflict with an importing country. In this way, export agreements are used to carry out governmental trade policy. MITI sometimes advises exporters to enter into an export agreement fixing a price or setting a quantity with a threat that if its advice is ignored it will promptly invoke compulsory export control as provided for in the Export Order.[49]

Article 28 of the Transactions Law authorizes MITI to issue an order binding export prices, quantity, or other terms of business when an agreement entered into among exporters is not sufficient to establish orderly export conditions. This provision is invoked when an exporters' agreement is not effective due to activities of outsiders or when the terms of business set up by the agreement (export price or export quantity, and so on) are not satisfactory. Such an order is binding on every exporter, including the participants in the agreement, and is sometimes called outsider regulations. However, this is a misnomer, since insiders are bound by it as well. The order can be issued only after an export agreement has been entered into and proven to be ineffective. The fact that the governmental order is premised on a private agreement indicates that private agreements are regarded as a part of a broader governmental trade policy.

In the *Zenith* case,[50] some Japanese television manufacturers-exporters were challenged by two American manufacturers for alleged dumping and cartel activities. In connection with this case, MITI issued a statement that was submitted to the American court where the case was pending. MITI stated that it had advised these enterprises to enter into the export agreement concerning televisions to be exported to the United States, and that if its advice had not been honored it would have invoked an order under the Export Order. The result of such an order would have been similar to that achieved by the export agreement entered into under MITI's advice.

Export agreements under the Transactions Law have perhaps been MITI's most important policy tool in effectuating orderly marketing agreements with foreign countries, notably the United States. In 1968, officials of the U.S. government and Japanese representatives of the steel industry informally discussed the voluntary export restraint to be exercised on the Japanese side. This informal restriction was put into effect by means of an export agreement entered into by the Japanese exporters of steel to the United States.[51] In 1974, the U.S. International Trade Commission (ITC) decided that the domestic specialty steel industry had been injured by imports from foreign countries, and the U.S. government took measures to restrict the quantity of imports of specialty steel.[52] The Japanese government advised the exporters to enter into a voluntary restraint agreement to supplement the U.S. import control. Also in 1977, the ITC determined that the U.S. television industry had been injured by imports of televisions from abroad.[53] President Carter, instead of accepting the tariff increase recommended by the ITC, chose to negotiate with the Japanese government to obtain a voluntary restraint of exports.[54] MITI advised television exporters to enter into an agreement fixing a maximum quantity to be exported to the United States (the maximum amount was 1,700,000 sets a year for three years). The agreement between the U.S. government and the Japanese government stated that the Japanese government would use the Transactions Law and the private agreement entered into under it as a means of achieving the purpose of this governmental agreement.

Even though export cartel agreements are formally private in nature, there is usually a strong government hand involved, and realistically we can say that the Transactions Law is one of the important policy tools available to MITI in enforcing export controls.

Import Control

There are several major laws designed to control imports: the Control Law, the Transactions Law, and the Customs Tariff Law. Moreover, the Tariff Law provides for procedures relating to imports and the collection of duties. In addition, there are also a number of laws that prohibit or restrict importation of some products into Japan.

The Control Law

Article 52 of the Control Law provides for an import approval system. It states "In order to ensure healthy development of foreign trade and national economy, any person desiring to effect imports may be required to obtain approval therefore as provided for by Cabinet Order." It should be noted that unlike Article 47 and Article 48(2), which concern export control, this Article contains no language that requires that import controls be kept within the limits dictated by "the maintenance of the balance of international payments and the sound development of international trade or national economy." Although the language in Article 52 authorizing import controls "in order to ensure healthy development of foreign trade and national economy" may suggest that an import control exercised for a purpose other than that of ensuring of healthy development of foreign trade and national economy is *ultra vires,* the outer limit of the government's power to control imports is not as clearly defined as it is for export controls. The legislative purpose of the legal structure pertaining to import controls may be interpreted to mean that the freedom to import is not emphasized as much as the freedom to export.

It should also be noted that there is no explicit requirement of a finding of injury to a domestic industry before an import control under the Import Order can be initiated. However, since Article XIX of the GATT does require such a finding before import controls are invoked, and since Japan is a signatory of the GATT, the Japanese government should find an injury to a domestic industry before it enforces an import restriction on a particular item.

Under Article 52 of the Control Law, MITI is authorized to establish an import quota system (IQ). If an IQ system is established for a specific item, a person desiring to import this item must obtain MITI's approval before applying for an import license for the product. In the 1950s and 1960s this IQ system was widely used to restrict imports of many kinds of items. However, since the late 1960s, the number of items under the IQ system has dropped sharply, due to the trend toward liberalization.[55] Some items are still controlled: (1) meat and dairy products, (2) marine products, (3) miscellaneous beans and oil-stuff seeds, (4) fruits, vegetables, and preparations containing them, (5) cereals, (6) coal, and (7) hides and leather products.[56] Import control under the Control Law is exercised for various purposes, among which the most important is the protection of domestic industries.

In addition to the Control Law, there are a number of laws regulating or prohibiting the importation of certain items, as specified in each statute. In 1982 the number was twenty-seven.[57] The names of some of the more important laws are: the Plant Quarantine Law, the Forest Seedling Law, the Law for the Prevention of Infectious Diseases in Domestic Animals, the Wildlife Preservation and Game Law, the Food Sanitation Law, the Fertilizer Control Law, the Drugs, Cosmetics and Medical Instruments Law, the Narcotics Control Law, the Stimulant Drugs Control Law, the Staple Food Control Law, the Tobacco Monopoly Law, the Alcohol Monopoly Law, the High Pressure Gas Control Law, the Explosives Control Law, and the Consumer Product Safety Law.

Some of these laws contain a provision that restricts or prohibits the importation of the item covered by the law. Others only set up standards of quality to be observed by the sellers of the item in question, whether it is domestically manufactured or imported. Still others require the sellers of such items to obtain a license from public authorities. However, they all affect imports in one way or another.

The Transactions Law

The Transactions Law permits importers of a commodity to enter into an import agreement fixing a purchase price, limiting the maximum quantity to be purchased, setting a minimum standard for quality, or restricting channels of import. (For example, the members of an import agreement may designate one of them as the sole import agency.) Unlike an export agreement, an import agreement can be entered into among importers of a commodity only if one of the following requirements is satisfied: (1) there is a substantial restraint of competition or a monopoly in the country or place that is exporting the commodity in question; (2) an import agreement is necessary to carry out an agreement between the Japanese government and the government of the exporting country; or (3) it is necessary to pool the demand for a raw material through an import agreement in order to make sure that there is a sufficient demand in Japan for the raw material to be exploited in a foreign country, thereby facilitating the exploitation and development of that raw material in the foreign country.[58]

When importers wish to enter into an import agreement they must file the agreement with MITI and obtain its approval.[59] As it does for export agreements, MITI often advises importers to enter into an import agreement. Thus an import agreement under the Transactions Law is also a foreign trade policy instrument for MITI. Import agreements of this type are deemed exempt from Japanese antimonopoly laws. If necessary, an import order under the Transactions Law, which binds both insiders of a cartel and outsiders, may be invoked.[60]

As compared with export agreements, there are few cases in which import agreements under the Transactions Law have been used. However, it is expected that import agreements among importers under administrative guidance of the government will be important in the future, since some Japanese industries are losing comparative advantages vis-à-vis some developing countries. Some form of import regulation may be urged by domestic interests.

Two important examples of import agreements should be mentioned. The first is the scrap-iron case. In 1974, under the Export Administration Act, the United States introduced an embargo on the export of scrap-iron, in the face of a domestic shortage. MITI initiated a corresponding import control under the Control Law. When the United States lifted the embargo, MITI dropped its import control and advised the importers of scrap-iron to establish an import agreement so that purchases would not rise to the point where they could touch off new export controls on the American side.[61]

The second and perhaps the most important case is that of Chinese silk fiber. Due to a loss of comparative advantage, the Japanese producers of raw silk had lost their market share to Korean and Chinese producers. To cope with this situation an amendment to the Silk Price Stabilization Law was adopted and a government corporation given the exclusive right to import raw silk from abroad. However, foreign producers could easily avoid this import regulation by processing the silk slightly and converting it to semiprocessed fiber (which, however, was very easy to convert back to raw silk).[62] MITI, which was concerned that the import of this product would damage the Japanese producers, advised importers of semi-processed silk to enter into an import agreement that would limit the amount of purchase below a certain level. At the same time, an order (outsider regulation) was invoked to make sure that every importer of the product would import it within the amount allocated to it.[63]

The government entered into an orderly marketing agreement with the Korean government whereby Korea agreed to enforce a voluntary export restraint on the product.[64] However, since the Chinese government refused to restrain exports, MITI used the Transactions Law to effectuate an import agreement among importers, based on an informal understanding with China.[65]

The import control exercised under the Silk Price Stabilization Law has been challenged by necktie producers in Japan. As has been explained, the law gives a government corporation the exclusive right to import raw silk from abroad. The corporation sells imported raw silk in the domestic market at the price prevailing there, which is higher than the international price. Therefore, Japanese producers of neckties purchase raw silk (the material for ties) at prices higher than those paid by foreign producers. Since Europe has no such import control system for raw silk, the price in Europe is much lower than in Japan. European producers purchase raw silk at a lower price, produce ties, and export them to Japan. Thus the Japanese tie producers have lost some of their market. They have brought a lawsuit against the government alleging that the Silk Price Stabilization Law was designed to protect only the domestic producers of raw silk, and for this reason was unduly discriminatory against the producers of ties, and also consumers. In addition, they argued that the import controls under the law violated provisions of the Constitution.[66] As of October 1983, the suit was still pending in the Kyoto District Court.

The Customs Tariff Law

Another important statute concerning import trade is the Customs Tariff Law. This law provides for such things as customs valuation, antidumping and countervailing duties, and tariff quotas. Some of the most important provisions of this law will be briefly mentioned here.

Article 4 provides for customs valuation. According to this provision, the government shall use the transaction value as the basis for tariffs. *Transaction value* is defined as the sum of money actually paid by the importer to the exporter when the import transaction took place.

Article 7 provides for a retaliatory tariff. The government is given the right to impose a special surcharge in addition to the regular tariff on a product imported from a country in which Japanese ships, airlines, or commodities are unfavorably discriminated against as compared with ships, airlines, and commodities from another country.

Articles 8 and 9 are, respectively, the provisions for countervailing duties and antidumping duties. These provisions and the amendments that were made to them as a result of the Tokyo Round will be explained later, in the section entitled Implementation of the Tokyo Round Agreements in Japan.

Under Article 9-2 an emergency tariff is authorized. When a sharp decline in price or other unforeseeable changes in the exporting country causes or threatens a sudden increase in imports of a commodity to Japan, causing material injury to a Japanese industry that competes with the imported commodity, the government may levy a special tariff in addition to the regular tariff. The tariff may amount to as much as the difference between the value of the imported commodity for the purpose of regular tariff and the appropriate wholesale price of the same or a similar commodity produced in Japan.

These tariffs or surcharges are called special tariffs because they are different from regular tariffs in that they are designed to cope with some specific situations, as defined in each provision.

Article 9-3 also provides for tariff quotas (TQ). The government can set a maximum quantity of imports of a product on which a certain level of tariff is applied. When the quantity of import exceeds that level, a higher tariff is levied on the excess.

So far not much use has been made of these special tariffs, except for tariff quotas. The major reason is that until the late 1960s the Japanese market was guarded by an import quota system, and accordingly there was little need for protective tariffs. Moreover, since liberalization took place, Japanese commodities (especially industrial products) have enjoyed a high level of international competitiveness. However, these protective tariffs may well be used in the future, in view of the fact that the international competitiveness of some Japanese industries is dwindling due to high labor costs, overhead costs, and energy costs, and the suffering industries may pressure or petition the government for relief.

Implementation of the Tokyo Round Agreements in Japan

In negotiating the Tokyo Round, the following ministries were in charge: MITI, MOF, MFA, MAFF, EPA, and occasionally some other agencies. Depending on the subject, one or several of the ministries took the responsibility of formulating requests and offers and of deciding governmental attitudes toward the issues. MITI was in charge of such areas as subsidies and countervailing duties, antidumping duties, standards, import licensing, and aircraft. MOF was active in such areas as government procurement, subsidies and countervailing duties, customs valuation, and tariff reduction. MFA participated in the subsidy and countervailing duty area, and took the lead in the area of the framework negotiations. MAFF was in charge in such areas as dairy products and bovine meat.

Representatives from these ministries made up the Japanese delegation, which consisted of vice-ministers, counsellors and bureau chiefs of the ministries. Whenever these representatives had different views on a matter, interministerial conferences were held to discuss the problem and iron out a solution before the government's view was presented in the negotiations. Each ministry also met with representatives of Japanese industries that would be affected as a result of the negotiations in order to arrive at an understanding with the industries in question.[67]

Most of the MTN agreements were introduced in the National Diet for its approval. The codes on tariff reduction, subsidies and countervailing duties, antidumping, import licensing, customs valuation, technical barriers to trade, government procurement, and civil aviation were all approved and promulgated on April 25, 1980.[68] On the other hand, the agreements on dairy products and bovine meat were not introduced in the National Diet for approval, but were signed as executive agreements.[69]

Generally speaking, the codes that were submitted to the Diet were those that required some changes of domestic laws, or regulations for implementation. However, one exception is the code on import licensing. Although the government did not think it necessary to change a domestic law or regulation in order to implement it, this code touched on a fundamental principle of the GATT and it was therefore considered advisable to submit it to the National Diet for its consideration and approval.

In order to implement the MTN agreements in Japanese law, some amendments to domestic laws and regulations were considered necessary. This was the case in the areas of: (1) customs valuation, (2) countervailing duties, (3) antidumping duties, and (4) technical standards. The implementation of the Government Procurement Code required some changes in the regulations, but not in the basic law. It was not necessary to amend the existing law to reduce the Japanese tariff in compliance with the Geneva Protocol. However, since this code was approved by the National Diet as a treaty, some changes were made in the Tariff Special Measures Law to reduce tariffs from the existing rate. (These changes will be explained later, under the heading Tariff Reduction.)

In the areas of import licensing, framework, agriculture and dairy, bovine meat, and aircraft, it was considered unnecessary to amend or enact new laws or regulations to implement the MTN agreements domestically.

Tariff Reduction

In the process of the Tokyo Round negotiations, the Japanese government was rather active in proposing tariff reductions. The government submitted an offer of tariff reduction to the Secretariat of the GATT on January 18, 1978. Moreover, on March 4, 1978, the government made an advance reduction of tariffs on 125 items in order to facilitate the negotiations. It signed the Geneva Protocol on July 27, 1979, as soon as the Cabinet decided that Japan would accept it. In total, the government made tariff concessions on 2,600 items in industrial products and 200 items in agricultural products.[70] The reason tariff concessions were made on many more industrial than agricultural items is probably that Japan is more internationally competitive in industrial products than in agricultural products. On the other hand, few concessions were made for industries that have some structural problems, such as textiles, leather goods, and nonferrous metals.

It was not necessary to change a Japanese domestic law in order to conform to the tariff reductions agreed upon in the Tokyo Round since Article 3 of the Tariff Law[71] states that tariffs shall be imposed as provided for in the Tariff Law or in the Customs Tariff Law, and that if there is a special provision for a tariff in a treaty to which the Japanese government is a party, a tariff shall be imposed in accordance with that provision. Since the National Diet approved the Geneva Protocol, it is a treaty in the sense of the Constitution, and accordingly, Article 3 of the Tariff Law applies.

However, because tariffs on many items were reduced in advance in 1978, the effective Japanese tariff rate was in many cases lower than the rate agreed upon in the Tokyo Round. Therefore, if the Japanese government carried out reductions according to the staging in the Tokyo Round, at first it would not be reducing tariffs *in compliance with the Geneva Protocol,* since at the early stages the rate agreed upon would be higher than Japan's then current effective rate. The government's view was that this situation was not desirable, since the Japanese government had actively proposed tariff reductions. Accordingly, it decided to reduce tariffs below the effective rate of the protocol. For this purpose, it was necessary to amend the domestic law, and the Tariff Special Measures Law, as amended, brought this into effect.[72]

Customs Valuation

Japan is a member of the Brussels Convention on Customs Valuation and has enforced its valuation system in accordance with the principles set forth in that Convention. There was, however, some difference between the language used in Article 4 of the Customs Tariff Law, which provided for customs valuation, and the language contained in the Customs Valuation Code, and Article 4 was amended to make its language identical to the code's. This amendment became effective as of January 1, 1981.[73]

Under Article 4, customs valuation was based on the price of an imported product at the port of importation, which price existed between the seller and the purchaser who were independent from each other at the time of notice of importation, if such price was decided under a condition of perfect competition. Based on this general principle, detailed methods for calculating customs value were provided. The Customs Valuation Code is based on a different principle, and thus the changes in Article 4 were necessary.

Under the amended Article 4, customs valuation is based on the transaction value of an imported commodity—that is, the price actually paid or payable by the purchaser to the seller for the imported goods in the import transaction relating to the goods, plus the cost of transport and some other costs to the extent that they are not included in the price actually paid for the goods. If the transaction value cannot be determined, customs valuation is based on the transaction value of the same or a similiar commodity exported on the day on which the imported commodity was exported, or some other day close in time.

If neither of these two values can be determined, customs valuation is based on a price arrived at by calculating backwards from the domestic sales price or a price arrived at by adding manufacturing costs and other costs. If that method cannot be used either, customs valuation will be based on a price determined by procedures provided for in a cabinet decree. It seems that under the new valuation system the value of an imported commodity is not necessarily lower than the value of the same commodity under the old system, since the new system is based on the price actually paid by an importer of an imported commodity and the old system was based on a hypothetical price that would have prevailed if there had been the condition of perfect competition. As long as the price that was actually paid is not lower than the price that would prevail under perfect competition, under the new system the tariff would not be lower than that under the old system.

However, one advantage of the new system is that it is a stable way of setting the value of an imported commodity, and thus should make importing easier. Under the old system, government officials engaged in valuation had more discretion concerning the value on which tariffs would be based, since the hypothetical price that would prevail under the condition of perfect competition could be manipulated by those who were in charge of calculating it. Under the new system, the actual price paid by an importer of a commodity is the basis for valuation, and government officials have much less discretion in the matter.

There had been some complaints about the older customs valuation practices. The Trade Study Group Report[74] states that there had been a feeling among foreign exporters that "customs uplifts" had caused buyers to be uncertain about their customs and commodity tax obligations. A U.S. congressional report also mentions arbitrariness in determining the value of the imported commodity.[75] The new valuation system should contribute toward a more transparent valuation process.

Countervailing and Antidumping Duties

As yet, the Japanese government has issued neither a countervailing nor an antidumping duty order. There are various reasons for the lack of cases in those areas. As already mentioned, until 1960 the quota system and other import controls tightly shielded the Japanese economy from penetration by foreign imports. In such circumstances it was not necessary to use countervailing or antidumping duty orders. Another possible reason was that by the time of liberalization of imports most Japanese industries had already acquired enough international competitiveness to make special tariffs unnecessary.

In addition, there were other regulatory means of import control, i.e., the Control Law, the Transactions Law, and also the important role played by the administrative guidance of government agencies. The government agencies that were the most sensitive to the suffering of domestic industries in industrial and agricultural goods were probably MITI and MAFF. However, the power to carry on an investigation in countervailing and antidumping matters was primarily vested in MOF. This may explain the lack of enthusiasm on the part of MITI and MAFF to push forward the enforcement of the countervailing and antidumping duty laws.

However, now that some sectors of the Japanese economy are losing international competitiveness due to rising wages, land prices,

prices of raw materials, and other factors, some industries (depressed industries such as petrochemical and textile industries) may well attempt to petition the government to initiate proceedings under the countervailing or antidumping duty laws.

As compared with some other tools for import control, such as the Control Law and the quota system provided for under it, the countervailing and antidumping duty laws are easier for private industries to use. The Control Law does not provide for a formal procedure a private enterprise can use to petition the government to invoke import controls, but there are such provisions in the cabinet decrees on countervailing and antidumping duties.[76] Private enterprises or labor unions that feel their interests are adversely affected by imports may petition the government for relief even though these laws do not grant private parties the right to require that the government start a formal proceeding.

On December 27, 1982, the Japan Spinning Industry Association filed antidumping and antisubsidy complaints against Korean and Pakistani cotton textiles with the Minister of MOF. It claimed that Korean textiles had been imported to Japan from Korea at a price lower than that which prevailed in the Korean home market, thereby causing material injury to the domestic industry in Japan. It also claimed that the Pakistani government provided export subsidy to Pakistani exporters of cotton textiles in the form of rebates to exporters of a portion of the export price, tax exemption of income earned from exports, and preferential export financing.

Discussions between the Japanese and Korean industries took place and resulted in an agreement between the Japanese and Korean industries that the Korean industry and the government would effect a voluntary export restraint on cotton textiles to be exported from Korea to Japan. The complainant thereupon decided to withdraw the complaint, and investigation was not initiated.

As to the Pakistan Subsidies Case, an investigation was initated by the Japanese government on April 20, 1983. The investigation is under way at the time of this writing and should come to the end within one year.

On the whole, it may be said that during the Tokyo Round the Japanese government's attitude toward countervailing and antidumping duty matters was passive. Since the later 1960s, there have been many instances in which Japanese products were challenged in foreign countries as being dumped or subsidized. Those claims were most numerous in the United States, but there were similar ones in Europe, Canada, and Australia. Major areas of concern were steel, electronics, and more recently, automobiles. The aim of the Japanese government during the Tokyo Round, therefore, was to put forth a view on new international antidumping and countervailing duty codes that would narrowly limit the powers of the national governments in enforcing antidumping and countervailing duty statutes. The Japanese government was also handicapped by a lack of experience in enforcing antidumping or countervailing duty statutes, even though government and industries had a great deal of experience in dealing with antidumping or countervailing duty proceedings initiated by foreign governments. It should also be pointed out, however, that the government is aware of the possibility that in due course the Japanese laws concerning foreign subsidies and dumping may be used to protect Japanese domestic industries.

To take a long-range view, it is perhaps fortunate for the Japanese government that the new MTN Antidumping Code may have made it easier for national governments to impose antidumping duties than was the case under the 1967 GATT code.

Since the Subsidies-Countervailing Duty Code, and the Antidumping Code contain some provisions on procedural matters that the Customs Tariff Law did not provide for, that law had to be amended. These procedural amendments include provisions concerning: (1) a petition by an interested party and self-initiation; (2) the period of investigation; (3) undertakings; (4) provisional measures; and (5) the retroactive effect of an order.[77]

Countervailing Duties

Article 8 of the Customs Tariff Law is the relevant provision for the imposition of countervailing duties. To implement the Subsidies-Countervailing Duty Code, Article 8 and also the Cabinet Order Concerning Countervailing Duty have been amended. As amended, Article 8 provides that when the importation of a commodity directly or indirectly subsidized by a foreign government causes or threatens to cause material injury to a Japanese industry that produces the same commodity or a similar one, the government may, in accordance with a cabinet decree, impose a countervailing duty up to the amount of the net subsidy, wherever such measure is necessary to protect the industry. The language of Article 8 before and after amendment was very similar; however, since the term *material injury* was agreed on in the Tokyo Round, it was written into the Customs Tariff Law.

As already mentioned, there was no specific provision in Japanese law for petitions by interested parties. Accordingly, an amendment was necessary in order to implement the Subsidies-Countervailing Duty Code. Under Article 2(1) of the Cabinet Order, a person requesting the initiation of a countervailing duty investigation shall file with the Minister of Finance a written petition and sufficient evidence. The Minister transmits a copy to the Minister of MITI. The government may initiate a proceeding when a petition is supported by evidence or when the government has acquired evidence that a subsidy and an injury exist.

Article 8(6) limits the investigation period to one year, in principle. This is in accordance with the code and prompted by the fact that a prolonged investigation may cause unreasonable uncertainty in the terms of trade. Under Article 8(7) the government in the exporting country or the exporter can propose an undertaking to offset the subsidy and the Japanese government can accept such an undertaking and terminate the investigation. Under Article 8(9) the Japanese government may effectuate a provisional measure before an investigation has concluded, whenever a subsidized commodity has been imported, it is possible to infer that a Japanese industry has been materially injured thereby, and a provisional measure is necessary to protect the industry.

In addition, Article 8(2) provides for a retroactive application of countervailing duties in three instances. When a subsidized import has materially injured a Japanese industry, a countervailing duty may be imposed with regard to imports during the period during which a provisional measure was effective. When a violation of an undertaking to offset a subsidy has caused material injury to an industry in Japan and a provisional measure has been taken, a countervailing duty may be imposed with regard to imports during the period between the day which is ninety days prior to the day on which the provisional measure was taken or the day on which a violation of the provisional measure took place, whichever is later, and the day before the day on which a decision to impose a countervailing duty was entered. When, because of a large quantity of subsidized imports, a countervailing duty is necessary to prevent irreparable damage to a Japanese industry from recurring, it may be imposed with regard to imports during the period between the day which is ninety days prior to the day on which a provisional measure was taken and the day before the day on which a decision to impose the countervailing duty was entered.

Whenever the Minister of MOF, the minister of the ministry in charge of the industry in question, or the Minister of MITI deems it necessary to initiate an investigation, each minister is to notify the others, and, in the process of an investigation, the three ministers are to stay in touch with one another. Whenever an important matter has to be decided, the decision is to be made after a discussion of these three Ministers has been held.

When, as a result of an investigation, it becomes clear that a final measure or a provisional measure is necessary, the Minister of MOF may impose a countervailing duty after having referred the matter to the Tariff Council.

Antidumping Duties

Japan has ratified as treaties both the GATT and the Antidumping Code of 1967. To implement the 1967 code and Article 9 of the Customs Tariff Law, a Cabinet Order Concerning Dumping was issued. However, when in the course of the Tokyo Round a new international agreement was made on antidumping matters, the Japanese government decided that it would be appropriate to amend Article 9 of the Customs Tariff Law and issue a new order to implement the new code. The amendments to Article 9 and the Cabinet Order were made effective on May 25, 1980.

As newly amended, Article 9 provides that when the import of a dumped product causes or threatens to cause material injury to Japanese industry or to materially retard the establishment of an industry in Japan, an antidumping duty may be imposed whenever it seems necessary to protect the industry concerned. The imposition of such a duty must be made as prescribed by a cabinet order. An antidumping duty is in addition to the regular customs duty, and the amount of the duty is equal to or less than the difference between the normal value and the dumped price of the product.

Dumping is defined as the export to Japan of a commodity at a price less than normal value, which causes material injury to a Japanese industry. *Normal value* is defined as follows: (1) the sales price of a commodity similar to the exported commodity sold in the normal process of commercial transactions for consumption in the country of export; (2) the export sales price to a third market of a similar commodity; and (3) a constructed value of such a commodity. Prices described in (2) or (3) can be used as a standard for price comparison only if the price described in (1) cannot be used because there is no domestic sale of the article or the domestic price reflects a peculiar situation in the country of export which makes that price improper as a standard for comparison.

In computing normal value, factors like stages of transaction, quantities of sale, or others that may result in differences of prices and comparisons of prices must be considered, and necessary adjustments made. If an export price is not appropriate for the purpose of price comparison because the exporter and importer are related entities, the price of the commodity charged to a first purchaser who is related to neither the exporter nor the importer is used as the basis for comparison.

There are provisions for a test of material injury, retroactive application of an antidumping duty, petitions filed by interested parties, investigation procedures, price undertakings and so forth. However, these procedures and requirements are essentially similar to those for imposing a countervailing duty.

Technical Barriers to Trade

Technical barriers to trade in Japan have given rise to many complaints by foreign exporters and Japanese importers of foreign products. Some of the barriers seem real, others imaginary. Moreover, some of the technical standards reflect special circumstances in Japan and cannot easily be removed even if they create trade problems. Emission controls, labels that protect consumers, and other standards for the protection of public health and welfare are some examples.

It will be useful here to give a total picture of the alleged barriers to trade in Japan.[78] Generally speaking, the comment has been made that the Japanese standards for product safety, health requirements, inspection practices, and government approval are more stringent than those in foreign countries. These standards and requirements are designed not to discriminate against foreign products but to meet domestic necessities. However, because Japan and foreign countries establish and enforce such standards in different ways, it may sometimes be difficult for foreign products to penetrate the Japanese market. A Special Progress Report of the United States–Japan Trade Study Group (TSG) states:[79]

> With the exception of quotas, government procurement and buy "local" practices, most of the Japanese regulations, procedures and practices which pose a problem for U.S. and other exporters were not created with a specific intent to discriminate against foreign goods. Very often, the core of the problem is that the exporter does not have sufficient information or ability to influence decisions affecting his interests to operate effectively in Japan.
>
> This problem has resulted from the paternalistic relationship between the Japanese government and business since the Meiji period (1867–1912). In contrast to the United States, Japanese industry was initially created largely by government initiative as an instrument to ward off foreign domination. Therefore, from the start, the government has taken a much more dominant role in economic decision-making than in the United States. Among other things, the government has gone to great lengths in protecting the public from dangerous or defective goods by setting strict standards, testing requirements and health and safety regulations. It was impossible for the government to rely on voluntary efforts or standards to the same extent as in the United States or in Europe because private standards-making groups did not exist in the initial period of Japanese modernization.

> As a general matter, the Japanese government has set very strict (though often ambiguous) basic rules in establishing technical relations, but has given the administrative officials who deal directly with the public wide discretion to relax regulations in individual cases. This practice has given the bureaucracy a combination of firm control plus the flexibility to deal with changing technology and economic circumstances. Unfortunately, this approach has tended to work to the disadvantage of foreigners, who usually have not had the experience or relationships necessary to take advantage of the system's flexibility.

Let us first review some major laws and regulations on technical standards and the agencies that enforce these laws. The Pharmaceutical Affairs Law provides for approval and testing of pharmaceuticals, and various related matters. Cosmetics are also covered by this law. The Poisonous Substances Control Law provides for control of poisonous substances. The Food Sanitation Law requires food producers, sellers, and importers to meet various standards in sanitation, safety, and related matters. The Law for the Prevention of Infectious Diseases in Domestic Animals provides for inspection of imported foods. The Law for Standardization of Agricultural Products and the Improvement of Their Representation provides for representation and labeling of the dates of manufacture of imported foodstuffs. The Law to Promote Mechanization of Agriculture authorizes the inspection of tractors for agriculture. The Agricultural Chemicals Control Law provides for registration of agricultural chemicals. The High Pressure Gas Control Law provides certain standards for containers of high pressure gas substances, and for the testing of such containers. The Consumer Product Safety Law provides for safety standards for various consumer products. The Electrical Appliances Control Law provides for approval of products and for various safety standards for them. The Law Concerning the Examination and Regulation of the Manufacture of Chemical Substances provides for testing and approval of chemical substances. The Metric Law provides for representation of weight, length, and other dimensions. The Industrial Standardization Law establishes the JIS (Japan Industrial Standard) mark. The Road Transportation Vehicles Law provides for the approval of models of cars and the inspection of performance of, for example, emission standards.

This list by no means includes all the laws and regulations concerning technical standards that may affect the import of foreign products. However, it does provide examples of major laws that have been the object of some concern in trade conflicts between Japan and foreign countries.

These laws are enforced through various agencies. For example, the Ministry of Health and Welfare enforces the Pharmaceutical Affairs Law, the Food Sanitation Law and the Poisonous Substances

Control Law. MAFF regulates agricultural products under the Law for the Prevention of Infectious Diseases in Domestic Animals, the Law for Standardization of Agricultural Products and the Improvement of Their Representation, the Law to Promote Mechanization of Agriculture, and the Agricultural Chemicals Control Law. The High Pressure Gas Control Law, the Consumer Product Safety Law, and the Electric Appliances Control Law are enforced by MITI. The Metric Law and the Industrial Standardization Law are also enforced by MITI. The Road Transportation Vehicles Law is enforced by the Ministry of Transportation.

Some Complaints about Technical Barriers to Trade, and Improvements Made to Ease Them

There have been various complaints against the enforcement of Japanese technical standards under the laws and regulations just described.[80] Some of them stated that there was not enough opportunity for foreign enterprises to participate in the formulation of technical standards. Others stated that the Japanese procedures for inspection under these laws and regulations were too cumbersome, and that the Japanese agencies would not readily accept the results of foreign tests of product safety and related matters. Still others complained that labeling requirements were so stringent that they effectively prevented foreign products from entering the Japanese market.

According to a survey conducted by the *Japan Economic Journal,*[81] the following five categories of complaints are raised by foreign and domestic enterprises engaged in importing products to Japan: (1) inspection procedures are too cumbersome and too detailed; (2) the results of foreign tests are not very well accepted in Japan (3) standards are too stringent in comparison with those generally accepted by most countries; (4) the enforcement of standards is arbitrary and capricious; and (5) sometimes foreign manufacturers cannot apply for an import license.

Some of these complaints are rather frivolous or not based on fact, but others are well founded. It has been felt in Japan that some improvements in these areas are indeed essential to make the Japanese market open. Many things still need to be improved, but the Japanese government has taken several steps to remedy the situation. Most of these measures do not necessitate any amendment to the laws themselves, but can be accomplished by changing the internal regulations of the enforcement agencies or simply changing administrative practices.

In order to give foreign enterprises the opportunity to participate in the formulation of standards, a cabinet decision containing the following procedural principles was made on May 22, 1979.

> When adopting or modifying standards, public notification of intention will be made, to the extent possible, sufficiently in advance.
>
> After such notifications are made, opportunity for interested parties, whether domestic or foreign, to submit their views will be provided as much as possible, and views submitted will be given due consideration. For this purpose, improvement in procedures shall be facilitated where necessary.

Following this decision, MITI has started to announce changes in standards in advance, in the *Daily Bulletin* published by the Japan External Trade Organization (JETRO).

One complaint was that Japan would grant an import license and an approval of sale only to a Japanese importer established in accordance with Japanese laws. The complainants alleged that when the amicable relationship between a foreign exporter and a Japanese importer is broken up, the foreign exporter found it difficult to obtain import licensing and approval for sales in Japan, since such licenses and approval were given only to domestic enterprises. On April 1, 1979, MITI took a step to remedy the situation by creating the "commissioned testing system for Category A electical appliances and materials," under which a foreign applicant may submit his products for testing by a "designated testing authority." After a successful test, he receives a certificate of test results. He then sends this certificate to his importer, who forwards it to the "designated testing authority" to obtain a "type test." After the "type test," the importer receives a successful test certificate and sends it to MITI, which then issues the "type authorization."[82] In short, under this system a foreign manufacturer or exporter can apply for testing and licensing of his product while located in a foreign country.

On May 25, 1983, a law was enacted which amends seventeen existing laws on technical standards of one kind or another to make it easier for foreign enterprises manufacturing products abroad to be exported to Japan to acquire from the Japanese government approval for new models. This legislation, which is entitled as "the Law to amend parts of the relevant laws for the purpose of facilitating the acquisitions by foreign enterprises of approval of models and related matters" (Law No. 57, 1983), amended such laws on technical standards as, inter alia, the Consumer Product Safety Law, the High Pressure Gas Law, the Electrical Appliances Control Law, the Pharmaceutical Affairs Law, the Road Transportation Vehicles Law, and others. In general, the laws were amended to enable foreign enterprises manufacturing products for export to Japan to register themselves in the Japanese ministry in charge and to acquire approval from the Ministry for new models. Hitherto it was a Japanese importer of a foreign product that acquired and held an approval from the ministry, and, if the relationship between the foreign exporter and the Japanese importer was broken up or terminated, the foreign exporter had to find a new importer who would apply for a new approval. This could be a time consuming and costly matter. The new legislation should remedy this situation if properly enforced.

Amendment to the Industrial Standardization Law

To comply with the requirements of the Tokyo Round Standards Code, an amendment was made to the Industrial Standardization Law[83] to permit foreign manufacturers or importers to affix a JIS mark on goods manufactured in foreign countries. Use of the JIS mark is voluntary, and it has no legal effect in Japan. However, because it carries prestige and authority, sometimes it is imperative for a seller to affix this mark on a product in order for it to be accepted by customers and government purchasing agencies. Moreover, some laws require that the products or parts used for certain purposes meet the requirements for JIS standards, as for example the Electrical Appliances Control Law and the Ship Safety Act. In such a case the use of this mark becomes essential for sales.

As the Tokyo Round negotiations progressed, the Japanese government felt that it was necessary to allow foreign producers or importers to put the JIS mark on foreign manufactured products under some conditions. In view of this, in September 1978, the Minister of MITI commissioned a task force of experts to study that issue. On November 13, 1979, this task force made a report to the Minister which, in essence, stated the following:[84]

1. In order to comply with the requirements of the Tokyo Round agreement, it would be necessary to open the JIS mark to foreign products.
2. Since, under the existing JIS system, a license to use the JIS mark was given to a factory that had been inspected and had proven to the government that it possessed sufficient technical and productive facilities to maintain a certain level of quality of industrial products, it was desirable to open the use of the JIS mark to foreign products on the condition that technical and productive facilities of the factory that manufactured the foreign products imported into Japan be examined. This would meet the requirement of the Standards Code that a supplier of imported products be accorded treatment no less favorable than that accorded a supplier of domestically produced products.
3. The JIS mark should be reviewed once every five years instead of once every three years.

After this report, MITI established a working group to investigate legal problems and draft an amendment bill. MITI's conclusion was that there should be an amendment concerning the application of the JIS system to foreign products, and a change in the review period. It took about a year to make the necessary adjustment and to reconcile the differences of opinion expressed by industries and other ministries[85]

On December 20, 1979, the Cabinet decided to amend the Industrial Standardization Law, and on the following day an amendment bill was introduced in the National Diet. The amendment passed and was promulgated on April 25, 1980. It stated that the JIS marking system would now be applicable to foreign manufacturers and processors under the following procedures.

1. A JIS mark may be used on a product produced in a foreign factory specifically approved by the minister who has authority over that particular product.
2. In granting such approval, the competent minister shall treat the foreign factory concerned exactly the same as a domestic factory producing the same product. In examining foreign factories applying for JIS mark certification, the same criteria will be used as for domestic factories—namely, quality control methods, maintenance of production facilities and testing of equipment at an appropriate level, handling of materials and products, and so on. The minister conducts an examination of the foreign factory applying for the JIS mark; usually two examiners are sent out.
3. Importers are allowed to sell products bearing JIS marks in the domestic market only if they have been produced in factories approved by the respective competent ministers.

The provision of the Industrial Standardization Law most relevant to permitting foreign manufacturers to affix the JIS mark to products imported to Japan is Article 25-2, which provides in part:

> When an application is made to the Minister in charge by a manufacturer of a designated commodity which carries on business in a foreign country, the Minister may grant an approval for such foreign manufacturer to affix the mark provided for in Article 19(1) [the JIS mark] on the designated commodity, package, vessel or invoice thereof manufactured by such manufacturer on the basis of an inspection of each factory or business located in such foreign country.

The Industrial Standardization Law adopts a factory inspection system rather than a product inspection system, according to which authorization to use the JIS mark is given after the factory that manufactures the products in question is examined and found to have sufficient technical and productive facilities. Under this system, the JIS mark is granted en bloc to products manufactured by a factory that has been inspected and proven to possess such facilities.

However, there is a special problem in applying this inspection system to foreign manufactured goods. Since the Industrial Standardization Law is a domestic law, its scope is in principle limited to products within Japanese territory. It is difficult to prohibit use of the JIS mark in foreign countries. Accordingly, the law adopts a system of controlling imports. An importer cannot sell a product on which the JIS mark is affixed if it was manufactured by someone who has not obtained a license or approval to use the mark from the minister in charge. It is impossible to enforce penalties for violation against a foreign manufacturer operating in foreign countries. Therefore, if such a violation occurs, approval to use the JIS mark is simply revoked. To enforce this system, Japanese government officials must inspect foreign factories. This, however, involves an extraterritorial application of Japanese domestic law, and is impossible if a foreign authority refuses to admit the official in charge of the inspection. So instead of stating that a Japanese government official may carry on an inspection in a factory located in a foreign country, Article 25-3 of the law provides that when a foreign manufacturer refuses an inspection approval to use the JIS mark may be denied or revoked.

Acceptance of the Results of Tests Conducted Abroad

There have been complaints that Japan has tended not to accept product testing conducted outside Japan, and as a result, imported products must also be tested in Japan to determine whether they meet Japanese requirements, a process which in some cases may take several years and involve considerable expense. The complaints stated that this resulted in undue delay in getting foreign products ready for sale in Japan. It has been alleged that this problem was compounded by foreign exporters' limited knowledge about the requirements to be met and their resulting difficulty in minimizing the expense of testing in Japan.[86] Although this problem has not been solved completely the Japanese government has made some significant moves to mitigate the difficulties by providing that the results of foreign testing will be accepted under some circumstances.

On May 22, 1979, the Cabinet decided to improve the procedures for adopting standards and test results made in foreign countries, in line with the Standards Code. This decision in part stated as follows:

> Cabinet Decision
>
> RE: Improvement of Procedures Concerning Technical Regulations and Standards (hereinafter "Standards") and Test Methods
>
> As Japan's position in the international community is becoming greater than ever, it is increasingly important for Japan to seek international

> standardization and simplification of procedures as well as non-discriminatory application of such standards and test methods as are generally employed in various countries.
>
> Japan intends to maintain its efforts to further improve its procedures concerning adoption and modification of standards and in testing procedures concerning imported goods. Thus it is hereby resolved that efforts for procedural improvements will be made in line with the following guidelines.
>
> Government affiliated agencies are given guidance to this effect.
>
> 1. When adopting or modifying standards, conformity with international standards will be sought as much as possible, while taking into account circumstances unique to Japan.
> 2. When adopting or modifying standards, public notification of such intention will be made, to the extent possible, sufficiently in advance.
> 3. After such notifications are made, opportunity for interested parties, whether domestic or foreign, to submit their views will be provided as much as possible, and views thus submitted will be given due consideration. For this purpose, improvements in procedures shall be facilitated where necessary.
> 4. When there is sufficient ground to regard foreign results as meeting in substance the requirements of Japanese standards, testing procedures in Japan should be simplified as much a possible.

Some progress has been made in accepting foreign test results for electrical appliances, pharmaceuticals, and agricultural chemicals.[87] For example, the administration of the Pharmaceutical Affairs Law has been changed.

Under Article 14 of the law, in order to import pharmaceutical products from abroad, it is necessary to obtain an approval from the Minister of MHW. Also, approval is given only after the effectiveness and other attributes of the pharmaceutical product in question have been examined. Some foreign countries (especially the European countries) had complained that the Japanese government would not approve the import of a foreign manufactured pharmaceutical product approved by the government of the country in which it had been manufactured unless an examination was conducted in Japan under the Pharmaceutical Affairs Law. The position of the government was that pharmaceutical products were examined differently in Japan and in foreign countries; that is, most of the foreign governments conducted an examination by a sample test, but Japan examined every unit of the product. The government also believed that foreign countries used more relaxed standards than Japan, and therefore the results of their examinations were not quite acceptable in Japan.

There have been several debates on this subject in the National Diet,[88] and some Diet members have questioned the wisdom of this treatment of foreign pharmaceutical products. For example, it was alleged that an examination by sample test is not necessarily more relaxed than a test in which every unit is examined.[89] However, government officials testifying in the National Diet reiterated the position of the government as explained above.

Finally, a decision was made to change the regulation under the Pharmaceutical Affairs Law and accept the results of the examinations conducted by the foreign authorities under some circumstances. On April 1, 1980, the Director General of the Pharmaceutical Affairs Bureau of MHW amended this regulation, providing that examinations of pharmaceutical products conducted in a foreign country may be accepted by the Japanese government as data to be used in conducting examinations in Japan.

New drugs must pass a stability test before they are approved for manufacture or importation. The regulation on this test was amended in order to simplify the administrative procedures for examining new pharmaceutical products for which approval is sought. The results of examinations conducted by foreign governments would be accepted, based on the premise that stability tests for new drugs are generally neutral in relation to cultural and dietary factors. Under the amendment, the Japanese government may accept the results of a stability test conducted by the relevant body of the foreign country concerned, as data in conducting its own examination. All test data and supporting documentation must be written in Japanese.

On January 14, 1982, a special task force established by the LDP, which had been commissioned to investigate nontariff barriers in Japan and suggest improvements, recommended that the enforcement of laws regulating the safety of various products be changed in order to accept the results of testing made abroad.[90] According to this report, sixteen items under the Pharmaceutical Affairs Law, two items under the Food Sanitation Law, and three items under the High Pressure Gas Control Law should be changed so that the results of tests conducted by foreign countries could be accepted. This should, at least, considerably ease the difficulties confronting foreign exporters, if not completely solve the problem.

Government Procurement

Views on Opening up Government Procurement to Foreign Companies

The Tokyo Round negotiation's conclusions on government procurement were probably its most controversial both in Japan and internationally. The central issue, however, was not whether Japanese government agencies should use an open tendering system that would make it possible for foreign enterprises to participate in bidding. The Japanese government was quite willing to make concessions on opening up the market consisting of government agencies. The core of the problem was whether some government-affiliated organizations (i.e., some public corporations) should also open their purchases to foreign bidders. This question was particularly debated in connection with purchase of instruments by Nippon Telegraph and Telephone Corporation (NTT). On this issue, there was a strong opinion in Japan that there should be no concession to open up to foreign bidding.

Views opposing an opening of NTT purchases are best summarized in the testimony of a leader of a labor union in the National Diet.[91] The first reason was that the communication system of a country is unified, and thus requires machines and instruments of uniform quality. Foreign-made goods could disrupt the efficient functioning of the Japanese communication system. The second reason was that many of the countries that participated in the Tokyo Round negotiations, notably some European countries, excluded electric communication instruments from the application of the Government Procurement Code. The third reason, which was probably the most important, was that of unemployment: if foreign producers were to participate in open tendering for NTT purchases of instruments, employment and business opportunities for small business would dwindle. According to this testimony, many small enterprises in Japan manufactured electric communication instruments or parts, and most of them were subcontractors of big entities like NTT. The testimony alleged that there were 180 small companies that were subcontractors of NTT, that they employed 70,000 workers, and that if 20 percent of NTT purchases was shifted to foreign producers those subcontractors would have to get rid of 14,000 workers.

A MITI official testified in the National Diet that some effort would be made to increase government purchases from small enterprises rather than from large companies under the Government Procurement Law, which provides that government agencies, including government-affiliated corporations like NTT, shall make reasonable efforts to increase purchases from small business, thereby redressing the hardships that might be caused by the concession.[92]

Of the various reasons advanced by NTT itself, labor union leaders, and some Diet members, the issue of employment was the most important.

Negotiations between the United States and Japan

In negotiating a code on government procurement, the basic position of the Japanese government was that it should apply to agencies that composed the central government. For this reason, the Japanese officer included only those government agencies in Japan to which the Accounts Law applied. However, the U.S. government strongly requested that some other government-affiliated organizations (especially NTT, the Japan Tobacco and Salt Corporation, and the Japan National Railway) be included. Considering this difference of opinion, the Japanese government felt it necessary to make some concessions, and in the Strauss-Ushiba Conference that took place in Washington, D.C., in March 1979, the government expressed its intention to improve its offer by including those corporations and some others. However, the view of the United States was that this offer was still not satisfactory, because some important instruments to be purchased by NTT were excluded from it. The Japanese government reached an agreement with participating governments other than the United States, and continued to negotiate with the U.S. government.

In December 1980, the two governments agreed that NTT would open up some more areas for open tendering, with some reservations. The Minister of Posts and Telecommunications was to issue administrative guidance to NTT in order to implement the agreement.

The Evaluation of NTT's Opening up of the Market

NTT initiated the new system of purchase in which foreign bidders can participate in bidding for sales of supplies on January 1, 1981. At first, there was a strong suspicion in the United States that the new system would be as closed as the previous one, despite the change. In fact, in the first year the agreement performed poorly, because NTT demanded extremely detailed information from firms seeking to qualify as bidders.[93] However, the Gibbons Report, published in December 1980, by the U.S. Congress (Congressman Sam Gibbons is Chairman of a subcommittee of the Ways and Means Committee of the House of Representatives), commented favorably on NTT's effort to purchase foreign instruments. A portion of the report reads:

> The Subcommittee on Trade has been very impressed, however, with the dedication of the new President of NTT . . . to make the Agreement work and truly to open up NTT. NTT has informed us that as of mid-August, four U.S. firms had won or were participating in contracts worth $1.5 million. While this would be rounded to zero in the trade balance figures between our two nations, it is a beginning. Furthermore, most big contracts will not be let until early next year, and it is reported that 8 to 12 U.S. firms will probably qualify as NTT bidders and that U.S. firms are reportedly being considered as suppliers of such major items as echo suppressors, car telephone contracts, etc. In short, while there has been little to show from the Agreement to date, the Subcom-

> mittee is impressed with the changes that are being made and in the new attitude at NTT.
>
> The NTT/Government Procurement Agreement is an important test case. The operation of the Agreement will be reviewed in about two years and if there have not been results, the Government Procurement Code Agreement between the United States and Japan will be terminated, thus ending the right of Japanese firms to bid on a number of U.S. contracts. Failure of the Agreement would be a serious blow to our bilateral relations.[94]

According to a press report of December 28, 1981,[95] the president of NTT sent a letter to the U.S. Department of Commerce and requested the Department to advise U.S. firms to use the new bid system adopted by NTT. This report stated that despite the opening of the NTT market, there has been insufficient participation of U.S. firms in supplying telecommunication instruments.

There are, however, again some complaints in the United States recently that, despite the opening up of the bid system, purchases of United States products by NTT has not significantly increased. At the time of this writing, whether the United States–Japan Agreement on this matter will be renewed or not remains to be seen.

The Legal System of Government Procurement in Japan

Until 1972, there was a provision in Imperial Edict No. 556 of 1964 that clearly stated: *"In order to promote use of domestically produced articles,* the Minister of each Ministry may use a single tendering in purchasing commodities as designated by the Minister of Finance." (Emphasis added.) In 1972, however, this provision was abolished in order to establish a more open system of government purchasing.

At present, there are one law and several orders concerning government procurement in Japan.[96] These are: (1) the Accounts Law, (2) the Cabinet Order Concerning the Budget, Auditing, and Accounting (Imperial Edict No. 165 of 1947, hereinafter referred to as the Order of 1947), (3) Special Provisions for the Cabinet Order Concerning the Budget, Auditing, and Accounting (Imperial Edict No. 558 of 1946, hereinafter referred to as the Special Provisions of 1946), (4) the Cabinet Order stipulating special procedures for government procurement of goods (Cabinet Order No. 300 of 1980, hereinafter referred to as the Special Cabinet Order), and (5) the Ministerial Ordinance stipulating special procedures for government procurement of goods (Ministry of Finance Ordinance No. 45 of 1980, hereinafter referred to as the Ordinance of 1980).

Because before January 1, 1981, the Order of 1947, the Special Provisions of 1946, and the Accounts Law included some provisions for procedures not identical to those set out in the agreement, some adjustments were required to implement the agreement. The Special Cabinet Order and the Ordinance of 1980 were thus issued to provide for special procedures and for the stipulations necessary in accordance with the Order of 1947 and the Special Provisions of 1946, so that the procedures applicable to the special procurement would be in full compliance with the agreement. In this way, the agreement has been incorporated into domestic law. Some essentials of the present procurement system are given below.

1. Notice of Proposed Purchase and Tender Documentation. The notice of proposed purchase by means of open or selective tendering procedures must be published in the *Official Gazette* (*Kampo*) at least thirty days prior to the day for submitting tenders.
2. Open and Selective Tendering Processes. Open and selective tendering procedures are adopted in accordance with the provisions of the agreement. Where selective tendering procedures are adopted, the invitation for participation in the tendering shall be issued on the same date as the publication of notice for the tendering.
3. Use of Single-Tendering Procedures. Use of single-tendering procedures is limited to those cases permitted under the agreement (Article 29-3 of the Accounts Law, Article 10 and 11 of the Special Cabinet Order).
4. The Lowest Bidder. Purchasing agencies award a contract to the supplier submitting the tender that offers the lowest price within the limits of the provisional value of the contract. Agencies may, because of the nature or objective of a contract, award a contract to the supplier submitting the most advantageous tender in terms of price and other factors.
5. National Treatment and Nondiscrimination. The principle of equal treatment for domestic and foreign suppliers is one of the bases for the new procedures for procurement in Japan, and the principle has been confirmed by the MOF Minister's directive entitled "With regard to the implementation of the Cabinet Order stipulating special procedures for government procurement of goods," issued on December 27, 1980.
6. Local Government. On January 23, 1981, MFA and the Ministry of Home Affairs sent to all the prefectural governments, the municipal or local governments, and some city authorities a joint letter describing the contents of the agreement, with particular reference to Paragraph 2 of Article I.

Single Tendering

Under the present system the basic principle in government procurement in Japan is open tendering, and if it is impossible to rely on open tendering, selective tendering, which is open to both domestic and foreign persons. As indicated above, the use of a single-tendering procedure is limited to some exceptional cases. Article 29-3 of the Accounts Law provides that single tendering shall be adopted where the circumstances (the nature or purpose of the contract concerned) do not allow the governmental entity concerned to adopt open or selective tendering procedures for a contract for procurement, when open or selective tendering procedures cannot be adopted because of extreme urgency, or when open or selective tendering procedures would be disadvantageous for the agency concerned. However, Article 29-3(5) of the Accounts Law provides that, notwithstanding the other provisions, a single-tendering procedure may be adopted in the cases specified by cabinet order. Article 99 of the Order of 1947 provides that a single-tendering procedure may be used when government agency purchases products directly from cooperatives composed mainly of small and medium-sized enterprises, or associations of such enterprises, in order to protect and foster them. By using this provision, the Japanese government can purchase products exclusively from small domestic enterprises. This is potentially an important leeway for the government agencies to use to avoid purchasing foreign products.

As already touched upon, to implement the Government Procurement Code some changes in domestic law and regulation were necessary. The implementation has mostly been effected through amendments to various regulations under the Accounts Law governing purchases by government agencies. The Accounts Law applies to purchases by agencies composing the national government, including both houses of the National Diet, the Supreme Court, the Prime Minister's office, and various ministries. In addition, some government-affiliated organizations are covered. These include, among others, the Japan National Railway, the Japan Tobacco and Salt Corporation, NTT, and twelve other financial organizations. As far as the Japan National Railway and NTT are concerned, the government entered into the Government Procurement Code on the following conditions: (1) the Japan National Railway is not obligated to comply with the terms of the code when purchasing equipment necessary to maintain safety standards in railway transportation; (2) NTT is not obligated to comply with the terms of the code for purchases of equipment and facilities for public communication or purchases by local establishments. However, in light of a joint announcement by the negotiator for Japan and the United States if those two governments reached an agreement by December 31, 1980, then NTT would be brought within the code obligations as to electronic communication equipment covered by such agreement. Such an agreement was reached on December 19, 1980.

Since the Japan National Railway, the Japan Tobacco and Salt

Corporation, NTT, and other government-affiliated financial organizations are not subject to the Accounts Law and regulations issued under it, implementation has been effected through administrative guidance of the ministries in charge and by amendments to the internal rules and regulations that govern the purchases made by those organizations.

Legal Remedies for Government Agencies' Violations of the MTN Codes

The issue to be dealt with at this point is the Japanese legal remedies available to private enterprises and citizens, domestic and foreign, when Japanese government agencies violate one or more of the MTN codes. For example, if a government agency refuses to grant a license to sell a product when the Japanese government is obligated under one of the codes to do so, what can the private enterprise or citizen who has suffered or will suffer economic disadvantage or damage do? Several types of legal remedies are available. Some of their basic features will be explored here.

Before discussing legal remedies, we should, however, mention that there are several organizations that are designed to handle complaints by foreign enterprises operating in Japan. In 1977, the TSG[97] was organized as a bilateral group of Japanese and American volunteers from the U.S. business community in Tokyo, the U.S. Embassy, MITI, JETRO, the Federation of Economic Organizations (*Keidanren*), the Japan–United States Economic Council, the Foreign Trade Council of Japan, the Japan Chamber of Commerce and Industry, and others from the Japanese business and government communities, all acting in an individual capacity. The work of the TSG has been concentrated on two related issues. The first is to identify, analyze, and make recommendations about Japanese laws, regulations, procedures, or practices that inhibit increased sales of U.S. goods and services in Japan. The second is to encourage efforts by U.S. companies to gain a position in the Japanese market by participating in specific trade promotion programs and to communicate directly or indirectly with U.S. businessmen about the nature and positive results of the work of the TSG.[98]

As noted, the TSG is a purely private organization composed of governmental and nongovermental members, all participating voluntarily, as private individuals. However, its remarks and recommendations have had some impact on changing governmental practices in regulating trade, and in this sense it has been quite successful. Moreover, its activities have been carefully evaluated by a U.S. congressional committee.

Faced with a huge trade deficit with Japan, the U.S. government felt that it would be necessary to create a common entity to ease the entry of American-made products into the Japanese market. Accordingly, a bilateral subcabinet meeting was held in early 1977. This meeting resulted in the establishment of the Joint United States–Japan Trade Facilitation Committee (TFC). The TFC is jointly composed of members of the U.S. Department of Commerce and MITI. When U.S. companies exporting products to the Japanese market complain to the U.S. government about barriers to market access, their complaints will be discussed in the TFC. Whenever there is a way of solving the difficulty, the Japanese government takes the necessary measure to remedy the situation. In this sense, the TFC is also an informal organization without any legal power. However, it has successfully handled many complaints and has contributed much to the easier entry of U.S. products into the Japanese market.[99]

The two organizations discussed so far are both informal in nature. They have, nevertheless, helped remove trade barriers.

In order to deal more effectively with foreign and Japanese exporters' complaints against Japanese trade barriers, the Cabinet, in a resolution passed on January 30, 1982, established a headquarters, or ombudsman, to help settle such grievances. The headquarters is called the Office of the Trade Ombudsman (OTO) and is composed of vice-ministers (of EPA, MFA, MOF, MITI, the Ministry of Education, MHW, MAFF, the Ministry of Transportation, the Ministry of Posts and Telecommunications, the Ministry of Home Affairs, and the Agency of Science and Technology), with the Vice-Minister of the Cabinet-Secretariat as the chairman. An executive board consisting of high-ranking officials of important government ministries and agencies has also been established. Under this system, complaints may be filed with the appropriate sections of these ministries and agencies and with Japanese embassies and consulates in foreign countries. When a complaint is filed specifying the complainant and the precise nature of the grievance, the relevant ministry or agency shall report to the complainant how the complaint is being considered within ten days and, as promptly as possible, inform him of the final result of the investigation and the remedy.

In formulating remedies, ministries and agencies are required to consider the following factors.

1. Technical standards under domestic laws should conform to internationally recognized standards, insofar as that is possible given circumstances unique to Japan.
2. The results of tests made in foreign countries regarded as reliable should be accepted.
3. Standards shall be clear, and quantities specified as much as possible.

4. Transparency in the domestic institutions shall be established as much as possible.

By March 1, 1982, eleven complaints had been filed with the relevant sections of the Japanese government. Among those, seven came from Japanese importers, three from U.S. exporters, one from an Irish exporter, and one from a state in the United States.[100]

The government can respond to complaints in one of four ways. It can take an affirmative measure to remedy the situation; it can tell the complainant that his complaint is based on a misunderstanding; it can continue considering the problem; or it can decide that nothing will change.

It is premature to judge whether this system will be the answer to trade barrier problems. However, it is expected that if it is used intensively it may be an effective tool to solve or mitigate them.

Legal Actions for Indemnification of Damages

Article 17 of the Constitution provides: "Any person can ask the State or a public body for the indemnification of the damage when he has sustained the damage by a tortious act of public official in accordance with a provision of a law." Under this provision, an individual's right to recover for damage sustained because of the wrongful conduct of a governmental official is recognized. Accordingly, a person whose property has unjustly been injured because a government official has violated one of the MTN codes should be allowed to recover damages. There is little doubt that a Japanese citizen can exercise his constitutional right to damages under this provision.

The question arises whether the same right is guaranteed when the property of a foreign citizen or enterprise is wrongfully injured due to an action of the Japanese government that is held to be a violation of one of the provisions of the MTN codes. The answer depends on whether or not "any person," as provided in Article 17, includes a foreign citizen or enterprise. Generally speaking, the term does include not only Japanese citizens but also foreign individuals. Thus there are some cases[101] in which the Supreme Court has held that foreigners are protected by the constitutional guarantee of human rights. However, Article 17 permits the recovery of damage caused by the tortious conduct of a government official *in accordance with a provision of a law*. The relevant law in this regard is the State Redress Law,[102] and Article 6 of that law provides that when a foreign person has sustained damage due to tortious conduct by a government official, he is allowed to recover the damage as long as there is a guarantee for reciprocity.[103] This means that a foreign person could recover for dam-

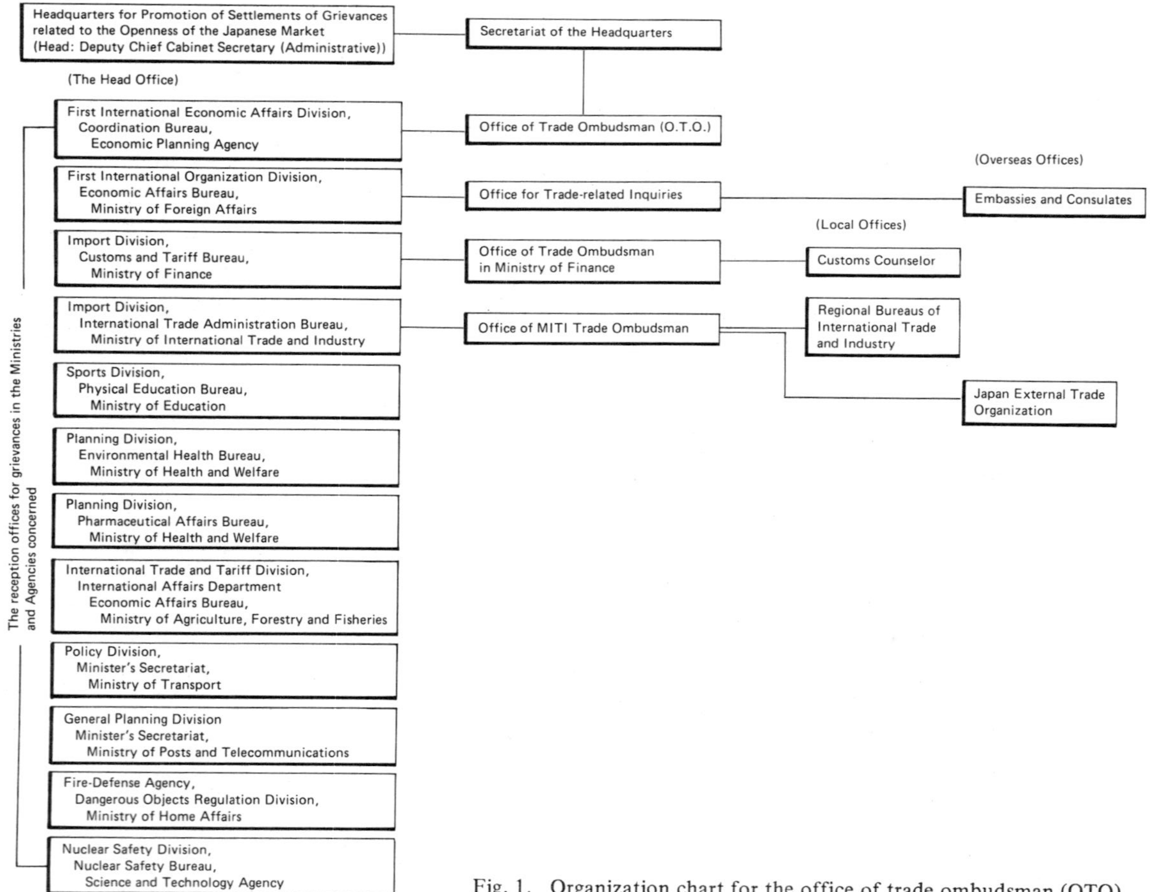

Fig. 1. Organization chart for the office of trade ombudsman (OTO)

ages if his own country allows Japanese citizens to recover damages caused by tortious acts of government officials of that country. In this sense, the application of state indemnification for a foreign person is limited by the rule of reciprocity, and there are some court cases that so hold.[104] However, some commentators argue that Article 6 is in violation of Article 17 of the Constitution, which holds that "any person" is entitled to recovery of damages caused by the tortious conduct of a government official.[105]

Even though there is some uncertainty about the reciprocity factor, it is at least clear that a foreign person can definitely seek to recover damages caused by a tortious act of the government when his home country grants such recovery to Japanese citizens. If we apply this rule to our situation, we can say that a foreign citizen or a foreign enterprise can bring a suit against the government on the basis of Article 6 of the State Redress Law and also Article 17 of the Constitution when his business interest has been adversely affected by a government action (for example, a refusal to grant a license to sell a product that violates one of the MTN codes). Since, as explained earlier, most of the MTN codes have been approved by the National Diet as treaties in the sense of Article 98(2) of the Constitution, it is clear that they override administrative actions of the government that are contrary to their contents.

To recover the damage, the plaintiff must prove that there was a malicious intent or negligence on the part of the government official who engaged in the tortious conduct. However, such proof should not be difficult as long as the official's conduct was contrary to the provisions of one of the MTN codes, since government officials should know the contents of the treaties to which the government of Japan is a party. Nevertheless, the plaintiff must prove the amount of damage he sustained, and show that the illegal conduct of the government official caused it.

The next question is whether a foreign citizen or enterprise can base a claim for the recovery of damages on the fact that the National Diet's failure to enact or abolish a law has kept the government's regulation of business from conforming to the obligations of the MTN codes. For example, a foreign enterprise may argue that it has suffered a loss of profit in Japan because of the existence of a discriminatory regulation that is contrary to the Standards Code, and that this regulation should either have been abolished or amended in order to fulfill the requirement of nondiscrimination incorporated in the code. In a court decision[106] where the issue was the National Diet's abolition of the home voting system for physically disabled persons, the Sapporo District Court stated that the existence of an unconstitutional law and the National Diet's failure to replace it with a proper one could be regarded as a tortious act of the government and could impose on it the duty to compensate for a loss suffered by a citizen as a result of such legislation. It is clear from this decision that under some circumstances, legislation or failure to enact legislation may be regarded as illegal conduct on the part of the government and may be used as grounds for seeking a pecuniary recovery for damage sustained by an individual.[107] The question here is whether we can equate the right of compensation under the State Redress Law with the voting rights that are regarded as most fundamental among the political rights of the people.

Generally speaking, the government is not held liable for pecuniary compensation of damage to individuals when the damage has been caused by its failure in economic policies, since formulating and executing such policies are discretionary on the part of the administrative branch of the government. There is a court decision[108] in which the plaintiff maintained that unusual price rises in consumer products, which caused pecuniary damages to consumers, were the result of mistakes committed by the government in formulating and executing policies, and that the government's failure to raise the interest rate on deposits in accounts in post offices was also a gross negligence that should subject it to the obligation to compensate for such losses. The Osaka High Court dismissed the claim on the ground that economic policies are entrusted to the administrative branch of the government and that the administrative branch has the discretionary power to decide what policies are wise.

A claim by a foreign enterprise or a domestic enterprise for the recovery of pecuniary losses caused by the National Diet's failure to amend a domestic regulation in accordance with a requirement of the MTN codes falls somewhere between a claim based on the right to vote that is guaranteed by the Constitution and a claim based on a failure of the government in handling economic policies. This claim, however, should be regarded as having more substance than a claim based on a purely economic policy matter, since most of the MTN codes are treaties in the sense of the Constitution. Therefore, they are clearly given a higher status than domestic legislation and regulations that are contrary to the contents of the codes. In a case where a domestic regulation or legislation is unequivocally contrary to the requirements of one of the MTN codes, the National Diet's failure to remedy the situation may constitute tortious conduct on the part of the government.

Legal Actions for Cancellation of Governmental Determinations

The Administrative Cases Litigation Law[109] (hereinafter referred to as the Litigation Law) provides for legal actions against the government aimed at cancelling wrongful governmental determinations. We shall examine here the conditions under which a foreign enterprise may challenge a governmental determination that has given it a business disadvantage, and the process for seeking a court decision that would nullify such a determination. The situation arises when, for example, an importer of foreign products or a foreign exporter to Japan is placed at a disadvantage as a result of the valuation of his products for customs purposes. As explained earlier, the Customs Tariff Law has been amended to base customs valuation on the transaction value of the imported product. Therefore, if a determination of customs value has been made on the basis of some other criteria, it is contrary to the Customs Tariff Law and also the Customs Valuation Code. What are the legal remedies in this situation?

Article 7 of the Litigation Law states that for matters not provided for in that law, provisions of the Civil Procedure Code will apply, and the Litigation Law contains no provision for a suit brought against the government by a foreign person or enterprise. Article 51 of the Civil Procedure Code is the applicable provision; it states: "An alien is deemed to possess the power to be a party in a litigation whenever he shall possess the power to be a party in a litigation according to the Japanese law, even though he has no such power according to the law of his home country." It is clear from this provision that a foreigner has the power to bring a suit against the government as long as he has the power to be a party in a ligitation under the provisions of the Civil Procedure Code and the Civil Code.

Under Article 3(2) of the Litigation Law, a person whose legal interest has been adversely affected by a governmental action may bring a suit against the government for cancellation of that action. In our situation a governmental decision like a refusal to grant a license to sell or to import is amenable to this suit as long as the action is contrary to the obligations imposed on the Japanese government by the MTN codes. A foreign party is entitled to bring such a suit if he is the addressee of a government decision. For example, if a foreign enterprise has applied for a license to sell a product in Japan, and the Japanese government issues a determination addressed to this party denying such a license, the foreign enterprise may bring suit under Article 3(2) of the Litigation Law. The plaintiff in such a litigation usually seeks a court decision that would cancel the determination; if a governmental determination is contrary to a provision of a treaty approved by the National Diet, the court handling the case must declare that the action is illegal and subject to cancellation.

However, to be qualified as a plaintiff in a suit against the government under Article 3(2), a party must have some legal interest in the issue. This is the question of standing, and it must be decided before the court addresses the issue of the illegality of the governmental determination. Article 9 of the Litigation Law provides that a person who brings a suit under that law must have a legal interest in the cancellation of the determination in question. However, if a foreign enterprise has been denied a license or approval of sale or import, there is little doubt that it has a legal interest in requesting a court to cancel the determination.

Article 3(5) of the Litigation Law provides for a legal action against the inaction of a government agency. For example, if an administrative agency is required to decide whether to grant an application for a license to sell within a reasonable period, it would be liable if it failed to make its decision within that period. Therefore, if a foreign enterprise has applied to an agency for approval to sell a certain type of product, and the agency has not acted for an unduly long period, it could be subject to suit under this provision.

However, whether a court will require the agency to act under Article 3(5) depends on the nature of the administrative action sought by the plaintiff. Some kinds of administrative actions are discretionary.[110] If an action falls within this category it is usually impossible to force the government agency to make a decision. However, some actions are regarded as ministerial, such as approvals or disapprovals of licenses given to products under the safety standards and laws. If an administrative action is of this type, it is usually possible to force the government agency to decide whether to take it.[111]

If an administrative inaction has been held illegal under Article 3(5), the government agency is required under Article 33 of the Litigation Law to make a decision on the matter in question. If, for example, the agency's inaction on an application for a license to sell a product under a law providing for a safety standard is held illegal, the agency must decide whether to approve the application.

Violation of the MTN Codes as a Defense

When a foreign enterprise is accused of violating a Japanese law or regulation that is contrary to the provisions of the MTN codes, the accused party can use as a defense the fact that the law or regulation under which he is being accused is in violation of a treaty and is null and void. This defense is possible when an enterprise is accused of a criminal offense for violating, for example, safety standards or some other standards incorporated in law. The party using the defense must of course prove that the law or regulation is contrary to a provision of a treaty. However, once this proof is established, the legal consequence is rather clear; that is, the court handling the case must decide that the treaty prevails over the domestic law or regulation that conflicts with it. After the criminal action has been dropped for this reason, the party may bring an action against the government for indemnification of the damage, if he can prove the damage.

Standing of Foreign Governments

As touched on earlier, only those whose legal interests have been adversely affected by an administrative action of the govenent have standing to sue the government in a suit to cancel the action. It seems, therefore, that there is no legal way for a foreign government to bring a court action in Japan to cancel an action of the Japanese government that violates the MTN codes. In a claim for damages under the State Redress Law there is no strict requirement of standing, and it is possible for any person to sue the government for tortious acts. However, the plaintiff has to prove both that he sustained damage and that the illegal conduct caused it. Except for unusual situations, it seldom happens that a foreign government suffers a property loss due to an action of a Japanese government official that violates the MTN codes. Thus there is little chance that a foreign government can use the State Redress Law as a basis for its claim.

Generally speaking, the role played by a foreign government in court litigation where the issue of a violation of the MTN codes by the Japanese government is raised is that of filing with the court an opinion stating its position on the action in question and its legality under the codes. It is up to the court to decide whether such an opinion should be accepted.[112]

Article 42 of the Litigation Law provides for a lawsuit against the Japanese government by a person or a body not having any legal interest in the court action. According to this provision, such an action is allowed only if there is a provision in a law to that effect. Therefore, if the MTN codes contained a provision permitting a foreign government to bring an action in a Japanese court, foreign governments would be given standing to challenge an action of the Japanese government that is contrary to the codes.

Article 89 of the Tariff Law provides for a procedure for petition with regard to tariff decisions. Under this Article, a person whose interests have been adversely affected by a decision of the director of Customs made under the authority of the Tariff Law or other laws related to tariff matters may file a petition with the minister of MOF. The minister then makes a decision revoking or affirming the decision of the director of Customs after consulting the matter with the Tariff Appeals Committee (Kanzei Fufuku Shinsakai). It is only after the decision of the Minister of MOF on this matter has been rendered that the petitioner may file a suit for cancellation of a tariff decision with a court.

Conclusions

It is probably fair to state that the MTN agreements and their implementation in Japan have contributed somewhat to the liberalization of Japan's international trade. Especially in such areas as technical standards and government procurement, considerable progress has been made in opening up some areas to foreign imports. There is, however, still some dissatisfaction with remaining trade barriers in Japan. Some of those allegations are real, but show a lack of understanding of what has happened in Japan in the past several years. Excluding new entrants in such areas as services, banking, the distribution system, and cartels have been pointed out in a 1981 U.S. congressional document.[113] It is the task of the Japanese government to see whether such allegations are justified, and whenever it finds undue restrictions and exclusions, to remedy the situation. At the same time, the Japanese government should make a major effort to demonstrate that the Japanese market is not as closed as it is believed to be in foreign countries.

On the export side, most of the important trade problems between Japan and the United States or European countries have been solved by orderly marketing agreements whereby the Japanese government and industries undertook to restrain exports of the products in question. Prominent examples are textiles, steel, specialty steel, televisions, and automobiles. The wisdom of solving trade problems in this way should be closely reexamined, and, even if this technique is used, it should be subject to international rules to guarantee fairness to everyone concerned.

Some of the alleged trade barriers in Japan have not been covered by the MTN agreements. For example, administrative guidance exercised by the Japanese government, the exclusivity in the Japanese distribution system, and the exclusivity in Japanese business groups were not addressed in the MTN negotiations.

More recently industrial policy exercised by the Japanese Government has become a hot issue in trade disputes between the Japanese government and the governments of other countries. "Industrial policy" is a general term that permits a considerable latitude for different meanings. However, as it is used in trade disputes, generally it means such practices as "targeting," that is, a policy of the government to select an industry that is potentially promising and aiding the industry to become competitive by such means as giving subsidies in research and development or grouping the enterprises into several groups under the leadership of government to avoid cut-throat competition. It also includes "negative targeting," that is, governmental measures given to structurally depressed industries to help them maintain artificially international competitiveness by such means as depression cartels or some other restrictive measures to dispose of excess capacity. Industrial policy is deeply rooted in the relationship between the Japanese government and industries. It is perhaps neither possible, nor desirable, to abolish industrial policy in Japan altogether. However, in view of the fact that industrial policy in Japan will cause some impacts on some industries in foreign countries, it should be exercised with prudence so that it will not result in undue hardships to them. Industrial policy has not been a traditional subject matter for international trade negotiation. However, since industrial policy should be exercised in the context of internationalization of the national economies, the time will come that this issue of industrial policy must be discussed in international trade negotiations.

Some of these alleged trade barriers are not legal barriers but arrangements made among private enterprises without government involvement. This raises an interesting question: Should nongovernmental arrangements initiated by private enterprises, trade-related cultural barriers, or business and social customs be the subject of trade negotiations? And, if so, how should the government go about changing those arrangements? It will be necessary to give some thought to this question in the future.

As has already been explained, there are some legal remedies available to domestic and foreign enterprises whose rights have been infringed upon by the Japanese government, if they can show that the government's action is contrary to one of the provisions contained in the MTN agreements to which the Japanese government is a party. It is recommended that foreign enterprises bring such legal claims to the Japanese government whenever they feel that their rights have been injured by its action. It is less likely that Japanese domestic companies will raise such claims, because they are less inclined to use legal actions to cope with troubles with the government. Although excess litigiousness may bring about inefficiency and unnecessary waste of time and energy, even in Japan, litigation can be an effective means to persuade governmental agencies that the MTN agreements should be strictly observed. It is worthwhile to give some thought to the possibility of using those legal remedies more fully, not only for securing the rights of foreign enterprises in Japan, but also for bettering Japanese society as a whole.

NOTES

1. KENPŌ (the Constitution of Japan) entered into force May 3, 1947. An English translation prepared by the Ministry of Foreign Affairs is reprinted in 9 CONSTITUTIONS OF THE COUNTRIES OF THE WORLD (A. Blaus-

tein & G. Flanz ed. 1973). [hereinafter cited as CONSTITUTIONS]. The following are some of the references on the Japanese Constitution that are available in English: S. FUJII, THE CONSTITUTION OF JAPAN: A HISTORICAL SURVEY (1965); D. HENDERSON, THE CONSTITUTION OF JAPAN, ITS FIRST TWENTY YEARS, 1947–1967 (1969). See also Bibliography, CONSTITUTIONS, *supra* following the text of the Japanese Constitution.

2. Article 98 of the Japanese Constitution reads: "This Constitution shall be the supreme law of the nation and no law, or ordinance, imperial rescript or other act of government, or part thereof, contrary to the provisions thereof, shall have legal force or validity. The treaties concluded by Japan and established laws of nations shall be faithfully observed." 9 CONSTITUTIONS, *supra* note 1, at 8.
3. In spite of the importance of this issue, there has been little writing on the extraparliamentary process in decision making in Japan. A recent book describes the details of this process. I. MURAKAWA, SEISAKU KETTEI KATEI (The Policy-Making Process) (1981).
4. *Id.* at 125–63.
5. Some interesting parallels to this Japanese practice may be seen in the fast-track procedure of U.S. law as it operated in the case of the 1979 Trade Act, see the section in chapter 4, entitled The "Fast-Track" Procedure for NTB Agreements, and the Drafting of the Trade Agreements Act of 1979.
6. MURAKAWA, *supra* note 3, at 128–29.
7. *Compare* three sections in chapter 4: Separation of Powers; Executive-Congressional Tensions; Congressional Power to Regulate Commerce; second, NTB Authority; Legislative Veto; "Fast-Track" Congressional Procedures; third, the "Fast-Track" Procedure for NTB Agreements, and the Drafting of the Trade Agreements Act of 1979.
8. Ashahi Newspaper, Mar. 4, 1981 (morning ed.), at 9.
9. Details on the textile negotiation and its result are available in NICHIBEI SENIKYOTEI NI KANSURU GYOSEI SOSYO KIROKU (Record of the Administrative Litigation concerning the Textile Agreement between the United States and Japan) (Seni Sangyo Renmei [Federation of Textile Industries] 1974). This report has been translated into English and can be found in the course materials on Japanese law at Harvard Law School (1977–78).
10. *See, e.g.,* INT'L TRADE REPORTER U.S. IMPORT WEEKLY (BNA) (hereinafter ITIM), Nos. 70–77 (Mar.–May 1981), and particularly No. 76, at A-1 (May 6, 1981).
11. Japan Economic Newspaper, Feb. 28, 1981 (morning ed.), at 3.
12. I. SATO, KENPOKAISHAKU NO SHOMONDAI (Problems in Constitutional Interpretations) 217 (1953); Sato, *Kokkai no joyakushoninken to kokankobun*" (The Power of the National Diet to Approve Treaties and Exchange of Notes), 19 JOCHI HOGAKU RONSHU, Mar. 1976, at 135.
13. Sato, *supra* note 12, (KENPOKAISHAKU) at 148, 154 et seq.
14. MFA Notification No. 275 of 1968.
15. MFA Notification No. 118 of 1970.
16. MFA Notification No. 259 of 1970.

17. Testimony of the Director of the Cabinet Legislation Bureau in *Hearing of the Committee of Budget of the House of Councillors,* Rec. Comm. Hearing No. 7, 67th Diet, 15 (Jan. 9, 1971).
18. *See* I. SATO, NIHONKOKU KENPŌ GAISETSU (A General Explanation of the Constitution of Japan) 467–69 (rev. ed. 1980).
19. Professor Sato takes this position. *Id.* at 469.
20. *Id.* at 467–68.
21. 13 Sai-han keishu (Supreme Court Criminal Cases Reporter) 3225 (1959).
22. In this case, a person was indicted for trespassing on a military installation of the U.S. Air Force in Japan. The indictment was made under the Criminal Special Measures Law (Keiji tokubetsu ho), which provided for the punishment of anyone who trespasses on the property of U.S. bases in Japan and was an implementation of the Status of Forces Agreement and the Security Treaty. The defendant's counsel alleged that this law, the agreement, and the treaty conflicted with Article 9 of the Constitution, which prohibits Japan from exercising military power for the purpose of solving international conflicts.
23. *See* cases cited *infra* note 25.
24. *See* the COCOM Decision, 20 Gyosei reishu (Administrative Cases Reporter) 842 (1969).
25. *See* Shimizu v. Japan, 26 Sai-han keishū (Supreme Court Criminal Cases Reporter) 586 (1955), *translated and reproduced* in J. MAKI, COURT AND CONSTITUTION IN JAPAN (1964). A translation of this decision is also included in the course materials on Japanese law at Harvard Law School (1977–78); Sumiyoshi v. Governor of Hiroshima Prefecture, (1975), *translated and reproduced in* 8 L. IN JAPAN 194–204 (1975). For a comment on this case in English, see Haley, *The Freedom to Choose an Occupation and the Constitutional Limits of Legislative Discretion—K.K. Sumiyoshi v. Governor of Hiroshima Prefecture,* 8 L. IN JAPAN 188–94 (1975).
26. In the case of Marushin Sangyo K.K. v. Japan, 26 Sai-han keishū (Supreme Court Criminal Decisions Reporter) 586 (1972), a company was indicted for having engaged in erecting a building with compartments and leasing the compartments to retailers. Under the Retail Business Adjustment Special Measures Law (Kouri shogyo chosei tokubetsu sochi ho), Law No. 155 of 1959, a developer of a building to be leased or assigned to small retail shopkeepers must file a report with the local government and obtain a license to do so. The law gives local governments the power to make conditions for the licensing of the building and leasing or assigning the building. The Osaka Prefecture conditioned such licensing on a new building for shops being at least 700 meters away from the existing building for such shops. This was designed to mitigate excessive competition among the existing shops and thereby to protect small Mom and Pop stores. The defendant built such a building and leased it to storekeepers without obtaining a license from the prefectural government, and the building was within 700 meters of existing buildings for small shops. The prefectural government brought a criminal accusation to the public pros-

ecutor's office, and the company was indicted. The company argued that the law and the zoning regulation enacted under it were contrary to Article 22 of the Constitution. The Supreme Court, however, stated that a decision on whether small shopkeepers need to be protected by such a legislation is best made by the National Diet, which is better equipped to investigate such matters than the judiciary, and the Court must defer to a judgment made by the National Diet on this type of matter. This would mean that, in matters relating to socioeconomic or industrial policy, the courts should adopt judicial passivism and refrain from exercising judicial review over the wisdom of such legislation.

27. S. Kiyomiya, Kenpō (The Constitution) 499 (3d ed. 1979); Sato, *supra* note 18, at 465.
28. Sato, *supra* note 18, at 467; Y. Takano, Kokusaiho Gairon (A General Theory of International Law) 84 (1969).
29. Sato, *supra* note 18, at 467. *See also, supra* note 2.
30. Y. Takano, Kenpō to joyaku (The Constitution and Treaties) 209 (1960).
31. What is referred to here is an international agreement which the National Diet has not approved and for which no authorizing treaty or law exists.
32. Gaikokukawase oyobi gaikokuboeki kanri ho, as amended, Law No. 228 of 1949.
33. Yushutsunyu torihiki ho, as amended, Law No. 299 of 1952.
34. Kanzei teiritsu ho, as amended, Law No. 54 of 1910.
35. Kanzei ho, as amended, Law No. 61 of 1954.
36. Shiteki dokusen no kinshi oyobi koseitorhiki no kakuho nikansuru horitsu, as amended, Law No. 54 of 1947.
37. Yushutsu hoken ho, as amended, Law No. 67 of 1950.
38. Yushutsu kensa ho, as amended, Law No. 97 of 1957.
39. On those laws, see *Japan's Import System,* in JETRO Exporters' Guide 16 et seq. (1979).
40. Yushutsu boeki kanri rei, as amended, Cabinet Order No. 378 of 1949.
41. The COCOM Decision, 20 Gyosei Reishu (Administrative Cases Reporter 842 (1969).
42. Article 1 of the Control Law states: "This Law has as its objective the sound development of the national economy together with the balance of international payments and currency stabilization, taking as its basic tenet the liberalization of foreign exchange, foreign trade, and other foreign transactions, based on the minimum restrictions necessary for the control or regulation of foreign transactions, to further the normal development of foreign transactions."
43. *See* Nichibei senikyotei ni kansuru Gyosei sosyo kiroku, *supra* note 9, for details on this case.
44. For articles written in English on administrative guidance from a legal standpoint, see Narita, *Administrative Guidance,* 2 L. in Japan 45 (1968); Sanekata, *Administrative Guidance and the Antimonopoly Law,* 10 L. in Japan 65 (1977); Smith, *Prices and Petroleum in Japan: 1973–1974—A*

Study of Administrative Guidance, 10 L. IN JAPAN 81 (1977); Davis, *Administrative Guidance in Japan,* 41 SOPHIA U. SOCIO-ECONOMIC INST. BULL. (1972); Matsushita, *Administrative Guidance and Economic Regulation in Japan,* 1 JAPAN BUS.L.J. 209 (1980).

45. *See, e.g.,* ITIM, *supra* note 10.
46. Art. 5(1), 11(1).
47. Art. 33(1).
48. Art. 5-2(1), 11(4).
49. In connection with Zenith Radio Corp. v. Matsushita Electric Industrial Co., Ltd., *In re* Japanese Elec. Prod. Antitrust Litigation, 513 F.Supp. 1100 (E.D. Pa. 1981), MITI issued a statement that was submitted to an American court, in which it claimed that it had "directed" the Japanese exporters of television sets to the United States that they should enter into an export cartel agreement fixing export prices. It also claimed that had the exporters failed to comply with this directive, MITI would have invoked a compulsory export approval mechanism at once. For details see Matsushita, *Export Control and Export Cartels in Japan,* 20 HARV. INT'L L.J. 103, 122–24 (1979).
50. *Japanese Elec. Prod.* 513 F. Supp 1100 (E.D. Pa. 1981), *supra* note 49.
51. This arrangement, however, was challenged in the United States by a consumer group. Consumers Union of U.S., Inc. v. Kissinger, 506 F.2d 136 (D.C. Cir. 1974), *cert. denied,* 421 U.S. 1004 (1975).
52. U.S. INT'L TRADE COMM'N, PUB. 756, STAINLESS STEEL AND ALLOY TOOL STEEL, REPORT TO THE PRESIDENT ON INVESTIGATION TA-201-5 UNDER SECTION 201 OF THE TRADE ACT OF 1974 (Jan. 1976).
53. U.S. INT'L TRADE COMM'N, PUB. 808, TELEVISION RECEIVERS, COLOR AND MONOCHROME, ASSEMBLED OR NOT ASSEMBLED, FINISHED OR NOT FINISHED, AND SUBASSEMBLIES THEREOF, REPORT TO THE PRESIDENT ON INVESTIGATION TA-201-19 UNDER SECTION 201(b) OF THE TRADE ACT OF 1974 (Mar. 1977).
54. President's Memorandum for the Special Representative for Trade Negotiations, 13 WEEKLY COMP. PRES. DOC. 761 (May 20, 1977).
55. *See* NIPPON NO HIKANZEI SHOHEKI (Nontariff Barriers in Japan) 130 et seq. (K. Komiya ed. 1972).
56. *Japan's Import System, supra* note 39, at 2 et seq.
57. *Id.* at 16 et seq.
58. Art. 7-2(1).
59. Art. 7-2(1).
60. Art. 30(1).
61. Japan Economic Newspaper, Jan. 8, 1975 (morning ed.), at 4.
62. *See* Ikeda, *Kiito-kinuseihin no yunyu chosei* (Import Adjustment of Raw Silk and Silk Products), 623 JURIST, Oct. 15, 1976, at 85 et seq.
63. MITI, TSUSHO HAKUSHO (White Paper on Foreign Trade), Kakuron (Itemized Discussion) 209–10 (1981).
64. Ikeda, *supra* note 62, at 91.
65. However, there was an informal understanding between China (a branch of the government dealing with foreign trade) and the Japanese govern-

ment corporation and the Import Association of Textiles as to the contents of import. *See* Ikeda, *supra* note 62, at 91.

66. This is a suit filed with the Kyoto District Court in January 1979 by eleven private individuals and companies engaged in the tie business. In their complaint, the plaintiffs allege that the amendment of the Silk Price Stabilization Law providing that the exclusive right of importing raw silk was given to the government corporation was contrary to Article 22 of the Constitution, which guarantees the freedom of trade and Article 25, which guarantees the right to livelihood.
67. There are a number of articles written in Japanese on the Tokyo Round Negotiations. Among them, the following books are the most comprehensive: HACHIJUNENDAI NO BOEKI RURU (Trade Rules for the 1980s) (N. Shinbunsha ed. 1980); TOKYO ROUND NO ZENBO (Total Picture of the Tokyo Round) (Kenkyukai ed. 1980).
68. *The Geneva Protocol,* Kampo (Official Gazette), April 25 1980 (Gogai [Special Issue]) at 2–59, 200–67; *Agreement on Anti-Dumping,* Kampo, (Official Gazette), May 23, 1980 (Gogai [Special Issue]) at 5–10; *Agreement on Countervailing Duty, id.* at 18–25; *Agreement on Customs Valuation, id.* at 41–50; *Agreement on Technical Barriers to Trade, id. at 71–77; Agreement on Import Licensing, id.* at 89–91; *Agreement on Civil Aviation, id.* at 95–100; *Agreement on Government Procurement, id.* at 110–29.
69. *Agreement on Dairy Products,* Kampo (Official Gazette), April 25, 1980 (Gogai [Special Issue]), at 1–8; *Agreement on Bovine Meat, id.* at 3–5. The decisions on framework are reported neither in the *Official Gazette* nor in any other reporter. It is, however, certain that they have been accepted by the Japanese government.
70. For details on tariff concessions, see MTN Office of MITI International Trade Bureau, *Tokyo Round kosyo no jishitsuteki daketsu nitsuite* (The Substantive Conclusion of the Tokyo Round Negotiation), 705 JURIST 39, 40–42 (Dec. 1, 1979).
71. Kanzei ho, as amended, Law. No. 61 of 1954. *See infra* note 72.
72. *See* Amano, *Tokyo Round kosho no daketsu nitomonau wagakuni kanzeikankeihorei no seibi nitsuite* (On Adjustment and Administration of Laws Relating to Tariff Following the Conclusion of the Tokyo Round Negotiation) 721 JURIST 84 et seq. (July 15, 1980).
73. Kanzei teiritsu ho no kaisei nikansuru horitsu, Law No. 5 of 1981.
74. UNITED STATES–JAPAN TRADE STUDY GROUP, A SPECIAL PROGRESS REPORT 17 (1980) (hereinafter cited as SPECIAL PROGRESS REPORT).
75. *United States-Japan Economic Relations: Hearings Before the Subcommittees on Asian and Pacific Affairs, and International Economic Policy and Trade of the House Committees on Foreign Affairs,* 96th Cong., 2d Sess. 156 et seq. (1980).
76. See the discussion below in the subsections entitled Countervailing Duties and Antidumping Duties.
77. A detailed explanation of the implementation in this respect is given in Amano, *supra* note 72, at 84 et seq.

78. Some of the difficulties encountered by foreign exporters with regard to technical standards and inspections are described in Weil & Glick, *Japan—Is the Market Open? A View of the Japanese Market Drawn from U.S. Corporate Experience,* 11 L. & POL'Y INT'L BUS. 845, 865–79. (1979). *See also* SPECIAL PROGRESS REPORT, *supra* note 74, at 13 et seq. The report contains comments on the experience of foreign exporters in this area.
79. SPECIAL PROGRESS REPORT, *supra* note 74, at 4–5.
80. *See id.* at 6; Weil & Glick, *supra* note 78 at 865–79.
81. Nihon Keizai Shinbun, Jan. 4, 1982 (morning ed), at 7.
82. SPECIAL PROGRESS REPORT, *supra* note 74, at 13 et seq.
83. The most comprehensive work on the Industrial Standardization Law is KOGYOGIJUTSUIN HYOJUNBU HYOJUNKA, KAISEI KOGYO HOYJUNKAHO—CHIKUJO KAISETSU (The Industrial Standardization Law, As Amended—Article-by-Article-Comments), Nihonkikaku kyokai (1980).
84. *Id.* at 20 et seq. where the entire text of this report is reprinted.
85. *Id.* at 26 et seq.
86. *See* SPECIAL PROGRESS REPORT, *supra* note 74, at 13 et seq.
87. *Id.*
88. See generally the following report: MINISTRY OF INTERNATIONAL TRADE AND INDUSTRY, TRADE AND TARIFF SECTION, TOKUSHUKANZEITO NIKANSURU KOKKAI GIJIROKU (Records of the National Diet on Special Tariff System and Related Matters) (1981). This is a compilation of the National Diet debates on tariff and trade matters collected by the Tariff and Trade Section of MITI (hereinafter cited as RECORD).
89. *Id.* at 271–72.
90. Nihon Keizai Shinbun, Jan. 15, 1982 (morning ed.), at 8.
91. Testimony of Komori Masao on March 14, 1980, RECORD, *supra* note 88, at 253.
92. RECORD, *supra* note 88, at 278.
93. SUBCOMM. ON TRADE OF THE HOUSE COMM. ON WAYS AND MEANS, 97th CONG., 1st SESS., REPORT ON TRADE MISSION TO FAR EAST 11 (Comm. Print 1981).
94. *Id.* at 12.
95. Nihon Keizai Shinbun, Dec. 28, 1981, at 7 (morning ed.).
96. The most comprehensive writing on the legal system of government procurement in Japan is SEIFUCHOTATSU NIKANSURU KYOTEI TO KANCHO KEIYAKU SEIDO (The Government Procurement Code and the Government Contract System) (Sumiya ed. 1981). The explanation in the text largely relies on this book.
97. SPECIAL PROGRESS REPORT, *supra* note 74.
98. *Id.* at 1–3.
99. For details of the TFC activities, see Weil & Glick, *supra* note 78.
100. Announcement of the Economic Planning Agency, March 29, 1982.
101. 11 Sai-han keishū (Supreme Court Criminal Cases Reporter) 3377 (1957); 903 Hanrei jiho 3 (1978).
102. Kokka baisho ho, Law No. 125 of 1947.

103. A detailed account of the applicability of the State Redress Law to foreign persons is made in E. Shimoyama, Kokka baisho ho (The State Redress Law) (1972).
104. 8 Kakyu minshu (Lower Court Civil Cases Reporter) 931 (1957); 18 Kosai minshu (High Court Civil Cases Reporter) 188 (1965); 582 Hanrei jiho 81 (1969).
105. 2 T. Miyazawa, Kenpo (The Constitution) 456 (rev. ed. 1974); Takada, Kihonho kom mentar kenpō (The Basic Law—Commentary—Constitution) 75 (Arikura ed. 1970); Hashimoto, Nihonkoku kenpō (The Japanese Constitution) 374 (1980).
106. 762 Hanrei jiho 9 (1974). In this case, the plaintiff argued that the abolition of the home voting system for physically disabled persons and the failure of the government to enact a law restoring this system was unconstitutional, and the government was liable to compensate the damage. The court held for the plaintiff.
107. For similar cases, see 766 Hanrei jiho 76 (1974); 914 Hanrei jiho 29 (1979); 953 Hanrei jiho 18 (1980); 972 Hanrei jiho 79 (1980).
108. 924 Hanrei jiho 34 (1979).
109. Gyosei jiken sosyo ho, Law No. 139 of 1962.
110. For example, a decision on whether the government should effectuate a price control, raise or lower tariff, or tighten import controls on some commodities would be regarded as discretionary, and the failure of those measures would not be grounds for a lawsuit by a private individual.
111. 909 Hanrei jiho 27 (1978); 948 Hanrei jiho 44 (1979).
112. Article 310 of the Civil Procedure Code states: "If the court deems it necessary, the court may request . . . a foreign government or a foreign public body to render an expert opinion."
113. Subcomm. on Trade of the House Comm. on Ways and Means, 97th Cong., 1st Sess. Report on Trade Mission to Far East 11 et seq. (Comm. Print 1981). On Japanese trade barriers, see generally Subcomm. on Trade of the House Comm. on Ways and Means, 95th Cong., 2d Sess., Task Force Report on United States–Japan Trade (Comm. Print 1979); Subcomm. on Trade of the House Comm. on Ways and Means, 96th Cong., 2d Sess., United States–Japan Trade Report (Comm. Print 1980); *United States–Japan Trade and Economic Relations: Hearings Before the Subcomms. on Asian and Pacific Affairs, and International Economic Policy and Trade of the House Comm. on Foreign Affairs,* 96th Cong., 2d Sess. 156 et seq. (1980); Weil & Glick, *supra* note 78.

CHAPTER 4

United States Law and Implementation of the Tokyo Round Negotiation

John H. Jackson

Like the other legal systems considered in this book, United States law creates considerable complexity for Multilateral Trade Negotiations implementation, and constrains policy makers and diplomats. The United States legal system, however, is different in important ways from the other two systems explored in this book. Some of these differences can be mentioned at the outset.

First, the parliamentary branch in the United States (i.e., the Congress) appears to be considerably more powerful than its counterparts elsewhere. This imposes a number of limitations on officials of the executive branch, and in some cases makes it nearly impossible for certain types of changes in the international rules to be carried out, or even negotiated.

A second, related point is that the U.S. legal system provides a great opportunity for individual citizens or citizen groups to challenge official action. One of the ways in which Congress limits the power of its rival, the executive branch, is to create procedures private interests can use to challenge official decisions by administrative process, by appeal to the courts, and in some cases by appeal to the Congress itself.

Third, although it is not so prominent as it was in the first century of the republic, there still remains some slight ambiguity about the distribution of powers between the states and the federal government. Even where the legal issues are clear (generally meaning the central government prevails), practical political constraints sometimes prevent the federal government from acting in an area traditionally subject to state government control.

In this chapter we will explore these and other themes and provide some tentative conclusions about them. The section of this discussion entitled Constitutional and Legal Framework of U.S. Government International Trade Relations outlines the basic structure of the U.S. constitutional system as it relates to international economic relations, and places the General Agreement on Tariffs and Trade (GATT) in this legal setting.

The section entitled Post–Kennedy Round and U.S. Law: Events Leading up to the Trade Act of 1979 then discusses the legal events that occured after the Kennedy Round and that led up to the Tokyo Round negotiations. Primarily, this section focuses on the important Trade Act of 1974.

Subsequent sections deal with the legal and government structure of U.S. participation in the Tokyo Round negotiations. Discussed in turn are the three critical issues that underlie much of the comparison undertaken in this book, namely, the legal and governmental structure for U.S. participation in the negotiation, the legal authority for U.S. government representatives to accept the MTN agreements as a matter of international law obligation, and finally the legal and governmental processes for actually implementing within U.S. borders the obligations undertaken in the MTN agreements.

Constitutional and Legal Framework of U.S. Government International Trade Relations

Constitutional Aspects—Introductory Concepts

It is well known that the draftsmen of the U.S. Constitution distrusted government and concentration of power. Consequently, they built into the Constitution the principle of separation of powers, explicitly distributing powers among three principal branches of the federal government (the presidency or executive branch, the Congress, and the courts) and between the federal government and the state governments.[1] This principle, wise as it may be, has resulted in constant tension between the Congress (legislative branch) and the executive branch (presidency).[2]

Beginning with the crises of the 1930s, the U.S. presidency grew considerably stronger. A 1936 Supreme Court case, *United States v. Curtiss-Wright Export Corp.*, even propounded the theory that the President has certain inherent powers over foreign affairs that do not depend on the Constitution.[3] Although many scholars reject this theory,[4] for practical reasons the presidency has developed a preeminent role in the conduct of foreign affairs, stemming partly from various clauses in the Constitution.[5] However, in international *economic* affairs, the Congress can point to particular clauses in Article I, Section 8, of the Constitution, which grants to the Congress the power to "regulate Commerce with foreign Nations . . . ," and to "Pay and collect Taxes, Duties, Imposts . . . ." Consequently, the Congress feels that it has a special power over matters of international trade, and it likes to remind the executive branch of this special power.[6]

The foreign affairs power of the presidency was particularly enhanced by the necessities of World War II and in the postwar period this power continued to be great. Nevertheless, in 1952 the U.S. Supreme Court, in the case of *Youngstown Sheet & Tube Co. v. Sawyer,*[7] held that President Truman had exceeded his power by seizing steel mills in order to keep them operating in the face of a strike. Language in that case has been relied upon for arguments limiting presidential power in matters relating to both domestic and foreign affairs. Although there have been few subsequent cases in which the Supreme Court has limited presidential powers over foreign affairs, some lower court cases have suggested the possibility of further limitations.[8]

The Vietnam War and the Watergate crisis caused Congress to reassert its powers, especially in international affairs. In the last decade, the Congress has taken a number of actions that have imposed restraints on the President's foreign affairs authority,[9] and consequently arguments are currently heard that the President's authority is too circumscribed for the good of the nation.[10]

For many years, the Congress persisted in its exercise of the explicit constitutional power to set tariffs. The 1930 Tariff Act, which has become infamous, was an example of the problems this exercise created.[11] After the Roosevelt administration came into office in 1933, Secretary of State Cordell Hull persuaded the Congress to pass the Reciprocal Trade Agreements Act of 1934.[12] Under this act, the Congress delegated authority to the President to enter into international treaty agreements that would call for the mutual reduction of tariffs within certain specified statutory limitations, and to implement those agreements without further reference to Congress. Using this authority, or renewals of it, the President entered into thirty-two reciprocal trade agreements during the next decade (1935–45).[13] It was under the authority of the 1945 renewal (for a three-year period) that the GATT was negotiated and accepted by the United States.[14]

The U.S. Constitution requires that "treaties" be submitted to the Senate for "Advice and Consent" (requiring a two-thirds affirmative vote) before the President can enter into them on behalf of the United States.[15] Nevertheless, over two centuries of constitutional history, alternative forms of approval of international agreements have developed. United States practice divides international treaty agreements into treaties in the constitutional sense (which must be submitted to the Senate) and executive agreements.[16] There are several ways in which executive agreements can be approved under constitutional practice.[17]

1. Executive agreements can be submitted to the Congress, for approval by the passage of a statute that grants the President the authority to accept the international agreement.

2. The Congress can pass a statute that authorizes the President, in advance, to negotiate, enter into, and accept for the United States an international agreement (and to implement it). (This is the approach of the trade agreement acts for tariff agreements.[18])
3. A treaty may give the President advance delegated authority, within limits, to accept an executive agreement designed to implement a treaty.[19]
4. There are some executive agreements the President can enter into on his own inherent authority under the Constitution, without any participation by the Congress or the Senate either before or after the negotiation.[20] These must be agreements that are authorized by explicit constitutional grants of authority to the President (such as his authority as Commander in Chief of the Armed Forces), or that can be inferred to be part of presidential authorities under the Constitution (such as his executive power).[21]

Even though the Congress has been reasserting its powers in connection with foreign affairs, the presidential powers are formidable, and still dominant. The President has authority to negotiate international agreements and to carry on international diplomacy. Consequently, as indicated earlier, he can enter into some executive agreements on his own constitutional authority, although only a rather small number fall in this category. More significantly, however, over the years the Congress has delegated to the President a wide variety of powers relating to international affairs. Since the President is the chief actor in international affairs, he can sometimes interpret these delegations expansively and effectively excerise great power.[22]

Federal-State Division of Constitutional Powers

Since the structure of the U.S. government under its Constitution is federal in nature—that is, it consists not only of a central government but also of state governments that have considerable independent authority and sovereignty—it might be thought that the division of powers between the federal and state governments would be an important constraint on the scope of federal government action in the area of foreign affairs. Indeed, at the outset of the republic, the states were first independent sovereignties after obtaining independence from Great Britain. It was these states that joined together, first into a confederacy, and later into the United States under the Constitution of 1788.

There has been a long and extraordinarily detailed history of constitutional evolution and accommodation between state powers and the federal powers.[23] However, as to the division of these powers in foreign affairs, the Supreme Court has had relatively few occasions on which to pronounce. Furthermore, in domestic affairs, the evolution of U.S. constitutional law has been generally in the direction of concentrating power in the federal government. It is reasonably well established today that the federal government has supremacy, if it chooses to exercise it, over almost all issues that have any commercial overtones. The most recent Supreme Court pronouncement in favor of reserving certain powers to the states is *National League of Cities v. Usery, Secretary of Labor,* in which the Supreme Court held that a federal fair labor standards act governing minimum wage and overtime pay matters could not be applied to the employees of state governments, since the regulation of the terms of employment of state government employees was part of the essential attributes of sovereignty reserved to states under the Constitution. However, some feel that this particular approach of the Supreme Court has not been nor is it likely to be carried very far.[24] A more recent case held that a federal statute could be applied to the terms of employment of employees of a railroad owned by a state government.[25] This case evaluated three criteria by which it would judge whether a federal statute made too great an incursion on the sovereignty reserved to states, namely:

> First, there must be a showing that the challenged regulation regulates the States as States.
>
> Second, the federal regulation must address matters that are indisputedly attributes of state sovereignty.
>
> And third, it must be apparent that the States' compliance with the federal law would directly impair their ability to structure integral operations in area of traditional functions.

In foreign affairs, there is virtually no Supreme Court opinion that rules against the exercise of federal power on the grounds that it conflicts with state power, as long as the exercise of federal power was itself otherwise constitutional.[26] Thus, although the Supreme Court has held that state powers sometimes prevail over international treaties (such as in the offshore oil cases), the basis for this decision was itself an exercise of federal power, namely an act of Congress.[27]

The courts and federal authorities can rely on a number of clauses in the Constitution in arguing that the exercise of federal power will prevail over state power in the areas of foreign relations. Such clauses include the commerce clause, the supremacy clause, the treaty clause, and clauses on presidential power, including his power to receive ambassadors, and his authority as Commander in Chief.

To the knowledge of this author, the only situation in which the problem of states rights under the Constitution seems to have had some relevance to the extent of the federal government's authority to negotiate in the Tokyo Round was that of government procurement. It might be argued that purchases by state governments is a matter so intimately connected with normal sovereign and administrative authority reserved to the states that the federal government would not have the authority to enter into an international agreement that constrained or interfered with that sovereignty. Indeed, some states have enacted statutes or regulations that require preference to be given to the purchase of goods made in the United States, as compared to foreign goods. Such state-originated rules have been challenged both by political persuasion from Washington and through litigation in some courts.[28] The litigation has been generally inconclusive. A lower-level California court held that the state's buy-American statute was unconstitutional, because it encroached on the subject of international trade reserved to federal government regulation.[29]

Another case, decided by the New Jersey Supreme Court,[30] held that state rules regarding procurement that related to a water supply were not in violation of the GATT (and implicitly ruled that such were not unconstitutional and not preempted by federal government action). Both of these cases, however, recognized that if the federal government had acted in a way that was explicitly *inconsistent* with state regulations or rules, the federal government action would prevail.

During the Tokyo Round, extensive negotiations were held on government procurement (resulting in the Government Procurement Code). In this portion of the negotiations, the negotiators did consider whether the international government procurement rules of the new code should apply to governmental subdivisions of a federal state. This author has been told that the U.S. government was prepared to accept some such rule, and that the negotiators were of the opinion that the federal government had the authority to do so. It was apparently the objection of *foreign* government negotiators that caused the proposal to be dropped. Certain other governments had considerably more difficult constitutional problems on this issue that did the United States. (For example, the German Länder have much autonomy, and the constitutions of Canada and Australia raise important questions in this connection.[31])

In short, one can say with considerable but not perfect assurance that in the area of foreign affairs, and particularly in economic affairs, it is hard to conceive of an action taken by the U.S. federal government that would not be supported by the Supreme Court in the event of direct conflict with state actions. This would be true whether the action was administrative or legislative, whether it was accomplished by an international agreement duly approved by the Congress, the Senate, or the President under his authority, or whether it was accomplished by other types of actions authorized by the Constitution or statutory delegations of power.

The GATT in U.S. Law

The theory of U.S. participation in the original 1946–47 GATT negotiations (and of U.S. acceptance of the 1947 Protocol of Provisional Application implementing the GATT) was that the GATT, under U.S. constitutional law, was an executive agreement authorized by the 1945 extension of the Trade Agreements Act. Consequently, the President accepted the GATT without further reference to Congress. Some members of Congress were angered by this procedure, arguing that the GATT was not a valid international agreement of the United States.[32] For several decades the Congress officially refused to recognize the GATT,[33] although in the Trade Act of 1974 it seems clear that Congress has recognized it as a U.S. international legal commitment.[34] Nevertheless, this history of congressional hostility to the GATT has affected U.S. international trade relations and its relationship to the GATT over the years.

As mentioned in chapter 1, the original concept for the GATT was that it would be merely a multilateral agreement appended to the new International Trade Organization (ITO) when the latter came into being. The GATT itself was not designed to be an international organization, and indeed U.S. representatives avoided any connotations that it was an organization at all, because the authority of the President to enter into the GATT would likely not have extended to entry of the United States into an organization. When the ITO draft charter was completed at Havana in 1948, it was submitted to governments for acceptance. However, by 1950 it was clear that the Congress would not approve the ITO and consequently the President withdrew it from congressional consideration.[35] Effectively, the ITO charter was then dead, and the GATT had to fill the gap.

Within the U.S. government, the GATT developments described above effectively resulted in a substantial shift of power to the President. With the de facto role of the GATT as the central international organization for trade, more and more trade issues tended to find their way into the GATT forum for discussion and resolution. The GATT provided the only overall systematic code of conduct governing the way many nations regulated their international trade. In addition, because of the relationship of the GATT to the U.S. statutory framework for tariffs, with the GATT agreement providing the authority for the application of a lower tariff on most goods, the GATT became an essential pillar of U.S. international trade policy. If the GATT were somehow to be extinguished, the legal effect in the United States would be that U.S. tariffs *could* bounce back to the 1930 statutory rates—an action that would be a devastating blow to international trade relations.[36]

Post–Kennedy Round and U.S. Law: Events Leading up to the Trade Act of 1974

The Kennedy Round and U.S. Law: Problems of Implementation

After the Kennedy Round negotiations were completed in June 1967, there was something of a backlash in U.S. political attitudes toward international trade. The portion of the Kennedy Round results that required approval by Congress for U.S. acceptance was submitted to Congress but the Congress refused to authorize such acceptance.[37] The Antidumping Code, negotiated in the Kennedy Round and accepted by the President, was strongly criticized in Congress by members who felt the President did not have authority to agree to that code.[38] The U.S. balance-of-payments problem and the surge of imports into the country toward the end of the 1960s led some labor unions, joined by a number of regional and other industrial interests, to urge the Congress to enact restrictions on imports.[39] The President's authority under the 1962 Trade Expansion Act to negotiate for reductions in tariffs had expired at the end of June 1967.[40] There was no renewal of the authority until the 1974 Trade Act. (This was the longest hiatus in Presidential tariff agreement authority since the 1934 Trade Agreements Act itself.)

In 1970 the President appointed the Williams Commission to investigate and report on recommendations for U.S. trade policy. The Commission reported in 1971,[41] with a number of recommendations that became the intellectual basis for much of the new legislation on U.S. participation in international trade negotiations.

The Trade Act of 1974

Although earlier attempts had been made to get the Congress to adopt new trade legislation, in 1972 preparations began in earnest for the formulation of a new trade bill. This bill was finally sent to Congress in April, 1973[42] (after a second effective devaluation of the dollar in early 1973). The new bill was the most comprehensive yet submitted to the Congress on the subject of international trade. It not only concerned the renewal of presidential authority for trade agreements but also contained provisions on the Generalized System of Preference (GSP) for developing countries, extension of the Most Favored Nation (MFN) treatment to certain Communist countries, amendments to the antidumping and countervailing duty laws of the United States, and a number of other matters.

As the Congress began to consider the trade bill, the Watergate crisis was stirring around the presidency. Nevertheless, in the fall of 1973, the House of Representatives approved a bill that was remarkably liberal-trade-oriented.[43] But the oil price crisis intervened, and when the Senate began considering the bill in early 1974 its mood was not nearly so generous. Furthermore, as the Watergate crisis deepened,[44] it became clear that the Congress was reluctant to enact trade legislation that would have delegated powers to a President it distrusted. Congressional interests viewed the Vietnam War as an abuse of presidential powers also.[45] Consequently, the mood of the Congress was to reassert its own authority in matters of international affairs, particularly on trade. It was only after President Nixon resigned and President Ford came into office and strongly supported the completion of the congressional work on the Trade Act that the Senate began in earnest to finish the work. The bill was finally passed in the closing days of the 93rd Congress, on December 19, 1974, after a number of compromises. The act was signed by the President on January 3, 1975, and came into force then.[46]

In 1972 and 1973 it was recognized by many that the seventh trade negotiation round in the context of the GATT had to concern itself with the increasingly troublesome nontariff barrier (NTB) issue. Tariffs would also be dealt with, but a number of nontariff matters required priority. However, under the U.S. constitutional system, presidential negotiation on nontariff barriers was considerably more difficult than on tariffs. Because of the complexity and subtlety of the negotiations and because of the difficulty of establishing limitations on delegated authority, the Congress was unwilling to grant the President advance authority to negotiate, accept, and implement international NTB agreements. On the other hand, other nations were unwilling to negotiate with the United States if the results of all negotiations had to be submitted to the Congress for approval through the normal procedures.[47] Congressional failure to approve part of the results of the Kennedy Round influenced those nations.

One idea for escaping this dilemma was the legislative veto approach, under which the President would negotiate and complete a tentative international agreement, consult extensively with the Congress, and then submit a final agreement and implementing legislation to the Congress. Under the concept of this procedure, if the Congress did not veto the action, the President's submittals would be approved and his proposed legislation would become law. The House of Representatives accepted this approach in 1973, but in 1974 the Senate refused, arguing that the approach was unconstitutional and extended too much power to the presidency.[48]

A search then ensued for a compromise position. The results can be seen in Sections 102 and 151 of the Trade Act of 1974, sometimes called the "fast-track" NTB authority. Under these provisions, the President would negotiate on various NTB matters, and ninety days before entering into international agreements on them, would notify the Congress and consult with the key congressional committees about the proposed agreements. After consultation, the President would complete the international agreements and submit them to the Congress along with proposed legislation for authority to approve them and implement them into U.S. law. The submittal would be in the form of a normal bill, requiring the usual constitutional action of both houses of the Congress, with the signature of the President. However, the 1974 Trade Act "fast-track" procedure established (in the rules of the House and the Senate) three important procedural modifications: (1) a requirement for automatic discharge from committee consideration, so that the bill would necessarily have to be considered by the full House and Senate within a certain period; (2) a prohibition on any amendments to the bill; and (3) a limitation on the debate on the floor of the House and the Senate. Thus, within a reasonable period—normally about sixty days of legislative session—the Congress would act on the negotiation results.[49]

It was under this new procedure that most of the MTN results were approved and implemented during 1979.

The Congress intended amendments in the 1974 act relating to the countervailing duty law to reduce the amount of executive branch discretion in the administration of that act by forcing action on complaints within a specified period, and by almost eliminating the discretion the Treasury previously had exercised in applying countervailing duties.[50] The Congress did grudgingly give a limited waiver authority to the executive branch.[51] Under this authority, in certain cases in which countervailing duties would be be required the Secretary of the Treasury could waive the duties if he made certain findings, including one that the trade negotiations would be jeopardized if the duties were imposed. This waiver authority expired, however, in four years.[52] The Congress contemplated that the new Tokyo Round of trade negotiations would result in a revision of the international rules on subsidies and countervailing duties, and that the 1974 U.S. law would force the negotiators to give this matter priority.[53] (Countervailing duties will be discussed later.)

The 1974 Trade Act included other important amendments to U.S. law, such as an overall revision of the escape clause provisions,[54] and the development of greater benefits for workers under the adjustment assistance provisions.[55]

United States Participation in the Tokyo Round

Authority to Negotiate

As stated earlier, in the U.S. constitutional system it is generally considered the prerogative of the executive branch to conduct foreign relations and negotiate on matters to foreign affairs.[56] Although it is true that there have been instances when certain members of Congress or certain congressional committees have had significant direct discussions with foreign government or nongovernment representatives that could be characterized as negotiations,[57] it is the executive branch that formally has both the responsibility and the authority to negotiate internationally. Indeed the President (with his officials) usually claims and is often considered to have authority to negotiate on any matter at any time. Whether he has authority to *accept* any negotiation results on behalf of the government is quite another matter. And clearly, as a practical matter, without authority to accept the results of a negotiation or to indicate to negotiating partners in some other way that the results of a negotiation have some reasonable chance of being accepted and implemented, the authority to negotiate itself is often meaningless.

The President's authority in areas of international trade and other economic relations is very circumscribed and most often depends on particular statutory delegations of authority. The executive branch's ability to participate meaningfully in the Tokyo Round MTN, therefore, depended heavily on the Trade Act of 1974, the major purpose of which was precisely to establish, channel, and circumscribe that authority. As a result of this act, the United States was able to participate in the MTN. Without it, it is doubtful that the United States could have done so in a meaningful way.[58]

Yet the act did not cover all the negotiating authority, and it took several different approaches to those it did cover. We can thus discern at least five categories of sources of negotiating authority for U.S. representatives at the MTN, three of which are contained in the Trade Act of 1974.

First, Section 101 of the act granted the President advance authority to negotiate *and to implement* certian specified tariff reductions.[59] This section basically followed the statutory pattern and language of the series of U.S. trade acts, beginning with the 1934 Reciprocal Trade Agreements Act.[60] It ended the 1967–74 hiatus in this authority that has been noted earlier. This authority was the most complete the President had—no further reference to Congress was needed. However, it expired on January 2, 1980, after being in effect for five years.[61]

Second, Section 102 of the act set forth an explicit authority to negotiate international agreements on "non-tariff barriers and other distortions of trade," and provided the "fast-track" method of Congressional approval for acceptence and implementation of these agreements.[62] This section was carefully worded to apply the procedure only when "the President enters into a trade agreement *under this Section.*" (Emphasis added.) It did not purport to require this procedure in all international NTB or "trade distortion" agreements, because doing so would have raised constitutional issues. In some cases, the President could claim that his own authority (whether originating in the Constitution or in prior statutes) allowed him to negotiate and perhaps even implement NTB or trade distortion ageements—that is, that in certain cases it was unnecessary to rely on Section 102. Also, the President always retained his general constitutional authority to negotiate an international agreement and submit it to the Congress or the Senate for approval under normal constitutional procedures (without benefit of the "fast-track"). However, since the largest and most important parts of the MTN involved nontariff distortions in trade, Section 102 authority, with the advantages of the "fast-track" procedure, was the most significant of all Presidential powers and probably a sine qua non for the success of the MTN.

Third, the Trade Act of 1974 implicitly recognized the authority of the President to negotiate on some matters. For example, Section 121 includes a list of reforms or other goals relating to the GATT and international trade rules, which the Congress wanted to see accomplished. A clause of that section specifically stated, however, that any agreement designed to carry out the stated reforms or goals had to be approved and implemented pursuant to authorities elsewhere provided—that is, that Section 121 did not itself grant any such authority. Section 121 referred to the "fast-track" procedure, but the section and its legislative history[63] recognized that certain other authorities for presidential action existed, such as that contained in some other statutes promulgating procedural regulations. For example, the congressional committee noted the existing authority of the Secretary of the Treasury to establish regulations for country of origin marks.[64] Likewise, it has been mentioned that as the chief executive the President has authority in carrying out diplomacy, to agree to various procedures regarding the settlement of disputes.[65]

Fourth, the President could always negotiate agreements that were not within the delegations of authority of the Trade Act of 1974, and then, if his own authority did not include power to accept or implement them, he could submit them for approval to Congress under normal constitutional procedures. For example, although the tariff agreement authority in Section 101 of the 1974 Trade Act limited tariff cuts to 60 percent from the tariff existing just before the act took effect, a deeper tariff cut could be agreed subject to later approval by Congress. (A few such agreements did occur.)[66]

Fifth, there was the possibility of the prior existence of presidential authority—inherent or delegated by statute—to negotiate, accept, and implement argeements. This was to some extent recognized in the 1974 Trade Act (and that recognition reinforced the President's legal arguments for certain authorities).[67] But even some authority not recognized by the act could supply a residuum of additional authority for the President and his officials for their MTN participation.[68]

The Structure of the United States Government for Participation in the MTN

For the most part, the governmental structure of U.S. participation in the MTN was simply the structure that existed for international trade policy matters generally, modified in certain ways to accommodate the particular demands of that major negotiation.

In the legislation that established the authority for U.S. participation in the Kennedy Round of trade negotiations between 1962 and 1967 (the Trade Expansion Act of 1962), Congress established the position of the Special Trade Representative (STR), with ambassadorial rank, reporting directly to the President. The STR was to take charge of the negotiations on behalf of the United States.[69] This act represented certain compromises, because before that time the Department of State (charged generally with foreign relations for the United States) and the Department of Commerce had competed for the principal authority to conduct international trade negotiations.

After the STR was established, the first incumbent assembled staff (including two deputies at the ambassador rank), and a structure of interagency committees was set up to advise the President and his chief officials on trade negotiations and other trade policy matters. The chief committee was the Cabinet-level committee called the Trade Expansion Act Advisory Committee, established by the Trade Expansion Act of 1962.[70] Under this were other interagency committees, including the Trade Staff Committee, which carried on most of the day-to-day work. Represented on these committees were appropiate level officals of the Departments of State, Commerce, Labor, Agriculture, and the Treasury. The committees were usually chaired by an official from STR. In later years, they sometimes included representatives from the Department of Justice's Antitrust Division, the Department of Defense, the

Council on International Economic Policy (CIEP), the National Security Council, and other agencies. If the various departmental representatives on this committee could agree, their position usually became the official U.S. position. However, if any department disagreed, its representative might cause his superior to require that the matter be brought to an interagency committee at a higher level. This could continue until ultimately an issue was taken to the President himself for a decision.[71]

Certain kinds of issues, such as escape clause cases, regularly require presidential action.[72] Consequently, there usually was some form of White House staff assistance and coordination for the President on the issue of international economic policy. This might be one person, or one person with several assistants, who merely coordinated the flow of paper to the President. In the early 1970s, the CIEP was developed, with an Executive Director and a more sizable staff, and charged with coordinating U.S. international economic policy. This structure existed when the drafts and positions that led to the Trade Act of 1974 were being formulated before Congress. However, members of Congress were increasingly critical of the structure, noting that the Executive Director of CIEP appeared to be in a superior position to the STR, but unlike the STR was not (until 1973) confirmed by the Senate (on the theory that he was a personal staff member of the President).[73] These and various other tensions and bureaucratic struggles finally led to the demise of the CIEP after the new Democratic adminstration took office at the beginning of 1977.

The Trade Act of 1974 did not change this structure fundamentally. However, during late stages of drafting the bill, the Senate inserted measures, accepted by the House, that upgraded the STR to Cabinet rank and permanently established his office as an agency within the Executive Office of the President.[74] Nevertheless, at that time the special additional expenses required for the STR to represent the U.S. at the MTN were controlled jointly by the STR and the Department of State.[75] In addition, matters relating to the GATT and international trade, other than those covered by the MTN, still fell within the jurisdiction of the Department of State. Consequently, there were two U.S. lines of authority at Geneva and to the GATT: first, the normal GATT mission with a minister responsible to State Department authority charged with the ongoing general GATT activities such as the annual Contracting Parties' sessions; and second, the Special Mission to the MTN, residing in Geneva and consisting of a deputy STR (at ambassador rank) and a number of STR officers, as well as officers from various other departments of the government assigned to the STR mission for the MTN. (Later, these lines of authority were merged under the STR.)

After the Kennedy Round negotiations, there had been much

criticism in Congress and in the private business sector that executive branch officials who had conducted U.S. participation in the negotiations had not adequately consulted with Congress or with the interested business sectors in formulating U.S. positions and strategy. Consequently, one of the most important changes the Trade Act of 1974 made in the structure of government participation in the GATT negotiation was the explicit expansion of congressional liaison and the measures taken for consulting with private business sectors in negotiating positions.[76]

Even in previous negotiating rounds it had been the practice to have a congressional delegation to the negotiations, consisting of two members of the Senate and two members of the House, officially accredited by the President as advisors to the U.S. negotiating team.[77] Senate and House members are busy, however, and cannot devote a great deal of time to this activity, and it was felt that something more was needed. The Trade Act of 1974 specified[78] that the STR was obligated to keep congressional advisors informed of the negotiations, and explicitly provided that the Chairmen of the House Ways and Means Committee and the Senate Finance Committee could designate committee staff members to have access to the information provided to official advisors. The act also provided for reports to be made regularly to the Congress. In carrying out these measures, the Senate and House committees hired additional full-time staff members to closely follow the progress of the MTN. These staff members traveled to Geneva from time to time, and followed the negotiations in order to keep the members of their committees informed, and in order to prepare for the time when results of the negotiations would have to be submitted to Congress. They were given access to official documents of the MTN as well as U.S. executive branch cables concerning the MTN, and were sometimes permitted to be present in the room during negotiating sessions.[79] They also occasionally met with representatives from other countries.

In order to establish better consultation and obtain advice from the private sector, the Trade Act of 1974 established an elaborate system of advisory committees for trade negotiations.[80] The act required the President to establish an Advisory Committee for Trade Negotiations for overall policy advice, chaired by the STR. In addition, it authorized the establishment of three general policy advisory committees, one for industry, one for labor, and one for agriculture. Finally, the President was authorized to establish sector advisory committees consisting of representatives of particular private sectors within industry, labor, or agriculture. Twenty-seven Industry Sector Advisory Committees (ISACs) were set up, including, for example, those for paper and paper products, food and kindred products, ferrous products, and consumer electronic products and household appliances. Likewise, several agricultural sector advisory committees were set up, including those for cotton, dairy, livestock and livestock products, and poultry and eggs.[81]

These committees existed throughout the negotiations, and met from time to time and provided information to U.S. negotiators. A special group of government officials was charged with looking after these committees, but in many cases when the negotiators themselves were in Washington they would meet with particular committees on one subject or another, and toward the end of the negotiations would present the outlines of proposed agreements to committees and obtain advice on them. The committees formulated a report at the end of the negotiations, presenting their views on its results.[82]

The issue of whether private citizen members of advisory committees would also have the opportunity to be present in the room with negotiators of foreign countries during actual negotiations was also explored during the drafting of the Trade Act of 1974, but it was decided not to go so far. It was stated, however, that the Advisory Committee members "can go up to the negotiating door. . . ."[83] It was a source of congressional concern, however, that certain foreign nations allowed very close liaisons between their negotiators and private industries.

Negotiating Tariff Reductions and the Role of the ITC

Before the Trade Act of 1974 was passed, there existed in the U.S. government, an agency known as the Tariff Commission. This agency had a series of statutory responsibilities that were particularly significant in relation to the injury test on antidumping matters and escape clause proceedings. The Trade Expansion Act of 1962 required the Tariff Commission to hold public hearings on possible tariff reductions and their impact on U.S. industry in all sectors. This information was a prerequisite to the authority of the U.S. negotiators and the President to conclude an agreement on tariff reductions and implement it. The Trade Act of 1974 continued this practice, but changed the name of the Tariff Commission to the International Trade Commission (ITC), recognizing that nontariff measures had become so important that the title of the agency should no longer suggest that its function had only to do with tariffs.[84]

Although the President had his most extensive authority for negotiations in the area of tariff reductions, as mentioned earlier he and his officials had to complete a number of explicit statutory procedures before entering into international agreements on the subject. The ITC was required to advise the President from time to time on any proposed trade agreement to be negotiated under the authority of the act. In particular, the President was required to submit a list of articles or products that could be considered in negotiations for changes in U.S. tariff duties. Within six months after receiving such a list the ITC was required to advise the President on how modifications of duties would likely affect each article. During this time, the Commission was charged with investigating and analyzing such information as it could obtain and holding public hearings. The result of the ITC's advice to the President influenced the actions of U.S. negotiators on tariff agreements with foreign countries during the MTN.[85]

In addition, advice from various executive branch departments on trade agreements was required, and the President himself was required to give interested members of the public an opportunity to comment on proposed trade agreements at open hearings. This particular mandate was carried out by the Office of the Special Trade Representative.[86] The statute explicitly made these public and interagency procedures a prerequisite for offering to change U.S. duties, restrictions, or other barriers to international trade.[87]

The Countervailing Duty Problem

One of the most perplexing issues of international trade policy is that of subsidies and their effects on international trade flows. The first problem is to determine what a subsidy is. In a broad sense, it can be any of a wide range of government policies pursued primarily for appropriate and legitimate domestic policy goals, which may also have some effect on international trade flows. For almost a century, it has been established practice in international trade that an importing country is entitled to impose countervailing duties on goods that are benefiting from foreign subsidies.[88] The theory is that the countervailing duty offsets the advantage the subsidy gives the imported goods. GATT Article VI continues this general approach, although it requires that the importing country establish that the subsidized goods are injuring competing domestic industries before it may use countervailing duties.[89]

The United States countervailing duty statute provided that the Secretary of the Treasury was to apply countervailing duties to imported goods that benefited from a "bounty or grant." This statute applied only to dutiable goods. Goods for which no duties were charged were exempt. However, the statute contained no injury test. Thus, even though GATT Article VI requires an injury test, under the so-called grandfather rights permitting deviation from GATT obligation in cases where previously exsiting legislation required it (see chapter 1), the United States was technically in compliance with

GATT obligations when it applied countervailing duties to goods without an injury test, because the U.S. statute dated from 1897.[90]

As tariffs were reduced through international negotiation under the sponsorship of the GATT over the past several decades, various other nontariff measures began to have a greater effect on international trade flows. Increasingly, the U.S. government found that domestic manufacturers were urging it to apply countervailing duties to imported goods. For a variety of reasons, however, the Department of the Treasury, which administered these duties, did so haltingly. Sometimes the Treasury simply held petitions or complaints for the application of countervailing duties for years without taking action on them. Members of Congress often expressed suspicions and complaints about Treasury actions on behalf of constituents who were trying to get it to apply countervailing duties. By the time the Trade Act of 1974 was being drafted, the subject had generated a considerable amount of ill will between the Congress and the executive branch. As a consequence, the Congress wrote into the act a number of measures designed to greatly circumscribe the administrative discretion involved in the administration of the countervailing duty statute. In particular, the statute imposed strict time limits within which the Treasury must act after receiving a complaint or petition for countervailing duties. It also required a complaint or petition for countervailing duties, and publication of the Secretary of Treasury's determination on such a petition. Finally, the statute explicitly provided for judicial review even of a negative determination by the Secretary (that no "bounty or grant" existed).[91] (Judicial review had been previously sought, but one court had decided that the Secretary's action was not reviewable by the courts, but was a matter of executive discretion.[92])

At the same time, at the request of the executive branch the Trade Act of 1974 extended the application of countervailing duties to nondutiable goods for the first time in U.S. practice. The argument was that nondutiable goods could harm competing manufacturers equally as well if they were subsidized. It was also noted that the establishment of the GSP for duties on certain goods from many developing countries would result in many of those goods being duty free. Therefore, although the discipline of countervailing duties was to be applied, they would often not be applied to the goods of developing countries, which, being duty free, would be subject to the injury test. On the other hand, since it was clear that the GATT grandfather rights did not extent to nondutiable goods, because the statute on those goods did not precede the GATT, the Congress agreed to include in the application of countervailing duties to nondutiable goods an injury test designed to fulfill the GATT obligations.[93]

It was feared that because the Trade Act of 1974 so greatly

circumscribed the discretion of the Treasury in administering countervailing duties, it would cause such duties to be applied to trading partners in a way that would destroy the possibility of a new round of trade negotiations by exacerbating the foreign trading partner's ill will toward the U.S. countervailing duty practice. (Some foreign countries argued that the United States was contravening the GATT in its actions.) The Congress was therefore reluctantly persuaded to include in the new countervailing duty provisions a temporary waiver provision, previously mentioned,[94] that would allow the government to suspend or waive the application of countervailing duties under certain conditions.[95]

The waiver authority, however, was to expire January 2, 1979 (four years after the enactment of the act). By midsummer of 1978, the main lines of the MTN were declared completed, but many details were still left open.[96] It was clear that the results of the MTN, including a potential new agreement on countervailing duties and subsidies, could not be completed before the January 2, 1979 deadline, and that consequently after that date the United States would be forced to apply countervailing duties to a number of goods, including dairy products from the European Economic Community (EEC).[97] Officials of the EEC stated that the application of such duties could cause them to refuse to conclude the MTN negotiations or approve the MTN agreements. They said that "we can't negotiate with this gun at our head."[98]

In the fall of 1978, the executive branch therefore attempted to persuade Congress to extend the deadline of the waiver authority. Unfortunately, however, the introduction of a bill to do that became an attractive focus for several amendments designed to achieve particular goals sought by various interest groups. For example, a textile group had introduced an amendment to another bill that would have withdrawn the whole textile sector from the negotiation,[99] and there was talk of putting this amendment on the waiver authority bill. In addition, certain business groups introduced legislation that would have broadened and extended the potential of "adjustment assistance for firms" (loan and tax measures for manufacturing firms who found themselves having difficulties because of competition from foreign imported goods).[100] The waiver extension was procedurally linked to this bill by an amendment. Despite a rather intensive scramble to sort out the problems, the Congress adjourned in the early hours of the morning of Sunday, October 15, 1978, without having extended the waiver authority.[101] Consequently, the executive branch was faced with the unhappy prospect of trying to mollify the European negotiators in the light of the potential application of countervailing duties after January 2. The Congress was not due to convene until January 15, so that at the very least there was a two-week gap during which countervailing duties could be applied. Even after convening, the Congress would take some months to organize itself, since 1978 was an election year and a new Congress would convene in 1979.

Interestingly enough, the solution was simply to tolerate a messy legal situation for several months until the matter could be rectified. Even though the waiver provision expired on January 2, 1979, it was understood that it would take some time for any administrative agency to act under the new legal conditions it faced, and obviously a creative bureaucracy knows ways to extend that time. The Treasury Department is, as some have commented, certainly creative in that sense. In the meantime, during the early months of 1979, the executive branch forcefully presented its case for the extension of the waiver authority to Congress. In March, Congress agreed to extend the authority until September 30, or until a bill to implement the negotiations was enacted or defeated, whichever was earlier.[102] In the meantime, no countervailing duties had actually been applied, and the legislation extending the waiver authority clearly absolved companies from any liability for the interim period.[103]

Sectoral Negotiations

One of the interesting provisions of the Trade Act of 1974, a provision that occasioned considerable congressional attention and much dispute among contending interest groups, and that was finally resolved only after extensive compromise negotiation, was Section 104, establishing a "sector negotiating objective" of the United States.[104] The basic thrust of this provision was to encourage the U.S. MTN negotiators to pursue negotiating techniques that would try to establish within "appropriate product sectors" equivalent competitive opportunities in the markets of all countries. Thus, a sectoral free trade agreement could be one result. Another might be the establishment, within a particular sector (such as steel), of the same level of protection in each of the major importing countries, whether such protection was afforded by tariffs or nontariff barriers.[105] Obviously this is a difficult negotiating objective and the groups urging various formulations of this objective on the Congress for the Trade Act of 1974 had a variety of motives.

Although some attempt was made in the MTN to pursue this approach for certain sectors (particularly steel, aircrafts, dairy, meat, and grains), on the whole it was not very influential in the overall results of the MTN. Perhaps the most significant sector result of the MTN was that for aircraft, in which basically a free trade agreement was reached for a limited number of participating countries.[106]

Accepting the MTN Results: U.S. Law

Legal Authority to Accept MTN International Agreements

In the traditional academic terminology, the United States embraces a type of dualist philosophy in the way it receives international legal obligations into its legal system (to be discussed below). Thus it is possible for the United States to be bound by an international legal obligation under international law but fail to observe that obligation in its domestic law (and then to be in noncompliance with its international obligation).[107]

In this part of our discussion we focus on the legal requirements and procedures that were necessary for the United States to accept the international law obligations of the MTN results, leaving for the next part the explanation of the implementation of and compliance with those obligations. Because the power to accept international obligations so vitally affects the effective power to negotiate, we have already dealt with a portion of this subject.[108]

In some cases the President had the authority, explicitly delegated by statute, to accept an MTN agreement (if it conformed to certain criteria). The most important illustration of this was the MTN tariff agreement, called the Geneva Protocol (1979) (along with the Supplementary Geneva Protocol).[109] Section 101 of the Trade Act authorized presidential acceptance and implementation of certain tariff concessions contained in protocols. The President's representative to the GATT correspondingly signed the protocols in Geneva on July 11, 1979, partly pursuant to that authority. Effectiveness was made contingent, however, on the passage of the Trade Agreements Act of 1979.[110] The reason for this contingency was that some of the proposed tariff concessions negotiated at the Tokyo Round went beyond the authority of Section 101 of the Trade Act and consequently required the procedures contemplated by Section 102 of the act. The President's Proclamation 4707 of December 11, 1979, implemented the tariff concessions in U.S. law, relying both on the authority of Section 101 of the 1974 act and on various sections of the 1979 act.[111]

The President probably had authority apart from the Trade Agreements Act of 1979 (to be discussed later) to accept certain other MTN agreements also. For example, the agreements on bovine meat and on dairy products basically only set up an international consultation mechanism, presumably a matter within inherent presidential authority.[112] The Licensing Code needed no legislation for implementation since the President had authority to regulate the procedure of licensing under existing legislation.[113] Consequently, it was also likely that the President had authority to accept the Licensing Code on his own authority, although analogous activity has been challenged.[114]

Except for the tariff agreements mentioned here, Section 2 of the Trade Agreements Act of 1979 provided explicit authority for the President to accept all the major MTN agreements and all the bilateral MTN agreements to which the U.S. was a party.[115] However, this statutory acceptance authority was qualified in three important ways.

First, because the textual versions of the agreements that were available to the executive branch and Congress at the time the 1979 act was enacted were not completely final (certain corrections or minor changes were expected), the statutory draftsmen were faced with the perplexing problem of how to authorize acceptance of agreements not precisely specified without giving the executive branch a carte blanche to enter into agreements not approved by the Congress. The uneasy solution was language authorizing the President to accept the "final legal instruments or text" of trade agreements approved by the Congress, if the differences between the final text and the text earlier submitted to Congress were only "rectifications of a formal character or minor technical or clerical changes," or if the changes were only in "annexes" to the agreement and the President determined that the balance of rights and obligations for the United States had been maintained.[116] One particular example of the use of this later authority was the Government Procurement Code. The United States and Japan continued to negotiate on the entities to be included in the annex to that agreement until December 1980, at which time agreement was reached and formalized through an exchange of letters. On December 23, 1980, the United States announced that it was accepting the Government Procurement Code, and the code went into effect on January 1, 1981.[117]

Second, the acceptance authority in Section 2 of the Trade Agreements Act of 1979 imposed the limitation that "no agreement accepted by the President . . . shall apply between the United States and any other country unless the President determines that such country—" (1) has accepted the obligations of the agreement in relation to the United States, and (2) should not be denied the benefits of the agreement because it has not accorded the adequate reciprocity to the commerce of the United States, that Section 126(c) of the Trade Act of 1974 requires of other industrial countries.[118] The latter condition is obviously more troublesome, but the problem must be distinguished from the Most Favored Nation (MFN) treatment. Even if the United States accepts an agreement but does not apply it to another country, it may still apply its own law implementing the obligations of the agreement, in a nondiscriminatory way, to trade of all other nations whether they are parties to the particular agreement or not.[119] Thus, in revising its antidumping law to conform to the new MTN Antidumping Code, the United States did not distinguish between trade from nations who were or were not parties to that MTN agreement. In other cases, however, the contrary is true, as we shall see later.[120]

The 1979 statute's reciprocity condition implies a legal mechanism under which the United States could accept a particular MTN agreement without applying it to other countries, some of whom were also parties to the same agreement. The obligation to apply an MTN agreement to nations that have *not* accepted the same agreement is a question either of the language of the agreement itself or of an MFN obligation in some other international agreement. The principal other source of such obligation is, of course, the GATT itself (MFN in Article 1), which indeed may apply in a number of such cases.[121] Other agreements, such as bilateral friendship, commerce and navigation agreements, could also give rise to an MFN obligation.[122]

In addition, however, some of the MTN agreements purport to be agreed interpretations of provisions in the GATT itself,[123] and as such could arguably be interpreted to imply an obligation to treat all other GATT members in the manner required by that specific MTN agreement. It is also theoretically possible (although not the case) that an MTN agreement could explicitly provide that parties to it would treat all GATT members, or all other nations (or some subset of them), in a manner required by that agreement.[124]

Nonapplication of a particular agreement to another party to that agreement is a seeming anomaly (which international law rules regarding reservations might in some cases legitimize)[125] that stems from the strong precedent of GATT Article XXXV, which allows (under certain circumstances) a GATT contracting party to give notice of nonapplication of the GATT between it and another GATT member.[126] An explicit cause in some of the MTN agreements allows this same type of action.[127]

Third, the final important qualification of the Section 2(b)(3) acceptance authority in the 1979 act prevents the President from accepting certain agreements (all the major multilateral agreements of the MTN except the tariff agreements) unless all "major industrial country" MTN participants also accept. The statute defines "major industrial country" as the European Communities (whose acceptance is deemed acceptance by the Member States for this purpose), Canada, Japan, and other countries designated by the President.[128] Despite the condition, however, the statute allows the President to go ahead and accept the agreement if: (1) only one "major industrial country" has not accepted and that country is not a major factor in the trade in products covered by the agreement; (2) the President has authority to deny the benefits of the agreement to that country and takes steps to do so; or (3) U.S. trade would benefit anyway and the President reports that it is in the national interest to accept the agreement.

Under this clause, some difficult situations arose concerning acceptance and implementation of the MTN agreements. The 1979 act made the United States the first major industrial participant of the MTN to obtain executive authority to accept the results. The U.S. then acted to accept conditionally.[129] The EEC delayed such action partly because of an internal constitutional dispute over which institutions or governments had the competence to authorize acceptance of the agreements. However, it accepted the agreements by the end of 1979.[130] Canada, also, first appeared to be delaying (partly because of an election) but also acted before the end of 1979.[131] This left Japan, which found itself totally unable to finish the acceptance procedure before 1980. A new Parliament was elected in October 1979, and needed time to organize.[132] The cabinet officials took the necessary steps to recommend approval of the MTN results, and the Parliament did finally act in April 1980.[133] The uneasy solution used in United States law was for the President to determine that

> (ii) in accordance with Section 2(b)(3) of the Act (93 Stat. 147), the acceptance of these agreements by Japan is not essential to the effective operation of the agreements for that period of time during which Japan is completing its Constitutional procedures to accept the agreements and in the light of the stated intention of the Government of Japan to act in the interim in line with the agreements within its existing powers; . . . .[134]

The "Fast-Track" Procedure for NTB Agreements and the Drafting of the Trade Agreements Act of 1979

For the United States to both accept and implement the major nontariff agreements of the MTN required congressional approval, and under the Trade Act of 1974 this was to be accomplished by normal legislation, which, however, was to be considered by the Congress under the "fast-track" procedure described earlier.[135] The procedures turned out to operate in a very interesting fashion, which is revealing of the United States governmental and constitutional processes.

Under the "fast-track" procedure, the President was required to notify the Congress ninety days before he signed any NTB agreements, and to consult with key congressional committees during that time. Congress had been kept informed generally throughout the course of the Tokyo Round negotiations, and key congressional committees had developed professional staff whose full time was devoted to following the course of the negotiations. When the President notified the Congress in early January 1979, about the tentative NTB agreements, his officials sent to the Congress detailed information about the status of the negotiations, including the tentative drafts of the various agreements that were contemplated.[136] Anticipating this, congressional staff, in consultation with key senators and congressmen, had designed a procedure for the consultation that closely paralleled the normal procedure followed in work on bills, except that in this case no bill had yet been introduced in the Congress.

When a committee of Congress begins to formally consider a bill that has been introduced and to prepare that bill for report to the floor of the whole House, its session is often called a *markup,* indicating that the committee is marking up the bill with its proposed changes. The consultations with the executive branch during the ninety days before completion of the international agreements were called *nonmarkup* sessions, and followed very closely this type of procedure. One important difference was that the sessions were not open to the public.

The principal committees devoting time to this subject were the Senate Finance Committee and the House Ways and Means Committee (particularly the latter's Subcommittee on Trade). These committees met extensively with executive branch officials, including the trade negotiators, and on some subjects entered into detailed negotiations about the matters that should be included in a statute implementing the international agreements. Particularly close attention was given to the antidumping and countervailing duty laws.[137] Perhaps most surprising, the members of Congress informed the executive branch that they desired to have their own staff (including the legal staff of the House and the Senate), develop the actual text of the bill the President would introduce.

Further procedures also indicated the parallel with normal legislative processes. On certain issues the Ways and Means Committee and the Finance Committee did not agree, so they held a "nonconference" joint session[138] at which they resolved their differences in order to present a united front to the executive branch. Throughout this process the executive branch officials participated, influenced the deliberations, and were in a position of some bargaining power, since it was understood that it was the President's bill that would be ultimately introduced and that could not be amended afterward.[139]

After the international agreements were initialed in Geneva, the executive branch prepared the bill that the President introduced to the Congress. Understanding the political realities, the President's officials took almost the exact text of the draft bill that had been prepared by the congressional committees and staff. The President then arranged to have the bill introduced in June 1979.[140]

Once the bill had been introduced, the basic substantive work was over, since it could not be amended. Thus, from the point of view of the Congress, the consultation period, including the nonmarkup and the nonconference, that went on before the bill was introduced was crucial in shaping the bill so that it would gain enough support in both houses of Congress to be able to pass. Thus, after the bill was introduced the normal procedures for enacting legislation were a formality. To no one's suprise, the bill passed.[141] What was surprising was the overwhelming vote in favor of the bill: 90 to 4 in the Senate, and 395 to 7 in the House.[142]

One interesting development in these congressional procedures for approval of the MTN agreements was the involvement of foreign nation interests. Early in the ninety-day consultation procedures, as the congressional committees' nonmarkup sessions began their work, officials of the EEC realized the significance and importance of what was going on in the Congress of the United States. It was recognized that the shape of the statute the Congress was formulating would have a profound effect on the practical implementation of the MTN agreements. Once the statute became U.S. law, it would be hard to persuade the Congress to change it. Thus, other nations would be likely to interpret or constrain their own implementation of the MTN agreements in accordance with the precedent in the United States. The fact that the United States procedures were moving faster than those of any other country would also be highly influential. Consequently, the EEC took the logical step: they hired professional (legal and economic) representation in Washington, D.C. to monitor as closely as possible what was going on in the congressional consultation with the executive branch officials. These representatives reported quickly and frequently to the EEC officials, and thus on certain issues EEC negotiators could raise questions with their American counterparts. If the EEC objected to a direction they saw the congressional-executive sessions taking, it could and did make it known that it would deem certain statutory formulations a breach of the international obligations assumed by both the EEC and the United States. One example of this was the phrasing of the injury test for the Antidumping Code and Countervailing Duty Code. U.S. law used only the word *injury,* not *material injury,* in its antidumping procedures. GATT Article VI required *material injury.* U.S. law preceded the GATT, so "grandfather" right exceptions could be argued. On the other hand, the 1967 Antidumping Code using *material injury* had been accepted by the United States. For more than a decade, foreign countries argued that the United States was not living up to its 1967 Antidumping Code obligations. The United States argued, however, that even though the U.S. statute used the word *injury* without the adjective *material,* in fact in all U.S. antidumping procedures the injury that was found was material. This is an exceedingly difficult proposition to refute (because it would require a de novo examination of the complicated facts).

In the MTN Countervailing Duty Code and Antidumping Code the word *material* was carefully included. Initially, however, the executive branch officials in their consultations with the Congress seemed to be willing to accept U.S. statutory formulations that did not include the word *material.* Presumably they felt they could continue to argue that a material injury test would be in fact fulfilled. The EEC negotiators let the United States know that they found this unacceptable, and that they felt it exceedingly important that the statute include the word *material.* As a result of these negotiations, and the presentation of these views to the committees, Congress finally accepted the word *material* for inclusion in the U.S. statute. Interestingly enough, however, the committee reports describing the meaning of the material injury test stated that the meaning (in antidumping law) was to be that which had been previously applied by the ITC in recent years under the injury test. Thus the Congress expressed its view that material injury had been the de facto criterion all along—that is, that the word *material* did not make any effective addition to the word *injury.*

The new injury test phrase will need to be applied a number of times before we are able to ascertain whether there has been an effective change in that fact. However, the whole incident pointedly demonstrates the direction of modern diplomacy, with participation of foreign representatives in seemingly internal domestic governmental procedures.[143]

In all this extensive consultation between the executive branch and the Congress, with the tugging and compromising that inevitably goes on in the legislative process, the testimony of participants was that the congressional committees were responsive to executive branch objectives that nothing be included in the U.S. statute that would require the United States to be in default of any of its international obligations under the MTN results. It appears that congressmen and senators were very careful to prevent any such measures from being included in the proposed statute. To confirm this observation, after the bill was forwarded to the Congress in final form there was an official statement by the EEC Commission to the effect that in the opinion of the EEC officials, on the whole, the bill reflected the spirit and the letter of the MTN agreements.[144]

Several aspects of this procedure for enacting the Trade Agreements Act of 1979 are particularly interesting and potentially significant. First, the Congress was evidently pleased with the procedure. The heavy involvement of the congressional committees in the drafting process gave the Congress confidence and a feeling of security that the executive branch was not trying to foist something upon Congress without giving it an opportunity to influence the results. For example, at one point in the consultative period before the international agreements were finalized, members of Congress voiced a particular criticism on behalf of small business constituents. They complained that the proposed Government Procurement Code would reduce their small business preference under existing U.S. law. U.S. executive branch negotiators sensed the importance of the issue as a potential problem in obtaining passage of the legislation, and also sensed that exempting small business from the reach of the agreement would not substantially affect the policies of the agreement nor the other countries involved in it. Consequently, the U.S. negotiators immediately approached other countries and obtained their approval to alter the proposed agreement in such a way as to take care of the problem.[145] The incident illustrated the value of the period of consultation required before the international agreement was completed.

The Congress' satisfaction with the procedure is evidenced not only by statements in the committee reports and other legislative history,[146] but more concretely by the fact that it extended by eight years the period prescribed for the procedure under the 1974 act.[147] In addition, in Section 3(c) of the 1979 act the Congress adopted virtually the same procedure for amending U.S. law implementing the MTN agreements when such amendments are necessary to fulfill a "requirement of, amendment to, or recommendation under such an agreement. . . ."[148] Thus, if an international disputes panel rules against the United States on a question of interpretation of an MTN agreement, and U.S. law prevented the executive branch from implementing the international interpretation, this procedure could be followed to change U.S. law.[149]

The "fast-track" procedure thus holds considerable potential for the future, as a means of accommodating the interests of both the executive branch in its international dealings and the Congress with its responsiveness to constituents. One might even hope that the rancor between these two branches of government over international trade policy during the past several decades may be considerably softened by the "fast-track" procedure. This could have important implications for the future of the GATT-MTN system.

The second interesting aspect of the procedures for enacting the 1979 act is a somewhat unusual problem concerning the techniques of interpreting it. Normally U.S courts are influenced in their interpretation of a statute by its legislative history. This history consists of, among other things, the committee hearings and debates, the committee reports, and statements on the floor of both houses while the bill was being considered. The theory is that the intent of Congress, when ambiguous in the statutory language itself, can sometimes be ascertained from the statements of the congressional participants in the drafting process. Under the "fast-track" procedure, however, a bill was introduced by the executive branch and could not be amended.

Thus the executive branch was in theory the draftsman, and its intent was arguably the intent of the draftsman. The executive branch sent to Congress, along with the drafted bill, a Statement of Administrative Action indicating its intentions in administering the new legislation.[150] Thus this statement is an important part of the legislative history, and arguably is the definitive source of legislative intent. However the actual history of the consultative process between the executive branch and Congress suggests a somewhat different approach, and the House and Senate Committee reports reflect that difference. Although these reports were formulated by the key congressional committees in reporting on the actual bill introduced, and thus came at a time when no amendments were permitted to the bill, the reports state:

> The committee emphasized that virtually all of the provisions of H.R. 4357 [which became the TAA of 1979] reflect the decisions of the House and Senate committees, as coordinated in the joint meetings noted above. The implementing bill was drafted in the offices of the House and Senate Legislative Counsel with the participation of staff members of the committees of jurisdiction in both Houses and representatives from the Administration. The bill reflects the understandings achieved on all issues, as explained in this report.[151]

Thus the report stakes out a claim to be considered as a prime source of legislative history, just as it would normally be for other legislation. Moreover it also presents a view of the role of the Statement of Administrative Action, and notes that those statements "are not part of the bill and will not become part of U.S. statutes. . . . They will not provide any new, independent legal authority for executive action."[152]

Finally, the role of the MTN agreements themselves in the legislative history must be considered. As will be seen below, it is clear that the agreements do not themselves become U.S. law, but the committee reports state, "This bill is drafted with the intent to permit U.S. practice to be consistent with the obligations of the agreements, as the United States understands those obligations."[153] Thus it seems fair to conclude that the trade agreements (and presumably *their* preparatory work) can be used as at least a secondary source of legislative history of the 1979 act when other sources fail to resolve an issue.

One additional aspect of the Trade Agreements Act of 1979 should be noted. The act clearly covers a number of matters not explicitly required by any of the MTN agreements or other negotiation results. Indeed, some of the matters contained in the act seem only remotely relevant to the MTN at all. For example, Section 1111 of the act makes some changes in Title V of the Trade Act of 1974 relating to the GSP. Among other changes, the President is authorized to designate OPEC members that meet certain requirements as beneficiaries of the GSP. Nevertheless, although the "fast-track" procedure purports to be a means of implementing and approving the trade negotiation results, since the form of the congressional action is that of a typical statute adopted through the normal constitutional procedures (and not through a procedure such as legislative veto or delegated regulations), the statute provides its own authority for even those matters that go beyond the necessities of implementing the MTN results. Thus, it seems impossible to challenge measures of the statute on the grounds that they are outside the authority of the "fast-track" procedure, as embodied in the Trade Act of 1974 and particularly Sections 102 and 151 of that act. This is an important feature of the stability and immunity from constitutional litigation provided by the "fast-track" procedure.[154]

U.S. Acceptance of the MTN Agreements

Once the Trade Agreements Act of 1979 became law (on July 26, 1979, upon the President's signature) the President then had the authority he needed to accept the MTN agreements as international law obligations of the United States.[155]

The President made most of the required determinations on December 14, 1979. His document authorized the signing and acceptance of seven of the agreements.[156] Six of them were signed and accepted by Deputy U.S. Trade Representative Michael B. Smith in Geneva on December 17, 1979, the opening day of the three-year signing period.[157] The Civil Aircraft Agreement was accepted on December 20, 1979. Two agreements, scheduled to enter into force January 1, 1981, were signed but not accepted at this time. The Government Procurement Code was not accepted because negotiations on entity coverage had not been completed, and the Customs Valuation Code was not accepted because the conditions in Section 2 of the Trade Agreements Act had not been met.[158]

The United States implemented the Customs Valuation Code in U.S. law effective July 1, 1980. The President's proclamation of the early implementation of the code was authorized by Section 204(a)(2) of the Trade Agreements Act, which required a determination that the EEC had accepted the obligations of the code.[159] A protocol to the Customs Valuation Code, designed to influence developing countries to adhere to the code, came into effect January 1, 1981. This agreement was implemented in U.S. law by a statute that amended one section of the Trade Agreements Act.[160]

The Government Procurement Code entered into force January 1, 1981, after the United States accepted it in December 1980.[161]

Implementing the MTN Results in U.S. Law

Source of U.S. Domestic Law

Although international agreements can be a direct part of the U.S. domestic law, it is not always the case that this is so. Thus the U.S. must be classified as dualist in the way it receives international law into domestic law.[162] In what form are the results of the MTN that the United States has accepted as international law obligations to be implemented into U.S. domestic law?

The general U.S. law on this subject depends heavily on the concept of self-execution, a well-established constitutional notion in U.S. jurisprudence. An international agreement (or part of one) that the courts find to be self-executing becomes directly a part of the domestic laws, and U.S. courts must apply it in specific cases.[163] In lieu of extensive analysis of this concept, suffice it to say that the U.S. courts determine whether an international agreement is self-executing by ascertaining whether the draftsmen intended it to be so, as manifested primarily by the language of the agreement itself and secondarily by the preparatory work. Since the concept of self-execution is a domestic constitutional question (often of little or no interest to other national parties to the agreement), it is not surprising that the courts tend to look at the intent of the U.S. draftsmen. For U.S. agreements that require approval of the Congress or Senate, the views of those bodies in giving approval become very important and perhaps determinative.[164] Often it is difficult to tell either from the language of the agreement or the preparatory work (legislative history) whether a particular international agreement is self-executing. If it is not, then whenever the international agreement obligates the U.S. to change its domestic law, the change must be brought about by other regular constitutional means, such as enactment of a statute, or, if the President or his officials have authority, the promulgation of a regulation.

U.S. law is quite clear on the question of self-execution and the source of implementing law for the MTN agreements. The Trade Agreements Act of 1979 has two clauses that address this subject, which, although not models of clarity themselves, are clarified by the relevant committee reports and Statement of Administrative Action. The clauses are Sections 3(a) and 3(f).

Section 3(a) states:

> SEC. 3. RELATIONSHIP OF TRADE AGREEMENTS TO UNITED STATES LAW.
>
> (a) United States Statutes to Prevail in Conflict.—No provision of any trade agreement approved by the Congress under section 2(a), nor the

> application of any such provision to any person or circumstances, which is in conflict with any statute of the United States shall be given effect under the laws of the United States.

Section 3(f) states:

> (f) Unspecified Private Remedies Not Created.—Neither the entry into force with respect to the United States of any agreement approved under section 2(a), nor the enactment of this Act, shall be construed as creating any private right of action or remedy for which provision is not explicitly made under this Act or under the laws of the United States.

The Statement of Administrative Action on the MTN agreements is unequivocal: "The Trade Agreements negotiated are not self-executing and accordingly do not have independent effect under U.S. law."[165] The Senate and House reports follow suit, saying that "the trade agreements are not self-executing."[166]

The Senate report goes on to say, "Implementation of obligations for the United States under the agreements can only be achieved as is provided in the Trade Act of 1974."[167] (This statement probably cannot be taken totally at face value.[168])

It seems clear that the Trade Agreements Act itself is the source of the U.S. domestic law that implements the major nontariff MTN agreements accepted by the United States under that act. This is true for the agreements on subsidies and countervailing measures, antidumping measures, custom valuation, government procurement, standards, and civil aircraft. Certain other MTN agreements are implemented through other legal actions, however. For example, most of the tariff agreements could be implemented under the authority of Section 101 of the 1974 Trade Act. This act (following the forty-year pattern of U.S. trade acts) explicitly authorized the President to enter into tariff change agreements (within specified limits). In a separate clause, it then authorized him to "proclaim such modification . . . of any existing duty, . . . [etc.] as he determines to be required or appropriate to carry out any such trade agreement."[169] It will be noticed that this statute exhibits the dualist philosophy. To the extent that the tariff obligations agreed to in the MTN exceeded the authority of Section 101 on the 1974 act, however, legislation of approval was necessary, and this is contained in Title V of the Trade Agreements Act of 1979.[170] Pursuant to both of these sources of authority, the President has proclaimed[171] the staged reductions and other changes in U.S. tariffs, and this proclamation is the direct source of domestic law applied by U.S. courts and customs officials.

In addition to those on tariffs, there were several MTN agreements (dairy, bovine meat, import licensing)[172] that the executive branch claimed, and the Congress agreed,[173] did not need implementing legislation. In these cases no U.S. statutes needed changing. The Dairy Products and the Bovine Meat "Arrangements" merely established international consultative procedures and normal U.S. diplomatic activities would embrace those functions. The President already had statutory delegations that authorized him or his officials to issue or change regulations in order to accommodate the merely procedural obligations of the Licensing Code.[174]

Some MTN agreements required no direct implementation in U.S. law because they did not require any particular U.S. action. The so-called framework agreements, which were approved as decisions of the GATT Contracting Parties[175] and not as independent international agreements, contained matters which, although potentially very important, did not call for specific actions by the U.S. except perhaps as it will conduct its diplomacy in GATT forums in the future. For example, one such matter apparently makes permanent the authority for GATT members to deviate from MFN so as to grant preferences to developing countries. No country is required to act that way, but this text, now a decision of the GATT Contracting Parties,[176] will effectively deprive a GATT member of the right to complain against other member nations in some cases.

While the Trade Agreements Act of 1979 thus implements in U.S. law the measures necessary for the U.S. to carry out its obligations under some agreements, one interesting facet of this concerns MFN obligations. Three of the 1979 statutory measures limit the effect of portions of those implementing measures so as to exclude their application to some nations, including some GATT nations.[177] Thus:

1. Section 101 of the act (introducing 19 U.S.C. Sec. 701) applies the new U.S. countervailing duty law, with its new injury test, only to countries that also accept the MTN Subsidies-Countervailing Duty Code (with exceptions for a few other countries).
2. Section 301 limits U.S. implementation of the MTN Government Procurement Code mainly to countries that also accept that agreement or provide appropriate reciprocal actions.
3. Section 441 limits certain procedural rights under the Standards Code to certain countries that reciprocate.

It appears that in implementing all other MTN agreements, whether required by international obligations or not, the U.S. has extended its law to all other GATT or MFN countries.

The three cases mentioned raise the issue of compliance with MFN obligations, a subject that will have to await more detailed study elsewhere. It should be noted that whether or not the U.S. law in Sections 101, 301, and 441 of the Trade Agreements Act is in full compliance with MFN obligations, including GATT Article I (and there are arguments in each case that compliance has been achieved), nevertheless the domestic law of the United States is that stated in the 1979 act (until superseded by a later domestic act), even if it is inconsistent with (i.e., in breach of) U.S. international obligations.

Executive Branch Reorganization

For many decades, the Congress has been critical of the way the executive branch carries out U.S. foreign international economic policy. Congress was distressed after the Kennedy Round, and felt that the United States had given up too much in those negotations.[178] Likewise, it had been increasingly critical of the executive branch's lack of effective organization in international economic matters. It felt that too many agencies were involved and that interagency conflicts had caused delays and mistakes in policy and had made it difficult for members of Congress or their constituents to know where to go with their complaints. The extraordinary vote in favor of the Trade Agreements Act of 1979,[179] suggests that some of these congressional concerns had been lessened by the particular procedures (including the extensive consultation with Congress) that were undertaken before the introduction of the bill. Some senators, however, wanted to go further. They strongly urged an executive branch reorganization of government functions relating to international economic affairs. Various ideas were suggested, including the establishment of a new department, to be devoted entirely to international trade matters, that would gather together the various executive branch agencies and activities relating to that subject.[180]

Part of the congressional concern also stemmed from decades of resentment at the way the Department of State handled international trade matters (it was alleged that the department tended to give too low a priority to international economic affairs, and to trade off U.S. economic interests for various political advantages). Congress also resented the way the Treasury Department had been administering the antidumping and countervailing duty acts.[181]

For a variety of reasons, the idea of a new department devoted to trade was deemed unacceptable both to the Congress and to the executive branch, but some reorganization of trade functions seemed necessary. Indeed, some senators and congressmen made this clear to the executive branch at certain points during the procedures on the Trade Agreements Act of 1979. They threatened to hold up that procedure unless some commitments were made on an executive branch reorganization.[182]

Consequently, after the Trade Agreements Act of 1979 was enacted, the President was committed to providing some reorganization, and he did so with Order Number 3 of September 25, 1979. Under a statute previously enacted by the Congress, the President had the authority to reorganize agencies of the United States, but he must do so by a reorganization order which he then laid before Congress for sixty days. If the Congress vetoed the order, the President would not be allowed to proceed with his reorganization. In this case, the reorganization order was laid before Congress and there was no veto, so on November 29, 1979, the order became law, authorizing the President to carry out the reorganization pursuant to its terms. He did so by Executive Order No. 12188 of January 2, 1980.[183]

The most important provisions of the reorganization were those that shifted the administration of the countervailing duty law and the antidumping law (newly and extensively amended by the Trade Agreements Act of 1979 in the light of the MTN agreements). These functions were shifted from the Treasury Department to the Department of Commerce.[184] In the Department of Commerce, a new International Trade Administration (ITA) was set up, with three principal divisions: one to handle antidumping and countervailing duty matters and to continue the Commerce Department function of export control administration; a second to be concerned with international economic policy; and a third to continue a now embellished function for the Department of Commerce, that of export promotion.[185]

In addition, the reorganization order took away from the Department of State a number of international economic functions, particularly authority for commodity agreements, and gave them to the office of the STR, renamed the Office of the United States Trade Representative (USTR). The reorganization also stated that the USTR Office would have primary international negotiating responsibilities on a number of economic matters, including matters relating to antidumping and countervailing duty law.[186]

MTN Implementation and the U.S. Regulatory Process

The Senate report, in stating that the MTN agreements are not self-executing in U.S. law, noted:

> Our trade laws are, and long have been, subject to administrative and judicial review processes. These processes both lead to and require greater precision in our law than the often vague terms of the agreements or implementing regulations of other countries. Furthermore, unfamiliar terms in the agreements, or terms which may have a different meaning in United States law than in international practice or another country's laws, need to be rendered into United States law in a way which ensures maximum predictability and fairness.[187]

In U.S. law there is much emphasis on individual citizen rights and fair and open procedures (sometimes criticized as overly legalistic). The process of implementing the MTN agreements did not stop with the 1979 statute, Presidential proclamations, or the reorganization of the government. In many cases the agencies concerned with the subject matter of a particular MTN code then undertook an elaborate exercise to revise or issue new regulations to further elaborate details of implementation within the borderlines provided by the statute.[188] For example, in the fall of 1979 the Treasury Department drafted and published new proposed regulations on the subjects of countervailing duties and antidumping duties. It held public hearings and solicited comment on those proposed regulations.[189] The reorganization shifted these two subjects to the Commerce Department as of January 1, 1980, and that department inherited the proposals.[190] After some further study the Commerce Department issued final regulations on both matters, following many of the proposals it had inherited.[191]

Likewise, the ITC issued a new set of regulations (also after public hearings and solicitation of comments on proposals[192]) to govern the injury determinations required in both countervailing and antidumping cases, and this subject received similar attention and efforts.

A significant part of the 1979 implementing statute itself was concerned with detailed procedures for administering the subjects of the MTN agreements. This was particularly true of the countervailing duty and antidumping duty laws. Elaborate provisions were included to govern the handling of private citizen complaints that imports were unfair. A series of time limits were imposed, and the opportunity for public hearings clarified and broadened.[193] Attempts were made to further insulate the administration of these subjects from influences of a political or international relations nature.[194] Finally, and very importantly, elaborate new statutory provisions on judicial review provided disappointed parties to the proceedings (foreign or domestic) access to the courts.[195]

Private Citizen Complaints and Section 301 Procedures: U.S. Export Access to Markets Abroad

Section 252 of the 1962 Trade Expansion Act provided a brief framework under which U.S. citizens could bring to the attention of the U.S. government activities by foreign governments in the conduct of international trade that were considered violations of the GATT or otherwise unfair.[196] This section then authorized the President to take certain countermeasures by way of retaliation, if after negotiating with the foreign government he could not obtain satisfaction for the U.S. citizens.[197]

This procedure was later revised and became Section 301 of the Trade Act of 1974. Section 301 sets up an explicit set of procedures and authorities designed to give a private citizen or businessman a channel through which he can complain to the United States government when he feels that foreign government actions are hurting his interests and are either unfair or in violation of international agreements like the GATT. Section 301 provides that the office of the USTR shall receive the complaints and shall on demand hold public hearings on their validity.[198]

The Trade Agreements Act of 1979 amended Section 301, but the procedure retains its basic goal of providing a channel for U.S. citizens to address their government in the field of trade. After consideration by the USTR (after public hearings have been held on a complaint), if the complaint is considered justified the President is required to take whatever action he can to redress the matter, and he is authorized to take a variety of countermeasures against the foreign government concerned, including trade restriction measures, if he is unable to obtain redress by negotiation.[199]

This procedure is interesting and indeed almost unique. It stems from a feeling of the U.S. public and its representatives in Congress that the individual citizen or businessman should have some right to redress when foreign governments are violating their international obligations.[200] It also stems from the Congress's distrust of the way the executive branch handles these types of complaints. Various proposals in the 1979 legislative process would have gone further in forcing executive branch action against foreign governments than did the provisions that were finally embodied in the statute. Nothing in the statute requires the President to take retaliatory actions, but the requirement of public hearings,[201] coupled with the requirement to state publicly on the record the reasons for not acting, make it politically difficult for the executive branch to ignore a citizen complaint against a foreign government when it appears to be reasonable and supported by the facts.

Summary and Conclusions: U.S. Law, the Tokyo Round Agreements, and the Future of International Economic Relations

The single most significant constraining influence of the U.S. Constitution on the ability of United States officials to negotiate international economic agreements, is, not surprisingly, the relationship of the executive and congressional branches of the government. This relationship colors every aspect of U.S. foreign relations, and particularly foreign economic relations, where the Congress has a special claim to jurisdiction due to the constitutional clause explicitly delegating authority over foreign commerce. In spite of this constraint, however, the Tokyo Round experience demonstrates that the executive-congressional relationship can be managed in a constructive way, to allow effective U.S. participation in international negotiations and subsequent agreements. The overwhelming vote in favor of the Trade Agreements Act of 1979, which authorizes U.S. acceptance of the Tokyo Round agreements, may, as some have alleged, be evidence of too many concessions by the executive branch to the Congress. Nevertheless, the close consultation between the executive branch and the Congress—in certain circumstances resulting in changes in the international negotiations, in other circumstances resulting in changes in congressional attitude—shows that the give-and-take of the process does work. This process, however, implies certain nontraditional diplomatic activities. For example, foreign nations make their presence felt on the Washington scene and follow executive-congressional activities closely. At appropriate times, they make representations to the government concerning potential congressional actions. This activity is obvious to persons with experience in government or business, but it seems, surprisingly, to have been overlooked by those who have been more involved in the theory of international law.

The U.S. system now seems to rely fairly extensively on the procedures provided in Section 301 of the Trade Act of 1974. The notion that a private citizen should have the right to almost compel his government to take action on his behalf in international forums seems to be very attractive to the Congress, especially in the light of its suspicions of the executive branch.

One aspect of the U.S. legal-constitutional processes of implementing the Tokyo Round is rather intriguing. Perhaps partly because of the system's rather elaborate legalistic approach, on several occasions certain legal dilemmas have been posed to the policy makers. For example, as described in this chapter, the authority for the President to waive countervailing duties in certain circumstances ran out before the negotiation was finished, and the application of such duties could have derailed the negotiations. Yet, in the end the messiness of the situation was simply tolerated, and the legal constraint was not allowed to override important policy goals. Likewise, the inability of Japan to formally ratify the results of the Tokyo Round posed certain legal problems for the U.S. administration and its desire to formally accept and implement the Tokyo Round agreements, but the lawyers for the administration were able to wiggle their way around the problem—albeit uneasily—with verbal formulas in the presidential findings document.

One might conclude, therefore, that to a certain extent the

lawyers were irrelevant, that whenever apparently formidable obstacles were posed by technical legal formulations, the approach was to ignore them or to tolerate technical illegality. One cannot, however, conclude that this approach would always work, particularly in a matter on which constituent groups in the United States differed strongly.

One of the problems inherent in the congressional-executive tensions is that of oversell, which arises when the executive branch is trying to persuade the Congress to accept and implement international agreements. In such a context there is a risk that executive branch officials will promise too much to the Congress and that later events will make it impossible to fulfill those promises. Perhaps the prime example of this was the Subsidies-Countervailing Duty Code. Executive branch officials made optimistic statements to the Congress, including some about pressure that the United States would exert on developing countries to abide by the basic principles of the code. It has proved very difficult, it not impossible, to fulfill these promises.

At least partly because of the characteristics of the American system that have just been reviewed, a feature of that system is its high degree of legalization. Congressional suspicions of executive branch actions, coupled with the Congress's realization that it cannot negotiate or administer the laws (even if the Constitution were to permit such activity), has led the Congress to pursue its goals through detailed legislation that limits the amount of discretion of executive branch officials. To help reinforce these limitations, the Congress has also mandated elaborate procedures designed to make the decisions open and transparent and to allow citizen and public participation at almost every stage. In addition, the Congress, particularly in the 1979 act, has provided elaborate court supervision of the administrative process through the many possibilities for judicial review.

All this legalization, of course, creates complexity and costs. Complexity and costs have in turn been challenged by foreign critics as trade barriers in themselves. To a certain extent this may be true, although this author has estimated the public and private annual costs of the U.S. regulatory system for imports (excluding the normal customs processes) to be less than 0.1 percent of the total value of annual imports to the country.[202] Yet it must be realized there are benefits in this system also. Its openness, and its comparative objectivity, comparative insulation from undue political influence, and comparative reliance on relatively detailed published criteria, give foreign parties interested in exporting to the U.S. a degree of predictable access to the market that may not be available in any other system. In the U.S. system it is hard for representatives of a domestic industry to privately boast that they will see to it that the government will exclude competing imports unless certain specified private criteria are met. Lawyers can give a measure of guidance both to domestic industry representatives desiring to exclude competing goods, and to importing interests, often eliminating the necessity of seeking any formal (or informal) government proceeding. It is at least possible to hypothesize that because of the public access to, transparency of, and stipulated criteria for the regulation of U.S. imports, more and better access to the U.S. market is available to foreign producers than is the case in most other markets. If liberal trade is the desired goal of the system, such legalization may more efficiently promote that goal than systems that rely more heavily on government discretion or nonpublic decision making.

In addition, legalization (as aggravating as it is sometimes) tends to reduce the power orientation of the system and nudge it more in the direction of rule orientation, as this author has elsewhere described.[203]

But there are other disadvantages to such a system. Clearly it is less flexible; indeed, that is its objective, for flexible generally means less predictable, and, possibly, more subject to influence by extraneous or unpredictable goals. One of the questions that has been appropriately raised in connection with the system is whether it can cope with the truly large cases, such as trade problems of the steel or automobile sector, which often are a result of important and painful trends of structural adjustment. If the rules are not adequately tuned to the massive problems of this type, they could, when inflexibly administered, create difficulties rather than solve them. One answer to this criticism would be to improve and change the rules. But when the world's procedures for such change (consisting of the intertwined national and international procedures as described in this book) are as difficult, lengthy, and inflexible as they are, rule changes do not occur easily. Thus rules sometimes become outdated, or are ambiguous or misdirected, because they result from difficult and elaborate negotiation processes. In such circumstances the rules tend to break down.

These reflections do not seem to be encouraging for the future of international economic relations. Yet improvisation by intelligent officials, coupled with the discernible trend of not only greater detail and complexity in rules, but also greater openness and predictability of the trade rules in the U.S., offers a longer-run prospect of greater stability in trade and economic relationships. If the rules can be steadily improved, and the experience with them used to further such improvements (a big if), then in the opinion of this author one is entitled to be modestly optimistic about the long-run prospects in international trade relations.

NOTES

1. *See generally* L. HENKIN, FOREIGN AFFAIRS AND THE CONSTITUTION (1972); L. TRIBE, AMERICAN CONSTITUTIONAL LAW chs. 2–6 (1978); THE FEDERALIST NOS. 47–51, 75 (A. Hamilton).
2. A. SOFAER, WAR, FOREIGN AFFAIRS AND CONSTITUTIONAL POWER (1976); D. CHEEVER & H. HAVILAND, AMERICAN FOREIGN POLICY AND THE SEPARATION OF POWERS (1952).
3. United States v. Curtiss-Wright Export Corp., 299 U.S. 304 (1936).
4. *See* Berger, *The Presidential Monopoly of Foreign Relations,* 71 MICH. L. REV. 1, 26–28 (1972); Levitan, *The Foreign Relations Power: An Analysis of Mr. Justice Sutherland's Theory,* 55 YALE L. J. 467 (1946); Fulbright, *American Foreign Policy in the Twentieth Century Under an Eighteenth Century Constitution,* 47 CORNELL L.Q. 1 (1961); Borchard, *Treaties and Executive Agreements—A Reply,* 54 YALE L.J. 616, 648 (1945); Lofgren, United States v. Curtiss-Wright Export Corporation: *An Historical Reassessment,* 83 YALE L.J. (1973); Schlesinger, *Congress and the Making of American Foreign Policy,* 51 FOREIGN AFF. 78 (1972).
5. Two constitutional clauses are pertinent. Article I, Section 2 states:

   > The President shall be Commander in Chief of the Army and Navy of the United States, and of the Militia of the several states. . . . He shall have the Power, by and with the Advice and Consent of the Senate, to make Treaties, provided two-thirds of the Senators present concur; and he shall nominate, and by and with the Advice and Consent of the Senate, shall appoint Ambassadors . . . .

   Article II, Section 3 states, "[H]e shall receive Ambassadors and other public Ministers; he shall take care that the Laws be faithfully executed. . . ."
6. *See, e.g.,* S. REP. NO. 1298, 93d Cong., 2d Sess. 14 (1974) [hereinafter cited as S. REP. NO. 1298], *reprinted* in 1974 U.S. CODE CONG. & AD. NEWS 7186, 7196; S. REP. NO. 249, 96th Cong., 1st Sess. 4 (1979) [hereinafter cited as S. REP. NO. 249], *reprinted* in 1979 U.S. CODE CONG. & AD. NEWS 381, 390.
7. Youngstown Sheet & Tube Co. v. Sawyer, 343 U.S. 579 (1952).
8. For example, in United States v. Guy W. Capps, Inc., 204 F.2d 655 (4th Cir. 1953), *aff'd on other grounds,* 348 U.S. 296 (1955), the Court of Appeals did not give effect to an executive agreement between the United States and Canada which had not been authorized by Congress and was contrary to a statute dealing with the same subject. In Consumers Union of U.S., Inc. v. Kissinger, 506 F.2d 136 (D.C. Cir. 1974), *cert. denied,* 421 U.S. 1004 (1975), the court held that voluntary restraint agreements that the executive branch entered into with foreign steel companies were not outside its constitutional powers. The discussion in *Consumers Union* suggests some potential limitation on presidential power.
9. *See, e.g.,* War Powers Resolution, Pub. L. No. 93-148, 87 Stat. 555 (1973) (codified at 50 U.S.C. §§ 1541–1548 (1976)); International Security Assistance and Arms Export Control Act of 1976, Pub. L. No. 94-329, 90 Stat. 729 (codified in scattered sections of 22 U.S.C.); the

Case Act (requiring transmission of international agreements to Congress), Pub. L. No. 92-403, 86 Stat, 619 (1972) (codified at 1 U.S.C. 11(2)(b) (1976); National Emergencies Act, Pub. L. No. 94-412, 90 Stat. 1255 (1979) (codified in scattered sections of Titles 8, 10, 16, and 50 of U.S.C.). *See generally* T. FRANCK & E. WEISBAND, FOREIGN POLICY BY CONGRESS (1979).

10. Cutler, *To Form a Government,* 59 FOREIGN AFF. 126 (1980).
11. *See* P. SAMUELSON, ECONOMICS 663 (11th ed. 1980); C. KINDLEBERGER, INTERNATIONAL ECONOMICS, 121 (5th ed. 1973); F. ROOT, INTERNATIONAL TRADE AND INVESTMENT 168–69 (4th ed. 1978); the 1930 Act raised tariffs to the highest level in U.S. history.
12. An Act to Amend the Tariff Act of 1930, Part III, Pub. L. No. 316, 48 Stat. 943 (1934); *see* JACKSON, LEGAL PROBLEMS OF INTERNATIONAL ECONOMIC RELATIONS, 29 (1977) [hereinafter cited as INTERNATIONAL ECONOMIC RELATIONS]
13. INTERNATIONAL ECONOMIC RELATIONS, *supra* note 12, at 396. See the list of the agreements reproduced in *Hearings on Extension of the Reciprocal Trade Agreements Act Before the House Comm. on Ways and Means,* 79th Cong., 1st Sess. 38, 636, 932 (1948).
14. *See* Jackson, *The General Agreement on Tariffs and Trade in U.S. Domestic Law,* 66 MICH. L. REV. 249, 255 (1967) [hereinafter cited as *GATT in U.S. Domestic Law*].
15. U.S. CONST. art. II, § 2.
16. U.S. DEP'T OF STATE, CIRCULAR NO. 175 (1955), *reprinted in* 50 AM. J. INT'L L. 784 (1956); Stevenson, *Constitutional Aspects of the Executive Agreement Procedure,* DEP'T STATE BULL. 840 (1972); L. HENKIN, *supra* note 1, at 173; McDougal & Lans, *Treaties and Congressional-Executive or Presidential Agreements: Interchangeable Instruments of National Policy,* 54 YALE L.J. 181, and 534 (1945).
17. See sources cited *supra* note 16.
18. See, e.g., Trade Act of 1974, § 101, Pub. L. No. 93-618, 88 Stat. 1978 (1975) (19 U.S.C. 2111 (1976)).
19. *See, e.g.,* North Atlantic Treaty, April 4, 1949, 63 Stat. 2241, T.I.A.S. No. 1964, 34 U.N.T.S. 243, and accompanying executive agreements, listed following the NATO treaty in U.S. DEP'T OF STATE PUB. NO. 9136, TREATIES IN FORCE (1980).
20. These are the most controversial. *See, e.g.,* L. HENKIN, *supra* note 1, at ch. 2; INTERNATIONAL ECONOMIC RELATIONS, *supra* note 12, at § 3.2; W. BISHOP, INTERNATIONAL LAW 101–04 (1971); U.S. DEP'T OF STATE CIRCULAR NO. 175, § 3(c) (1956).
21. See sources cited *supra* note 20.
22. *See* INTERNATIONAL ECONOMIC RELATIONS, *supra* note 12, at ch. 4, p. 199 n. 4.
23. *See, e.g.,* A.T. MASON & W.M. BEANEY, AMERICAN CONSTITUTIONAL LAW chs. 4, 5 (2d ed. 1959); W.B. LOCKHART, Y. KAMISAR & J.H. CHOPER, CONSTITUTIONAL RIGHTS AND LIBERTIES ch. 3, § 1 (5th ed. 1981).
24. National League of Cities v. Usery, Secretary of Labor, 426 U.S. 833

(1976). *See* Vanaskie, *The State Sovereignty Doctrine Since* National League of Cities v. Usery: *A New Constitutional Interpretation Under the Commerce Clause,* 81 DICK. L. REV. 599, 621–25 (1977); Note, *Redefining the* National League of Cities *State Sovereignty Doctrine,* 129 U. PA. L. REV. 1460, 1475–84 (1981).

25. United Transportation Union v. Long Island Railroad, 455 U.S. 678 (1982).
26. As noted *supra,* text accompanying note 8, there are very few Supreme Court cases concerning the exercise of federal government power in the area of foreign affairs. Those which have ruled that the government's action exceeded its authority under the Constitution, in cases other than those affecting civil liberties, are even fewer.
27. United States v. Louisiana, 363 U.S. 1 (1960).
28. Note, *State Buy-American Laws—Invalidity of State Attempts to Favor American Producers,* 64 MINN. L. REV. 389 (1980); Interview with Joel S. Spiro, Chief, Division of Special Trade Activities and Commercial Treaties, Department of State, in Washington D.C. (Oct. 23, 1979).
29. Bethlehem Steel Corp. v. Board of Comm'rs of Dep't of Water & Power, 276 Cal. App. 2d 221, 80 Cal. Rptr. 800 (1969). See discussion in J. JACKSON, INTERNATIONAL ECONOMIC RELATIONS, *supra* note 12, 174–80.
30. K.S.B. Technical Sales Corp. v. New Jersey Dist. Water Supply Comm'on, 75 N.J. 272, 280–81 (1977).
31. *See, e.g.,* I. BERNIER, INTERNATIONAL LEGAL ASPECTS OF FEDERALISM 153–58, 169–70 (1973).
32. *See GATT in U.S. Domestic Law, supra* note 14, at 268.
33. *See GATT in U.S. Domestic Law, supra* note 14, at 265–69. Note statutory formulas used before 1974.
34. See particularly the Trade Act of 1974, § 121(d), 19 U.S.C. § 2131(d) (1976), and the Trade Agreements Act of 1979, § 2(c), 19 U.S.C. § 2503(c) (Supp. III 1979), which approves a number of the MTN agreements.
35. U.S. State Dep't Press Release, Dec. 6, 1950, *reprinted in* 23 DEP'T STATE BULL. 977 (1950).
36. See § 125(e) of the Trade Act of 1974, 19 U.S.C. § 2135(e) (1976), which provides, however, that the trade agreement levels of tariffs can remain in effect for one year, pending petition to Congress to set the tariff levels, if an international trade agreement on which the rates rely is terminated.
37. Agreement Relating Principally to Chemicals, Supplementary to the Geneva (1967) Protocol to the General Agreement on Tariffs and Trade, GENERAL AGREEMENT ON TARIFFS AND TRADE, BASIC INSTRUMENTS AND SELECTED DOCUMENTS 8 (15th Supp. 1968) [hereinafter cited as BISD]. For a discussion of the aftermath of the Kennedy Round see J. EVANS, THE KENNEDY ROUND IN AMERICAN TRADE POLICY 299–317 (1971).
38. Agreement on Implementation of Article VI of the General Agreement on Tariffs and Trade, BISD, *supra* note 37, at 24 (15th Supp. 1968). *See* R. Long, *United States Law and the International Anti-Dumping Code,* 3 INT'L LAW. 464 (1969); Barcelo, *Anti-Dumping Laws as Barriers to*

Trade—The United States and the International Dumping Code, 57 CORNELL L. REV. 491 (1972). *See also* S. REP. No. 1385, 90th Cong., 2d Sess. Part 2 (1968), *reprinted in* 1968 U.S. CODE CONG. & AD. NEWS 4539.

39. For a history of these bills see F. ROOT, *supra* note 11, at 183–85. *See also Tariff and Trade Proposals: Hearings Before the House Committee on Ways and Means,* 91st Cong., 2d Sess. (1970); TRADE ACT OF 1970: REPORT TO ACCOMPANY H.R. 18970, H.R. REP. No. 1435, 91st Cong., 2d Sess. (1970); *Trade Act of 1970, Amendments 925 and 1009 to H.R. 17550 Social Security Amendments of 1970: Hearings Before the Senate Committee on Finance,* 91st Cong., 2d Sess. (1970); SOCIAL SECURITY AMENDMENT: REPORT TO ACCOMPANY H.R. 17550, S. REP. No. 1431, 91st Cong., 2d Sess. (1970).
40. Trade Expansion Act of 1962, Pub. L. No. 87-794, 76 Stat. 872 (1962).
41. COMM'N ON INT'L TRADE & INVESTMENT POLICY, UNITED STATES INTERNATIONAL ECONOMIC POLICY IN AN INTERDEPENDENT WORLD, REPORT TO THE PRESIDENT (July 1971) [hereinafter cited as WILLIAMS COMMISSION]. The Chairman of the Commission was Albert L. Williams of the International Business Machines Corporation. Its work has been collected in one volume of report and two volumes of staff papers.
42. H.R. 6767, 93d Cong., 1st Sess. (1973); Comm. on Ways and Means, 93d Cong., 1st Sess., Press Release and Other Material Relating to the Administration Proposal Entitled the "Trade Reform Act of 1973" (Comm. Print 1973).
43. H.R. 10710, 93d Cong., 1st Sess. (1973).
44. *See, e.g.,* C. BERNSTEIN & R. WOODWARD, ALL THE PRESIDENT'S MEN (1974); L. CHESTER ET AL., WATERGATE (1973); L. JAWORSKI, THE RIGHT AND THE POWER (1976).
45. War Powers Resolution, Pub. L. No. 93-148, 87 Stat. 555 (1973) (codified at 50 U.S.C. §§ 1541-1548 (1976)); H.R. REP. No. 287, 93d Cong., 1st Sess. (1973), *reprinted in* 1973 U.S. CODE CONG. & AD. NEWS 2346; S. REP. No. 220, 93d Cong., 1st Sess. (1973).
46. Trade Act of 1974, Pub. L. No. 93-618, 88 Stat. 1978 (1975) (codified at 19 U.S.C. §§ 2101-2487 (1976)); *see* House debate and action, 119 CONG. REC. 40,769 (1973), 120 CONG. REC. 41,796 (1974); Senate debate and action, 120 CONG. REC. 39,497, 41,629 (1974); H.R. REP. No. 571, 93d Cong., 1st Sess. (1973) [hereinafter cited as H.R. REP. No. 571]; S. REP. No. 1298, *supra* note 6; CONFERENCE REPORT, H.R. REP. No. 1644, 93d Cong., 2d Sess. (1974), *reprinted in* 1974 U.S. CODE CONG. & AD. NEWS 7367 [hereinafter cited as CONFERENCE REPORT].
47. In his testimony before the House Ways and Means Committee, Ambassador William R. Pearce, Deputy Special Representative for Trade Negotiations, said, "[O]ur trading partners are reluctant to negotiate with us until they have some assurance that agreements can be implemented, and implemented rather promptly. After all, when you put an offer on the table, you spend some political capital. You are offering to expose some part of the domestic economy to competition it hasn't had before, whether it is a tariff negotiation or NTB negotation. No country is willing

to do that—ourselves included—unless when we make an offer we have reasonable chance that, if accepted, it will result in agreement—and fairly soon." *Trade Reform: Hearings before the Committee on Ways and Means on H.R. 6767,* 93d Cong., 1st Sess. 394 (1973) (testimony of William R. Pearce).

48. There is an extensive constitutional debate in the United States, still continuing, about the constitutionality of the legislative veto. Such a veto procedure is embodied in a number of statutes, including several elsewhere in the 1974 Trade Act itself. Recent writing on the legislative veto includes: Abourezk, *The Congressional Veto: A Contemporary Response to Executive Encroachment on Legislative Prerogative,* 52 IND. L.J. 323 (1977); Bruff & Gellhorn, *Congressional Control of Administrative Regulation: A Study of Legislative Vetos,* 90 HARV. L. REV. 1369 (1977); Dixon, *The Congressional Veto and Separation of Powers: The Executive on a Leash,* 56 N.C. L. REV. 423 (1978); Henry, *The Legislative Veto: In Search of Constitutional Limits,* 16 HARV. J. LEGIS. 735 (1979); Miller & Bowman, *Presidential Attacks on the Constitutionality of Federal Statutes: A New Separation of Powers Problem,* 40 OHIO ST. L.J. 51 (1979); Miller & Knapp, *The Congressional Veto: Preserving the Constitutional Framework,* 52 IND. L.J. 367 (1977); Stewart, *Constitutionality of the Legislative Veto,* 13 HARV. J. ON LEGIS. 593 (1976); Volz, *Legislative Veto in the Arms Export Control Act of 1976,* 9 L. & POL'Y INT'L BUS. 1029 (1977). Watson, *Congress Steps Out: A Look at Congressional Control of the Executive,* 63 CALIF. L. REV. 983 (1975). *See also* S. REP. NO. 1298, *supra* note 6, at 75. The Court of Appeals for the Ninth Circuit ruled, in Chadha v. I.N.S., 634 F. 2d 408 (9th Cir. 1980), that the one-house veto provision in the Immigration and Nationality Act permitting an override of the Attorney General's decision to suspend deportation of an alien was unconstitutional. A similar legislative veto provision that allowed use of a one-house veto to disapprove a Federal Energy Regulatory Commission gas-pricing regulation was struck down in Consumer Energy Council of America v. FERC, 673 F. 2d 425 (D.C. Cir. 1982). Both cases were appealed to the Supreme Court, and on June 23, 1983, the court in I.N.S. v. Chadha, 51 LAW WEEK No. 49, p. 4907, affirmed and ruled that legislative vetos are unconstitutional.

49. 19 U.S.C. §§ 2112, 2191 (1976); *see* S. REP. No. 1298, *supra* note 6, at 74–77, 107–11; CONFERENCE REPORT, *supra* note 46, at 31.

50. 19 U.S.C. §§ 1303, 1516 (1976); *see* S. REP. No. 1231, 93d Cong., 2d Sess. 183–91 (1974) [hereinafter cited as S. REP. No. 1231]; H.R. REP. No. 571, *supra* note 46, at 73–77. The Court of Customs and Patents Appeals held, in the case of United States v. Hammond Lead Prods., Inc., 440 F.2d 1024 (C.C.P.A. 1971), that judicial review in the Customs Court was not available for negative countervailing duty determinations.

51. 19 U.S.C. § 1303(d) (1976); *see infra* text accompanying note 94.

52. 19 U.S.C. § 1303(d) (1976).

53. S. REP. No. 1231, *supra* note 50, at 186. *See also, infra,* text accompanying note 95.

54. 19 U.S.C. §§ 2251—2253 (1976). The 1974 act modified the rigid injury and causation tests that had been adopted in the Trade Expansion Act of 1962, Pub. L. No. 87-794, 76 Stat. 872 (1962). This was accomplished by "(1) removing the 'causal link' requirement that imports result in major part from trade agreement concessions and (2) requiring that increased imports need only be 'a substantial cause,' rather than 'the major cause,' of actual or threatened injury." S. REP. NO. 1298, *supra* note 6, at 120. *See also* H.R. REP. NO. 571, *supra* note 46, at 44–52. *See generally* INTERNATIONAL ECONOMIC RELATIONS, *supra* note 12, at ch. 11.3.
55. Adjustment assistance provisions had been included in the 1962 Trade Expansion Act, but had not been very effective. From 1962 until 1969 no workers were certified as eligible for the adjustment assistance benefits. After 1969, there were outlays for adjustment assistance but the levels of payment and the number of recipients were low. There were also delays in paying benefits. These factors combined to thwart the policy objectives of adjustment assistance. The 1974 act "provided a new adjustment assistance program with eased qualifying criteria and a streamlined petitionery process." S. REP. NO. 1298, *supra* note 6, at 131. The act raised the level of benefits from 65 percent to 70 percent of the workers' average weekly wage and increased the maximum level from 65 percent to 100 percent of the "average weekly manufacturing wage." 19 U.S.C. §§ 2271–2298, (1976); S. REP. NO. 1298, *supra* note 6, at 131–41; H.R. REP. NO. 571, *supra* note 46, at 52–60. *See generally* Cprek, *Worker Adjustment Assistance: Black Comedy in the Post-Renaissance,* 11 L. & POL'Y INT'L BUS. 593 (1979).
56. *See generally* L. HENKIN, *supra* note 1; Berger, *supra* note 4.
57. Examples of such activity would include "negotiations" with Japan over textiles in the early 1970s, discussed in I. DESTLER, H. FUKUI & H. SATO, THE TEXTILE WRANGLE: CONFLICT IN JAPANESE-AMERICAN RELATIONS 1969–1971 (1979) (see especially chs. 9 and 11), and "negotiations" with the Soviet Union over its emigration policy in 1973, discussed in P. STERN, WATER'S EDGE: DOMESTIC POLITICS AND THE MAKING OF AMERICAN FOREIGN POLICY (1979) (see especially ch. 4).
58. *See Trade Agreements Act of 1979: Hearings Before the Subcomm. on International Trade of the Comm. on Finance, United States Senate,* 96th Cong., 1st Sess. 393 (1979) [hereinafter cited as *Senate Finance Comm. Hearings* (1979)] (statement of Robert S. Strauss, Special Representative for Trade Negotiations).
59. 19 U.S.C. § 2111 (1976). *See infra* text accompanying notes 85, 109.
60. An Act to Amend the Tariff Act of 1930, Part II, Pub. L. No. 316, 48 Stat. 943 (1934) *See supra* note 12.
61. Certain residual clean-up authority continued for two years. *See* 19 U.S.C. § 2134 (1976). There is also limited authority to negotiate on tariffs under other statutory provisions, e.g., 19 U.S.C. § 2133 (1976). The President's authority under Section 124 expired on January 3, 1982. A bill (H.R. 4761) extending the President's authority for two additional years was approved by the House Ways and Means Trade Sub-

committee on February 2, 1982 but has, as of July 1982, not passed the full committee.

62. *See supra* text accompanying note 49.
63. S. Rep. No. 1298, *supra* note 6, at 87; 19 U.S.C. § 2112 (1976).
64. 19 U.S.C. § 1304 (1976). *See supra* note 63, *infra* note 67.
65. Statement of Administrative Action, H.R. Doc. No. 153, 96th Cong., 1st sess. Part II, at 526–27 (1979); H.R. Rep. No. 571, *supra* note 46, at 65; S. Rep. No. 249, *supra* note 6, at 232–35, 238.
66. *See infra* text accompanying notes 170, 171.
67. *See supra* note 64; 19 U.S.C. § 2131 (1976); S. Rep. No. 1298, *supra* note 6, at 86–87.
68. *See, e.g.,* Tariff Act of 1930, 19 U.S.C. § 1202 (1976), general headnote 11; S. Rep. No. 249, *supra* note 6, at 257–58; *infra* text accompanying notes 113, 114.
69. Trade Expansion Act of 1962, § 241, Pub. L. No. 87-794, 76 Stat. 872 (1962).
70. Trade Expansion Act of 1962, § 242, 19 U.S.C. § 1872 (1976) as amended. This section calls for a Cabinet-level advisory committee. Such a committee was established by regulation in 1963. It was called the Trade Expansion Act Advisory Committee, and the regulations were codified at 48 C.F.R. ch. 1 (1963). Regulations also established committees below the Cabinet level. These were (in descending order) the Trade Executive Committee, the Trade Staff Committee, and the Trade Information Committee. The regulations establishing these committees were codified at 48 C.F.R. ch. 2 (1963). Title 48 of the United States Code was vacated at the end of 1968. Chapter II of the regulations was transferred to Title 15, Chapter VI, but Chapter I was discontinued. The order vacating Title 48 does not disclose the fate of the Cabinet-level committee.
71. *See* Malmgren, *Managing Foreign Economic Policy,* 6 For Pol'y 42, 48 (1972).
72. Trade Act of 1974, §§ 201–203, 19 U.S.C. §§ 2251–2253 (1976), Trade Act of 1974, § 301 § 901, 19 U.S.C. § 2411 (1976), *as amended by* Trade Agreements Act of 1979, Pub. L. No. 96-39, 93 Stat. 144 (1979).
73. The position of Executive Director of CIEP, as established by the Section 208 of the International Policy Act of 1972, 22 U.S.C. § 2847 (1972), did not require Senate confirmation. However, in 1973, Section 208 was amended to provide for Senate confirmation. 22 U.S.C. § 2847 (a) (1976), (amending 22 U.S.C. § 2847 (1976)). The STR has always required Senate confirmation. Trade Expansion Act of 1962, § 241(a), 76 Stat. 878 (1962) as amended.
74. Trade Act of 1974, § 141, 19 U.S.C. § 2171 (1976); S. Rep. No. 1298, *supra* note 6, at 105. See also *Senate Finance Comm. Hearings, supra* note 58, at 442 for Senator Long's statement on why he fought to upgrade the position of the STR.
75. *See, e.g.,* An Act making appropriations for the Department of State, Justice, Commerce, Judiciary, and related agencies for the fiscal year

ending June 30, 1976, and the period ending September 30, 1976, and for other purposes, Title I—Department of State, International Organizations and Conferences, International Trade Negotiations, Pub. L. No. 94-131, 89 Stat. 611,614 (1975).

76. Trade Act of 1974, §§ 161-63, 135, 19 U.S.C. §§ 2211-2213, 2155 (1976).
77. Section 243 of the Trade Expansion Act of 1962 called for two members from each house of Congress to be accredited. Section 161 of the Trade Act of 1974 calls for delegations of five members from each house. 19 U.S.C. §2211 (1976).
78. Trade Act of 1974, § 161 (b), 19 U.S.C. § 2211 (b) (1976); *see* H.R. Rep. No. 571, *supra* note 46, at 43; S. Rep. No. 1298, *supra* note 6, at 113.
79. *See* S. Rep. No. 249, *supra* note 6, at 6, H.R. Rep. No. 317, 96th Cong., 1st Sess. 26 (1979) [hereinafter cited as H.R. Rep. No. 317].
80. Trade Act of 1974, § 135, 19 U.S.C. § 2155 (1976); *see* H.R. Rep. No. 571, *supra* note 46, at 38: S. Rep. No. 1298, *supra* note 6, at 101.
81. *See* Senate, Comm. on Finance, Subcomm. on International Trade, 96th Cong., 1st Sess., Private Advisory Committee Reports on the Tokyo Round of Multilateral Trade Negotiations (Comm. Print, 1979).
82. *Id.*
83. *Hearings on H.R. 10710, the Trade Reform Act of 1973, Before the Comm. on Finance, U.S. Senate,* 93d Cong., 2d Sess. 225 (1974) (statement of William Eberle, Special Representative for Trade Negotiations, March 5, 1974); S. Rep. No. 1298, *supra* note 6, at 104; H.R. Rep. No. 571, *supra* note 46, at 38-40.
84. 19 U.S.C. § 2231 (1976); *see* S. Rep. No. 1298, *supra* note 6, at 115.
85. Trade Act of 1974, § 131, 19, U.S.C. § 2151 (1976); 1977 U.S. Int'l Trade Comm. Ann. Rep. 15–16; 1979 U.S. Int'l Trade Commission Ann. Rep. 25–29.
86. *See, e.g.,* 40 Fed. Reg. 19,046; 23,546; 24,252; 34,649 (1975).
87. Trade Act of 1974, §§ 132-34, 19 U.S.C. §§ 2152-2154 (1976).
88. *See generally* Barcelo, *Subsidies and Countervailing Duties—Analysis and a Proposal* 9 L. & Pol'y Int'l Bus. 779 (1977).
89. The General Agreement on Tariffs and Trade Art. VI, *opened for signature* Oct. 30, 1947, 61 Stat. A3, T.I.A.S. No.1700, 55 U.N.T.S. 194.
90. 19 U.S.C. § 1303 (1976); *see* Dep't. of Treasury, Countervailing Duties *in* Williams Commission Papers 409 (1971); S. Rep. No. 1298, *supra* note 6, at 185.
91. Trade Act of 1974, § 321 (f) (1), 19 U.S.C. § 1516 (1976); *see* S. Rep. No. 1298, *supra* note 6, at 185.
92. United States v. Hammond Lead Products, Inc., 440 F.2d 1024, 1031 (C.C.P.A. 1971). (This discretion could be analogous to "prosecutorial" discretion, especially if the practice triggering the importing government's response is viewed as a breach of law or of international rules of "fair trade.") In the House Ways and Means Committee report, *Hammond Lead Products* is cited as the decision necessitating the amendment mentioned. *Supra* note 91, H.R. Rep. No. 571; note 46, at 76.

93. Trade Act of 1974, § 331 (a) (amending § 303 of the Tariff Act of 1930) 19 U.S.C. § 1303 (1976); *see* H.R. REP. NO. 571, *supra* note 46, at 74; S. REP. NO. 1231, *supra* note 50, at 185.
94. *See supra* text accompanying note 51.
95. These conditions included the following: (1) that there be a reasonable prospect for successful trade negotiations for reducing and eliminating barriers to international trade; (2) that adequate steps had been taken to substantially reduce or eliminate the adverse effects of a bounty or grant; and (3) that the imposition of such countervailing duty would be likely to "seriously jeopardize the satisfactory completion" of the negotiations. This authority was explicitly provided to last for a four-year period from the enactment of the act. It will be recalled that the general negotiating authority on tariffs, and indeed on nontariff barriers, had a duration of five years. The shorter duration of the waiver provision for countervailing duties was understood by the Congress to indicate its view of the importance of negotiating new international rules on subsidies and countervailing duties.

    Indeed, after the act was enacted, the Treasury received a number of new petitions for the application of countervailing duties, and in nineteen cases it felt necessary to exercise the waiver so as to prevent jeopardizing the negotiations. *See* S. Rep. No. 45, 96th Cong., 1st Sess. 8 (1979); T.D. 75-114, 9 Cust. Bull 229 (1975); 40 Fed. Reg. 21,720 (1975).
96. *See* INT'L TRADE REPORTER: U.S. Export Weekly (BNA) No. 214, C-2 (July 11, 1978) No. 215, at AA-1 [hereinafter cited as ITEX]; GENEVA FOCUS: A REPORT FROM THE INDUSTRY CENTER FOR TRADE NEGOTIATIONS," No. 5, 1 (1978).
97. Trade Act of 1974, § 331 (a), (amending) § 303 of the Tariff Act of 1930, 19 U.S.C. § 1303 (1976). *See supra*, note 95.
98. GENEVA FOCUS: A REPORT FROM THE INDUSTRY CENTER FOR TRADE NEGOTIATIONS, No. 5, at 3 (1978). *See also* European Community News Press Release No. 19/1978 (Oct. 16, 1978); Wall St. J., Oct. 20, 1978, at 22; ITEX, *supra* note 96, No. 235, at C-1 (Dec. 5, 1978). See chapter 2, *supra* text accompanying note 27.
99. See ITEX, *supra* note 96, No. 226 at A-9 (Oct. 3, 1978), ITEX No. 227 C-1 (Oct. 10, 1978), discussing the Hollings amendment to the Ex-Im Bank extension.
100. *See Hearings on H.R. 1147 Before the Subcomm. on Trade of the House Comm. on Ways and Means, 96th Cong., 1st Sess. 10-11 (1979)* (to extend temporarily the authority of the Secretary of the Treasury to waive the imposition of countervailing duties).
101. *See,* ITEX, *supra* note 96, No. 228, at A-11 (Oct. 17, 1978).
102. Pub. L. No. 96-6, 93 Stat. 10 (1979); *see* H.R. REP. No. 15, 96th Cong., 1st Sess. (1979); S. Rep. No. 45, 96th Cong., 1st Sess. (1979), *reprinted in* 1979 U.S. CODE CONG. & AD. NEWS 30; *Extension of Authority to Waive Countervailing Duties: Hearing Before the Subcomm. on Trade of the Comm. on Ways and Means,* 96th Cong., 1st Sess. (1979). For the notice of administrative action to be taken by the U.S. Customs Service during the period between the expiration of the waiver authority and the subse-

quent extension of the authority, see 44 Fed. Reg. 141 (1979), and the memorandum reprinted at p. 12 of the House Ways and Means Committee hearings, *supra.*

103. The amendment was effective as of January 3, 1979. Pub. L. No.96-6, 93 Stat. 10 (1979). See H.R. REP. No. 15, 96th Cong., 1st Sess. (1979); S. Rep. No. 45, 96th Cong., 1st Sess. (1979); 125 Cong. Rec. H. 1018 (daily ed. March 1, 1979); 125 CONG. REC. S3574 (daily ed. Mar. 28, 1979).

104. Trade Act of 1974, § 104, 19 U.S.C. 2114 (1976); *see* H.R. REP. No. 571, *supra* note 46, at 20-23; S. Rep. No. 1298, *supra* note 6, at 22–23, 78–79; *Executive Hearing on Sector Negotiations Before the Senate Comm. on Finance,* 93d Cong., 2d Sess. (1974); A. RIBICOFF, 93D CONG., 1ST SESS. STRATEGY FOR INTERNATIONAL TRADE NEGOTIATIONS: REPORT TO THE SENATE FINANCE COMMITTEE 9 (Comm. Print 1973).

105. *See* H.R. REP. No. 571, *supra* note 46, at 22; S. REP. No. 1298, *supra* note 6, at 79.

106. *See generally* Piper, *Unique Sectoral Agreement Establishes Free Trade Framework,* 12 L. & POL'Y INT'L BUS. 221 (1980).

107. *See* L. HENKIN, *supra* note 1, at 151; RESTATEMENT (SECOND) OF FOREIGN RELATIONS LAW OF THE UNITED STATES § 145 (1965); I. BROWNLIE, PRINCIPLES OF PUBLIC INTERNATIONAL LAW 610–11 (3d ed. 1979).

108. *See* the section of this chapter entitled United States Participation in the Tokyo Round.

109. Trade Act of 1974 § 101, 19 U.S.C. § 2111 (1976).

110. ITEX, *supra* note 96, No. 265, at C-4, and Special Supplement at 29 (July 17, 1979); GATT Doc. L. 4914/Rev.2 (July 23, 1980).

111. 19 U.S.C. §§ 2503, 1202, 2135, 2111, 2119 (Supp. III 1979). Proclamation to Carry Out the Geneva (1979) Protocol to the General Agreement on Tariffs and Trade and for Other Purposes, Proclamation 4707, 44 Fed. Reg. 72,348 (1979).

112. Arrangement Regarding Bovine Meat, BISD, *supra* note 37, at 84 (26th Supp. 1980) and International Dairy Arrangement, BISD, *supra* note 37, at 91 (26th Supp. 1980).

113. *See* S. REP. No. 249, *supra* note 6, at 257.

114. The challenge to the 1967 Antidumping Code included the idea that the President did not have the authority to change long-standing administrative practice without congressional approval. *See* S. REP. No. 1385, 90th Cong., 2d Sess. Part 2 (1968), *reprinted in* 1968 U.S. CODE CONG. & AD. NEWS 4539, 4551.

115. Section 2 (c) of the Trade Agreement Act of 1979, 19 U.S.C. § 2503 (c) (Supp. III 1979), lists the following agreements:

(1) The Agreement on Implementation of Article VII of the General Agreement on Tariffs and Trade (relating to customs valuation).

(2) The Agreement on Government Procurement.

(3) The Agreement on Import Licensing Procedures.

(4) The Agreement of Technical Barriers to Trade (relating to product standards).

(5) The Agreement on Interpretation and Application of Articles VI,

XVI, and XXIII of the General Agreement on Tariffs and Trade (relating to subsidies and countervailing measures).

(6) The Agreement on Implementation of Article VI of the General Agreement on Tariffs and Trade (relating to antidumping measures).

(7) The International Dairy Arrangement.

(8) Certain bilateral agreements on cheese, other dairy products, and meat.

(9) The Arrangement Regarding Bovine Meat.

(10) The Agreement on Trade in Civil Aircraft.

(11) Texts Concerning a Framework for the Conduct of World Trade.

(12) Certain Bilateral Agreements to Eliminate the Wine-Gallon Method of Tax and Duty Assessment.

(13) Certain other agreements to be collected in Schedule XX of the United States to the General Agreement on Tariffs and Trade, including Agreements—

(A) to Modify United States Watch Requirements, and to Modify United States Tariff Nomenclature and Rates of Duty for Watches,

(B) to Provide Duty-Free Treatment for Agricultural and Horticultural Machinery, Equipment, Implements, and Parts Thereof, and

(C) to Modify United States Tariff Nomenclature and Rates of Duty for Ceramic Tableware.

(14) The Agreement with the Hungarian People's Republic.

Note the exceptional ambiguity of item number 13.

116. Trade Agreement Act of 1979, § 2(b) (1), 19 U.S.C. § 2503(b)(1) (Supp. III 1979).

117. Determination Regarding Acceptence and Application of the Agreement on Government Procurement, 45 Fed. Reg. 252 (1980).

118. Section 2(b)(2) of the Trade Agreements Act of 1979, 19 U.S.C. § 2503 (b)(2) (Supp. III 1979), states:

No agreement accepted by the President under paragragh (1) shall apply between the United States and any other country unless the President determines that such country—

(A) has accepted the obligations of the agreement with respect to the United States, and

(B) should not otherwise be denied the benefits of the agreement with respect to the United States because such country has not accorded adequate benefits, including substantially equal competitive opportunities for the commerce of the United States to the extent required under section 126 (c) of the Trade Act of 1974 (19 U.S.C. 2136 (c)), to the United States.

Section 126 (c) of the Trade Act of 1974, 19 U.S.C. § 2136 (c) (1976), states

If the President determines under subsection (b) of this section that a major industrial country has not made concessions under trade agreements entered into under this chapter which provides substantially equivalent competitive opportunities for the commerce of the United States, he shall, either generally, with respect to such country or by article produced by such country, in order to restore equivalence of competitive opportunities, recommend to the Congress—

(1) legislation providing for the termination or denial of the benefits of concessions of trade aggrements entered into under this chapter made with respect to rates of duty or other import restrictions by the United States; and

(2) that any legislation necessary to carry out any trade agreement under section 2112 of this title shall not apply to any such country.

119. *E.g.*, Trade Agreements Act of 1979, §§ 101 (adding title VII to the Tariff Act of 1930), 106 (repealing the Antidumping Act, 1921 (19 U.S.C. §§ 160–171 (Supp. III 1979), and other amendments).

120. *See infra,* text accompanying note 177. One can ask, then, what difference these legal forms make. But if the United States unilaterally applies its own law to benefit another country under MFN, the other country may not be able to invoke specific dispute settlement or other procedures of the MTN agreement on the subject, when that *agreement* is not applied to it by the United States.

121. The United States does not apply MFN treatment in its implementation of the results of three of the MTN Agreements—the Subsidies-Countervailing Duty Code, the Government Procurement Code, and the Standards Code; *see* Agreement on Interpretation and Application of Articles VI, XVI, and XXIII of the General Agreement on Tariffs and Trade, BISD, *supra* note 37, at 56 (26th Supp. 1980); Agreement on Government Procurement, BISD, *supra* note 37, at 33 (26th Supp. 1980); Agreement on Technical Barriers to Trade, BISD, *supra* note 37, at 8 (26th Supp. 1980); GATT Article I; *infra* text accompanying note 177. *See also* Hufbauer, Erb & Starr, *The GATT Codes and the Unconditional Most-Favored-Nation Principle* 12 L. & POL'Y INT'L BUS. 59 (1980).

122. *E.g.* Treaty of Friendship, Commerce and Navigation, July 14, 1956, United States–Federal Republic of Germany, 7 U.S.T. 1839, T.I.A.S. No. 3593, *See* Walker, *Modern Treaties of Friendship, Commerce and Navigation,* 42 MINN. L. REV. 805 (1958). *See also* Trade Agreements Act of 1979, § 101 § 701 (b) (3), 19 U.S.C. § 1671 (b) (3) (Supp. III 1979), in which the term "country under the Agreement" is defined to include a country

with respect to which the President determines that—

(A) there is an agreement in effect between the United States and that country which—

(i) was in force on June 19, 1979, and

(ii) requires unconditional most-favored-nation treatment with respect to articles imported into the United States,

(B) the General Agreement on Tariffs and Trade does not apply between the United States and that country, and

(C) the agreement described in subparagraph A does not expressly permit—
(i) actions required or permitted by the General Agreement on Tariffs and Trade, or required by Congress, or
(ii) nondiscriminatory prohibitions or restrictions on importation which are designed to prevent deceptive or unfair practices.

The Senate Report lists agreements with seven countries which could potentially meet these requirements—Venezuela, Honduras, Nepal, North Yemen, El Salvador, Paraguay, and Liberia. S. REP. No. 249, *supra* note 6, at 45.

123. *E.g.* Agreement on Implementation of Article VII of the General Agreements in Tariffs and Trade (relating to customs valuation), BISD, *supra* note 37, at 116 (26th Supp. 1980); Agreement on Interpretation and Application of Articles VI, XVI and XXIII of the General Agreement on Tariffs and Trade (relating to subsidies and countervailing measures), BISD, *supra* note 37, at 56 (26th Supp. 1980); Agreement on Implementation of Article VI of the General Agreement on Tariffs and Trade (relating to antidumping measures), BISD, *supra* note 37, at 171 (26th Supp. 1980).
124. A search of the MTN agreements reveals no such provision.
125. Most of the MTN agreements prohibit reservations without the consent of all parties, *See, e.g.,* Agreement on Implementation of Article VII of the General Agreement on Tariffs and Trade BISD, *supra* note 37, at 171 (26th Supp. 1980) Art. 23 Agreement on Import Licensing Procedures § 18, BISD, *supra* note 37, at 154 (26th Supp. 1980); Agreement on Technical Barriers to Trade Art. 15.4, BISD, *supra* note 37, at 8 (26th Supp. 1980). *See* Bishop, *Reservations to Treaties, Hague Academy of International Law,* 103 RECUEIL DES COURS 245 (1961).
126. *See* J. JACKSON, WORLD TRADE AND THE LAW OF GATT 100–02 (1969).
127. *See, e.g.,* Agreement on Governmental Procurement Part IX, ¶9, BISD, *supra* note 37, at 33 (26th Supp. 1980); Agreement on Implementation of Article VI, ¶10, BISD, *supra* note 37, at 171 (26th Supp. 1980); Agreement in Interpretation and Application of Articles VI, XVI, and XXIII of GATT Art. 19, § 9, BISD, *supra* note 37, at 56 (26th Supp. 1980); Agreement on Trade in Civil Aircraft Art. 9.7, BISD, *supra* note 37, at 162 (26th Supp. 1980).
128. The Trade Act of 1974, § 126 (d), 19 U.S.C. § 2136 (d) (1976) defines *major industrial countries* as follows: "For purposes of this section, major industrial country means Canada, the European Economic Community, the individual member countries of such Community, Japan, and any other foreign country designated by the President for purposes of the subsection."
129. ITEX, *supra,* note 96, No. 287, at A-3 (Dec. 18, 1979).
130. Council Decision of Dec. 10, 1979, concerning the conclusion of the multilateral agreements resulting from the 1973–1979 trade negotiations, O.J. EUR. COMM. (No. L 71) 1 (1980). *See also* ITEX, *supra* note 96, No.

288, at A-5 (Jan. 1, 1980). About the constitutional dispute see the section in chapter 2 entitled The Preparation of the Conclusion in 1979: The Legal and Political Problems. *See also* ITEX, *supra* note 96, No. 283, at C-4 (Nov. 20, 1979).

131. *See* ITEX, *supra* note 96, No. 287, at C-2 (Dec. 18, 1979); ITEX, *supra* note 96, No. 288 at A-6 (Jan. 1, 1980).
132. *See* ITEX, *supra* note 96, No. 287, at A-3 (Dec. 18, 1979); INT'L TRADE REPORTER: U.S. IMPORT WEEKLY (BNA) No. 4, at A-11 (Nov. 28, 1979). [Hereinafter cited as ITIM.]
133. *See* the sections in chapter 3 entitled The Constitutions and Treaties, and Implementation of the Tokyo Round Agreements in Japan.
134. Determination Regarding the Multilateral Trade Negotiations and Acceptance and Application of Certain International Trade Agreements, 44 Fed. Reg. 74,781 (1979).
135. *See supra* text accompanying note 49; Trade Act of 1974 §§ 102, 151, 19 U.S.C. §§ 2112, 2191 (1976).
136. See COMMUNICATION FROM THE PRESIDENT OF THE UNITED STATES TRANSMITTING NOTICE OF SEVERAL TRADE AGREEMENTS REACHED IN THE TOKYO ROUND OF MULTILATERAL TRADE NEGOTIATIONS, PURSUANT TO SECTION 102(e) (1) OF THE TRADE ACT OF 1974, H.R. DOC. NO. 33, 96th Cong., 1st Sess. (1979), for a summary of the status of the negotiations at that time.
137. *See* House Ways and Means Committee, Press Release No. 14 (Mar. 19, 1979); Senate Finance Committee, Press Release Nos. 112, 115, 116 (Apr. 5, May 3, 8, 1979).
138. Joint Press Release No.1 (May 24, 1979). For normal bills, a conference committee session to resolve differences in the two houses is typical.
139. This was probably the most important feature of the "fast-track" procedure.
140. H.R. 4537, 96th Cong., 1st Sess. (1979).
141. The bill passed on July 23, 1979, and was signed on July 26, 1979. Pub. L. 96-39, 93 Stat. 144 (codified at U.S.C. §§ 2501 et seq.) (Supp. III 1979).
142. *See* 125 CONG. REC. S10,340 (daily ed. July 23, 1979); 125 CONG. REC. H5690 (daily ed. July 11, 1979). Destler notes that five of the eleven legislators voting against the act were from Wisconsin and that the dairy industry in that state objected to increases in cheese imports allowed in the U.S. concession. *See* M. DESTLER, MAKING FOREIGN ECONOMIC POLICY 202 (1980).
143. About the involvement of the EEC see BULL. EUR. COMM. (NO. 4) 15 (1975), where it is stated that prompted by rumors that the future American legislation implementing the code on subsidies would not interpret correctly the idea of material injury the Community has approached the American authorities. *See also* BULL. EUR. COMM. (No. 5) 75 (1975); N.Y. Times, Apr. 21, 1979, at 29; European Community News Press Release Nos. 14/1979 (Apr. 25, 1979), 28/1979 (July 16, 1979). For some comments on U.S. law and the material injury test see Ehrenhaft, *What the Antidumping and Countervailing Duty Provisions* [*Can*] [*Will*] [*Should*] *Mean for U.S. Trade Policy,* 11 L. & POL'Y INT'L BUS. 1361, 1421 (1979); Marks,

Recent Changes in U.S. Import Restrictions, and Albergen & Yerxa, *The Concept of Injury in United States Trade Law-The Role of the U.S. International Trade Commission,* in AIDES ET MESURES DE SAUVEGARDE EN DROIT INTERNATIONAL ECONOMIQUE (P. Demaret ed. 1980) 163, 179 (XXXIId Conference, University of Liege, Liege, Belgium, Oct. 18–20, 1979). Matthew J. Marks is a partner in the firm of Wender, Murase & White; William Alberger is a Vice-Chairman of the ITC.

144. "The European Commission notes that the texts agreed on in Geneva have not been transferred literally into this Act with all the accuracy that is required, but *on the whole, the American Act reflects the spirit and the letter of the agreements.* The Act alone does not provide a full guarantee that the United States will meet their commitments. Some texts lend themselves to several interpretations and some procedural provisions still have to be stipulated. The Commission therefore intends to follow very closely the way in which the legislation is put into practice, in compliance with the Geneva commitments." EUROPE: DAILY BULL. No. 2763 (Oct. 6, 1979) at 7 (emphasis added). *See also* the final report by the Commission in the MTN, where the Commission notes: "With the United States major agreements have been arrived at, both in the industrial and agricultural sectors. The United States customs tariffs will have fewer peaks and in the non-tariff field the United States will come into line with the GATT, particularly in relation to the criterion of 'material injury', for the application of countervailing duties, abolition of the American Selling Price and Final List systems of valuation, elimination of the discriminatory fiscal system of wine gallon assessment on alcoholic beverages, and significant changes in the application of the Buy American Act." BULL. EUR. COMM. (No.10) 7,8 (1979).

145. A front-page story in the Washington Post of March 14, 1979, led to criticism of the U.S. position in the negotiations on a government procurement code. The story stated that the United States would agree to a relaxation of preferences for small and minority businesses in its government procurement practices. Members of the Subcommittee on General Oversight and Minority Enterprise of the House Committee on Small Business expressed concern that small businesses would pay a price for benefits that would flow largely to multinational corporations. They criticized the STR for the lack of prior consultation with those in the executive and legislative branches involved with small and minority business concerns. Special Trade Representative Robert Strauss defended the administration's position in testimony before the Subcommittee on March 20, 1979. On March 22, the adminstration announced that Japan and the European Community had approved a change that would exclude United States set-aside programs for small and minority businesses from the coverage of the agreement. It appears that the inclusion of NASA in the U.S. entity list was part of the deal. *See* Washington Post, Mar. 14, 1979 at A-1, Mar. 21, 1979 at D-6, Mar. 23, 1979 at F-1; *Multinational Trade Negotiations: Hearings Before the Subcomm. on General Oversight and Minority Enterprises of the Comm. on Small Business—House of Representatives,* 96th Cong., 1st Sess. (1979).

146. *See* S. Rep. No. 249, *supra* note 6, at 5.
147. *See* Trade Agreements Act of 1979, § 1101 (amending 19 U.S.C. § 2112 (b) (Supp. III 1979)).
148. Trade Agreement Act of 1979, § 3(c), 19 U.S.C. § 2504(c) (Supp. III 1979).
149. *See* S. Rep. No. 249, *supra* note 6, at 36.
150. Trade Agreements Act of 1979: Statements of Administrative Action, H.R. Doc. No. 153, 96th Cong., 1st Sess. Part 2 (1979) [hereinafter cited as H.R. Doc. No. 153], *reprinted in* 1979 U.S. Code Cong. & Ad. News 665.
151. S. Rep. No. 249, *supra* note 6, at 6. *See also* H.R. Rep. No. 317, *supra* note 79, at 28.
152. S. Rep. No. 249, *supra* note 6, at 33.
153. *Id.* at 36; *see also* H.R. Rep. No. 317, *supra* note 79, at 41.
154. The importance of this point was underscored dramatically in June 1983, when the Supreme Court ruled in Chadha that legislative vetoes are unconstitutional. See note 48, *supra.* Title X and Title XI contain measures not necessary to implement the MTN results. Title X amends sections of U.S. law dealing with judical review of administrative decision. Title XI is entitled Miscellaneous Provisions and includes the following sections: § 1101 Extension of nontariff barrier negotiating authority, § 1103 Advice from private sector, § 1104 Study of possible agreements with North American countries, §1110 Study of export trade policy, and § 1111 Generalized System of Preferences.
155. Trade Agreements Act of 1979, § 2(b)(3), 19 U.S.C. § 2503(b)(3) (Supp. III 1979).
156. Determination Regarding the Multilateral Trade Negotiations and Acceptance and Application of Certain International Trade Agreements, 44 Fed. Reg. 74,781 (1979).
157. *See* ITEX, *supra* note 96, No. 288, at A-5 (Jan. 1, 1980).
158. Office of the Special Representative for Trade Negotiations—Determination Regarding the Application of Certain International Trade Agreements, 45 Fed. Reg. 1, 181 (1980).
159. Proclamation to Carry Out the Agreement on Implementation of Article VII of the General Agreement in on Tariffs and Trade (the Customs Valuation Code) and for Other Purposes, 45 Fed. Reg. 45,135 (1980).
160. Pub.L. No.96-490, 94 Stat. 2556 (codified at 19 U.S.C. § 2503), (Supp. III 1979) *amending* 19 U.S.C. § 1202.
161. ITEX, *supra* note 96, No. 287, at A-3 (Dec. 18, 1979).
162. *See* I. Brownlie, *supra* note 107, at ch. 2.
163. L. Henkin, *supra* note 1, at 156–61; Restatement, *supra* note 107, at § 154; W. Bishop, International Law: Cases and Materials 144–49 (1962).
164. In Diggs. v. Richardson, 555 F.2d 848, 851 (D.C. Cir. 1976), the court noted that in interpreting treaties courts must "look to the intent of the signatory parties as manifested by the language of the instrument, and, if the instrument is uncertain, recourse must be had to the circumstances surrounding its execution."

165. H.R. Doc. No. 153, *supra* note 150, at Part 2.
166. S. Rep. No. 249, *supra* note 6, at 36; H.R. Rep. No. 317, *supra* note 79, at 41.
167. S. Rep. No. 249, *supra* note 6, at 36.
168. As discussed earlier, the President has some authority not solely derived from that Act. *See supra* notes 44–49 and accompanying text.
169. 19 U.S.C. § 2111(a)(2) (1976).
170. Trade Agreements Act of 1979, § 503. 19 U.S.C. § 2119 (Supp. III 1979).
171. Proclamation 4707, 44 Fed. Reg. 72,348 (1979).
172. International Dairy Arrangement, BISD, *supra* note 37, at 91 (26th Supp. 1980); Arrangement Regarding Bovine Meat, BISD, *supra* note 37, at 84 (26th Supp. 1980); Agreement on Import Licensing Procedures, BISD, *supra* note 37, 154 (26th Supp. 1980).
173. *See* H.R. Doc. No. 153, *supra* note 150, at Part 2, 526, 527; S. Rep. No. 249, *supra* note 6, at 257–58; H.R. Rep. No. 317, *supra* note 79, at 148, 186.
174. *See* S. Rep. No. 249, *supra* note 6, at 257–58.
175. *See* Texts Concerning a Framework for the Conduct of World Trade, BISD, *supra* note 37, at 201 (26th Supp. 1980).
176. *The Tokyo Round of Multilateral Trade Negotiations,* Report by the Director-General of GATT (GATT/1979-3) Apr. 1979; *The Tokyo Round of Multilateral Trade Negotiations, Vol. II,* Report by the Director-General of GATT, (GATT/1980-1) Jan. 1980; BISD, *supra* note 37 (26th Supp. 1980).
177. Trade Agreements Act of 1979, § 101 (adding Title VII to Tariff Act of 1930, 19 U.S.C. § 701) (1976), §§ 301, 441, 19 U.S.C. §§ 2511, 2561 (Supp. III 1979); *See also, supra* notes 120, 121 and accompanying text.
178. *See* J. Evans, *supra* note 37, at 305.
179. *See supra* text accompanying note 142.
180. *See, e.g.,* Ribicoff-Roth Bill, S. 377, 96 Cong., 1st Sess. (1979); ITEX, *supra* note 96, No. 244, at M-1 (Feb. 14, 1979); Byrd Bill, S. 891, 96 Cong., 1st Sess. (1979); ITEX, *supra* note 96, No. 252, at P-1 (Apr. 10, 1979); ITEX, *supra* note 96, No. 262, at 0-1 (June 19, 1979).
181. *See* H.R. Rep. No. 571, *supra* note 46, at 40; S. Rep. No. 1298, *supra* note 6, at 183.
182. *See* Senate Finance Comm. Hearings (1979), at 390–93, 435. In 1983, the Reagan administration proposed a new reorganization that would establish a Department of Trade and Industry, see 8 ITIM, *supra* note 132, at 365 (June 8, 1983).
183. Reorg. Plan No. 3 of 1979, 44 Fed. Reg. 69,273 (1979); Exec. Order No. 12,188, 45 Fed. Reg. 989 (1980). The reorganization statute can be found at 5 U.S.C. §§ 901–912 (1976).
184. Reorg. Plan No. 3 of 1979 § 2, 44 Fed. Reg. 69,273 (1979).
185. *See* Undersecretary for the International Trade Administration, Authority and Functions, 45 Fed. Reg. 6,141 (1980); International Trade Administration, Organization and Function Order, 45 Fed. Reg. 36,427 (1980). *See also* ITIM, *supra* note 132, Reference File 92: 0103-0104;

ITIM, *supra* note 132, No. 5, at A-2 (Dec. 5, 1979); ITIM, *supra* note 132, at No. 9, A-2 (Jan. 9, 1980); ITEX, *supra* note 96, No. 289, at A-8 (Jan. 8, 1980); ITEX, *supra* note 96, No. 298, at A-3 (Mar. 4, 1980).

186. *See* Reorg. Plan No. 3 of 1979, 44 Fed. Reg. 69,273 (1979); Exec. Order No. 12,188, 45 Fed. Reg. 989 (1980). *See also* ITIM, *supra* note 96, No. 5, at A-2 (Dec. 5, 1979); ITIM, *supra* note 132, No. 9, at A-2 (Jan. 9, 1980). Reorganization issues were reopened in 1983 by a Presidential attempt to establish a Department of Trade that would merge functions of UTSR into those of the Commerce Department. *See, e.g.,* 20 ITEX 12 (Oct. 4, 1983).

187. S. Rep. No. 249, *supra* note 6, at 36.

188. Proposed Revision of the Customs Regulations Relating to Antidumping Duties, 44 Fed. Reg. 59,742 (1979); Procedures for Conference on Proposed Amendment to Antidumping and Countervailing Duty Regulations, 44 Fed. Reg. 59,762 (1979).

189. 44 Fed. Reg. 59,762 (1979).

190. The Treasury Department published proposed regulations in late 1979. 44 Fed. Reg. 59,742 (1979); 44 Fed. Reg. 57,044 (1979). After the transfer of international trade functions, the Commerce Department published final regulations at 19 C.F.R ch. III, Parts 353, 355 (1982).

191. *See* Dep't of Commerce, International Trade Administration, 19 C.F.R. Part 355 (1982), Countervailing Duties, 45 Fed. Reg. 4,932 (1980); Dept. of Commerce, International Trade Administration 19 C.F.R. Part 353 (1982), Antidumping Duties, 45 Fed. Reg. 8,182 (1980).

192. Procedures for the Conduct of Investigations of Whether Injury to Domestic Industries Results from Imports Sold at Less Than Fair Value or from Subsidized Exports to the United States—Proposed Rules, 44 Fed. Reg. 59,392 (1979); Final Rules, 44 Fed. Reg. 76,458 (1979). More recent regulations can be found at 19 C.F.R. ch. II, Part 207 (1982).

193. *E.g.,* Trade Agreements Act of 1979, § 101, adding §§ 702–706 and § 751 19 U.S.C. §§ 1671, 1675 (Supp. III 1979).

194. *E.g.,* Trade Agreements Act of 1979, § 101, in § 777(a)(3) 19 U.S.C. § 1677f(a)(3) (Supp. III 1979), which requires ex parte meetings in connection with antidumping and countervailing duty investigations. "[T]his provision is intended to insure that all parties to the proceedings are more fully aware of the presentation of information to the administering authority or the ITC." S. Rep. No. 249, *supra* note 6, at 100. *See also* 19 C.F.R. § 207.5 (1982), 19 C.F.R. § 355.16 (1982); 19 C.F.R. § 353.26 (1982).

195. Trade Agreements Act of 1979, Title X, 19 U.S.C. § 1516A (Supp. III 1979).

196. Trade Expansion Act of 1962 § 252, Pub. L. No. 87-794, 76 Stat. 872 (1962).

197. Section 252 was used in the "chicken war." *See* Walker, *Dispute Settlement: The Chicken War,* 58 Am. J. Int'l L. 671 (1964); United States v. Star Indus. Inc., 462 F.2d 557 (C.C.P.A. 1972).

198. 19 U.S.C. § 2411 (1976); Procedures for Complaints Received Pursuant

to Section 301 of the Trade Act of 1974, As Amended, 15 C.F.R. Part 2006 (1982).

199. Trade Agreements Act of 1979, Title IX, 19 U.S.C. § 2411–2416 (Supp. III 1979); Procedures for Complaints Received Pursuant to Section 301 of the Trade Act of 1974, As Amended, 15 C.F.R. Part 2006 (1982).

200. *See* S. REP. NO. 249, *supra* note 6, at 232; H.R. REP. NO. 317, *supra* note 79, at 173–74.

201. Trade Agreements Act of 1979, § 901, amending § 302(b)(2) of the Trade Act of 1974, 19 U.S.C. § 2412(b)(2) (Supp. III 1979).

202. This figure is based on annual U.S. government costs of approximately $68 million for trade agencies such as USTR, ITA, and others, plus very rough estimates of private lawyers' fees and inhouse corporate costs for procedures occurring under U.S. law. A total of $101 million annual costs estimated in this way can be compared with the 1981 total value of imports into the U.S. of $264 billion, and the resulting fraction is .04 percent. Allowing leeway for various estimating errors, it would seem almost certain that this ratio is less than .1 percent.

203. *See* Jackson, *The Crumbling Institutions of the Liberal Trade System,* 12 J. World Trade L. 2 (1978); Jackson, *The Birth of the GATT-MTN System: A Constitutional Appraisal,* 12 L. & POLICY INT'L BUS. 21 (1980).

CHAPTER 5

National Constitutions and the International Economic System

John H. Jackson, Jean-Victor Louis, and Mitsuo Matsushita

In the preceding chapters, we have examined the relationship of three national constitutional systems to the processes of negotiating and implementing international agreements. We have focused on the Tokyo Round negotiations in the context of the GATT as a case study, so as to add precision to our inquiries. However, we had no intention of simply chronicling the history of the Tokyo Round. Instead, it has been our purpose to examine the constitutional systems of the three major trading partners in the world today, with a view to understanding the effect of national constitutions on potential future international negotiations. As we write, it is not clear what the next major international economic negotiation will be. Preparations have begun in the GATT, however, for some further multilateral activity that could possibly lead to negotiations on certain subjects, such as international trade in services, or on international rules relating to merchandise trade, such as safeguards.[1]

In three different chapters, we have each explored the constitutional and legal constraints on international economic negotiations in each of three systems. The reader will realize by now that there are some substantial and interesting differences between those systems. In addition, it may be clear by now that lurking in the disparities between those systems are some potential problems for any international economic negotiations. In this chapter, we propose to draw some comparisons and formulate some tentative hypotheses about the significance of the differences between the national constitutional systems. As we indicated at the outset of this book, we view our study as only part of the total story. Clearly, a similar examination of national constitutional structures of a number of other countries would be interesting and valuable for a better understanding of the potential for international economic negotiations. It is our hope that other scholars will now adopt some of the same techniques we have used and address some of the same questions that we have explored. We hope to see articles about other national constitutional systems and their relationship to international economic negotiations published in various scholarly legal journals.[2]

We have divided the remainder of this final chapter into five sections. In the section entitled The Three Constitutions Compared, we will draw some conclusions and make some general comparisons of the three systems. In the section entitled Implications for Future Negotiations, we will discuss some of the implications of our findings for future negotiations. In the section entitled The Structure of the International Economic System, we raise a question that seems to be more and more frequently on the minds of statesmen and politicians—namely, whether the international economic structure for trade and other economic affairs is workable and fair. In the section entitled A Proposal for the Future-Direct Citizen Access to the International System of Economic Obligations, we make a proposal that could add to the workability and significance of international economic systems, although we do not have any illusions that it is likely to be adopted in the near future. Finally, the section entitled Conclusions brings the book to a close.

The Three Constitutions Compared

The three constitutions we have discussed are very different, and these differences obviously affect international economic relations. Japan's constitutional system is one of a highly centralized governmental structure, with a parliamentary system. In some respects, the Japanese constitutional system is rather new (dating technically from the post–World War II period). The European system is even newer. Here we have treated the system of the European Economic Community as a sort of national system for the purposes of our analysis. The constitution of the EEC is in a process of rapid change. Starting with the Treaty of Rome of 1957, that constitution includes the longest written constitutional document of any of the three systems examined. A number of changes have occurred in that written document, particularly because of the addition of new members. In addition, a number of changes in the way the document gets applied have been and continue to be occurring. In all three systems, power struggles among the various branches of the system occur and have considerable influence.

The United States has the oldest continuous government of the three bodies treated here, based on a written constitution two hundred years old and a large supply of Supreme Court opinions interpreting it. However, the Supreme Court has spoken relatively infrequently about international economic relations under that constitution. Despite its long history, the United States Constitution still leaves a number of issues having to do with multinational relations open.

Some brief comparisons (others have been made in the preceding chapters) can be grouped under two headings: the distribution of power, and the legal process of implementing the Tokyo Round agreements.

The Distribution of Power

A prime attribute of any constitutional system is the way it distributes power. Power can be distributed among various branches of a national government, and it can also be distributed in a federal system between the central government and the subordinate units of government (such as the states).

Subordinate Units of Government

Questions of power distribution between the central government and the subordinate units of government are least significant in Japan and most significant in the EEC. The Japanese government is highly centralized, and we could not find that problems of power distributed to or held by local units have any significant implications for international economic negotiations.

In the United States, questions of distribution of powers between the states and the federal government still have some potency, although not nearly so much as they did a century ago. Today the federal government can generally negotiate and fulfill almost any international agreement that it feels it can obtain and that is approved through the constitutional processes of the federal government. However, there are some political implications for the processes of negotiating and approving international agreements that stem from the federal system. For example, it seems reasonably clear that if the nations that are parties to the Tokyo Round Government Procurement Code had provided in the code that it would apply also to governmental purchases by government subdivisions like states in the United States, the U.S. federal government would have had the power to require the states to follow the international agreement. However, there were at least some perceptions during the negotiations that some members of Congress might have opposed approval of an international government procurement code designed to apply to state government purchases. We do not know the degree or extent of that potential opposition, since the issue was never put to Congress. Indeed, the U.S. negotiators were at one point probably willing to try to have the international agreement embrace state government purchases, but negotiators from other nations did not desire that move.

The EEC has the most serious problems with distributing powers between central government institutions and member government states or subordinate government units. There continues to be a considerable power struggle between the central institutions of the EEC and the Member State governments (such as the United Kingdom or France). Extraconstitutional mechanisms like the European Council have been set up to enable national government officials to participate at the highest level, and this has tended to strengthen the retention of power by the Member States, as opposed to the EEC institutions.

Some of the Member States of the EEC also face important internal federalism questions. For example, in West Germany, the Länder retain certain significant rights and powers that have had and will continue to have some influence on international economic negotiations.

More specifically, within the EEC the degree of centralization varies with the subject being considered. The general subject of commercial policy, which is deemed to include tariffs and trade and most GATT matters, is delegated to the central institutions of the EEC in Article 113 of the Treaty of Rome. However, a number of other subjects are not—at least not explicitly—so delegated. For example, monetary policy tends to remain with the Member States. Some have argued that at least some provisions of the codes concerning government procurement or standards touch on matters that are within the power and jurisdiction of the Member States. This problem may have clouded certain phases of the Tokyo Round negotiations, but in the end the actions of the EEC and its Member State governments have tended to confirm the proposition that these activities as negotiated in the Tokyo Round are covered by the commercial policy delegation of authority to the EEC. In future international economic negotiations, however, it will be necessary to examine fairly closely whether a subject to be taken up is definitely within the jurisdiction of the EEC institutions. For example, it has often been stated that the next phase of GATT multilateral discussions and potential negotiations will embrace trade in services (insurance, shipping, tourism, and so on). It has been argued that power to regulate and enter into international negotiations concerning trade in certain types of services remains with the Members States, or at least is not under the authority of Article 113. If true, this could suggest the need for different negotiating procedures.

Central Government Institutions

Power is also distributed among institutions at the central or federal government level. Problems caused by such arrangements are most significant in the United States. The relationship of the executive branch (the President) and the Congress is the single most important factor in U.S. participation in international economic negotiations.

This relationship has a number of difficulties. Although it is usually argued that the President has authority to negotiate on anything in an international context, it is clear under the Constitution that the President does not have sole authority to approve or finally commit the United States to an international agreement on many subjects. In commercial matters, Congress feels that it has the preeminent reserved power, and that the President has only those powers that have been delegated to him by the Congress. This imposes effective restraints on the President's ability to negotiate in the international context, since negotiators from other countries are not likely to be willing to negotiate with him on matters for which they feel he cannot obtain approval. Thus executive branch officials tend to be more willing to enter into international negotiations on subjects they feel are within the powers already delegated to the President. Otherwise, it would be necessary for the President to obtain additional statutory delegations from the Congress before the negotiations or to take results of a negotiation back to the Congress for approval under one procedure or another. In connection with a major international economic negotiation, a great deal of time, effort, and thought will go into managing these relationships between the executive branch and the Congress.

In the EEC, the power distribution among the various central institutions is also highly significant. To a certain extent, the power relationships mirror the problems encountered in the relationships between the EEC institutions and the Member States. The EEC has a Commission on the one hand, and a Council on the other. The Council is composed of representatives of the Member States. This institution is reluctant to yield power to the Commission which is considered to reflect a more general EEC perspective. There is also a European Parliament, now selected by popular suffrage, but its powers are extremely limited, at least at this juncture. The other very important central institution is the Court of Justice (sitting at Luxembourg). This court has the final say about legal matters interpreting the Treaty of Rome, and therefore is the arbiter of disputes about power distribution within the EEC—both those involving the central institutions and those involving the relationship of those institutions to the Member States.

In the Japanese government, the problem of distribution of power among the national institutions is not so great. In a parliamentary system, the executive branch is headed by a cabinet that is largely drawn from the parliament itself, so at least in theory there is no significant tension between the parliament and the executive. In Japan, the power distribution questions at the central level are rather different in nature from those in the United States or the EEC. This makes comparison somewhat difficult. Many of the problems of power distribution in the Japanese government have to do with rivalry between ministries such as the Ministry of Foreign Affairs (MFA) and the Ministry of International Trade and Industry (MITI). More specifically, the relationships between powerful ministries and between ministries and the Liberal Democratic Party (LDP), and the pressures exerted by some powerful interest groups (for example, agricultural groups) may affect future negotiations. When looking at the different constitutional systems of the three trading partners, to make effective comparisons and analyze the power distribution questions one has to look at different information in Japan. The information is often not easily available, because it is rarely embodied in such things as Supreme Court cases or statutes and explicit regulations that are available to the public. Nevertheless, there are some significant power distribution questions in Japan that could affect future negotiations, and have affected past negotiations.

Finally, in this comparison of power distribution, one must look at the role of the courts. In the United States, the Supreme Court has an extraordinarily powerful role in arbitrating the allocation of power among units of government. It also has an important role in enforcing statutes and regulations and the Constitution itself. Consequently, many issues in the United States tend to become judicial issues, and this gives the court system a more significant role in the total process of international economic negotiations than the judiciary would probably have in the other two constitutional systems explored here. In the EEC, the Court of Justice also proves to be very prominent. Indeed, the analogies between the Court of Justice and the U.S. Supreme Court are strong, and many people have commented upon them. Even though the governments of many EEC Member States have not traditionally had a constitutional system that placed considerable power in a judicial body, the EEC does have such a system, which could evolve in the direction of the U.S. Court.

In Japan, courts, including the Supreme Court, have the power of judicial review, and at least in theory could play a role as arbiters of the allocation of actions enforced by the ministries under the Constitution or laws. However, in reality the Japanese courts have rarely exercised this power in foreign trade matters. This is probably due to the paucity of court actions raised by government agencies and private individuals, which in turn reflects the nonlitigiousness of the national character.

Implementation of the Tokyo Round Agreements in National Legal Systems

There is virtually no uniformity in the way the results of the Tokyo Round were implemented under the three constitutional systems examined here. In the United States, as we have seen, the Congress generally reserved the power to approve most of the final Tokyo Round agreements before the United States became committed to them. The statute adopted by Congress to grant this approval, and to implement the agreements, clearly provides that the agreements themselves will not be self-executing in U.S. law. This means that the agreements do not become part of the domestic law of the United States. Therefore, a citizen must look to the implementing statute adopted by Congress for the source of his rights and for judicial and administrative application of the agreements in the United States. On the other hand, the statute adopted is quite long and quite detailed. It takes much of the language of the international agreements and applies it verbatim as part of U.S. law. In addition, administrative agencies charged with implementing various parts of that statute have issued regulations that are even more detailed. Thus, there is a vast, elaborate, explicit body of written rules that is part of U.S. jurisprudence and designed to implement the Tokyo Round agreements. Individual citizens have the right to invoke those rules, and to use the court system to assist them in doing so.

In the EEC, the situation is considerably more confused. It is not entirely clear whether the international agreements negotiated in the Tokyo Round will be considered to have direct effect as part of the jurisprudence of national government institutions, including the courts, in the EEC, although a very recent Court of Justice decision seems not to exclude that some provisions of the MTN agreements could have direct effect. In some cases, the EEC has issued a regulation on the subject concerned; such a regulation becomes part of domestic jurisprudence in the Member States of the EEC. In other cases, the EEC has issued a directive that directs Member States to take implementing action. The directive would not normally lend itself to being treated as part of domestic jurisprudence, but a private person can rely on the provisions of a directive that has not been implemented, or has been implemented incorrectly, by a Member State. He can invoke the directive against this state. Finally, in some situations, implementation of the Tokyo Round agreements has simply been left to the Member States. Entry into the agreement by the EEC institutions imposes a legal requirement on the Member States to follow and implement the international agreement.

In Japan, as long as the international agreements negotiated in the Tokyo Round have been approved by the National Diet, they are regarded as treaties in the sense of the constitutional provision, and as such are given not only the power of law but also overriding effect upon domestic law that conflicts with them. As touched upon earlier, such approval has been given to most of the agreements negotiated in the Tokyo Round. Whenever there are differences between the approved international agreements and domestic laws, it has been the practice of the Japanese government that the Cabinet proposes legislative bills and the National Diet enacts them into laws in order to make the language of domestic laws conform to the language of the agreements. This has been done for some of the international agreements negotiated in the Tokyo Round. With certain limitations, individuals have the right to invoke the rules contained in the agreements and to seek cancellation of administrative actions, regulations, or laws that are contrary to these rules, and also to seek recovery for damage sustained due to actions or inactions of the government officials contrary to the rules enunciated in the agreements. Here again, however, the likelihood that such suits will be brought is rather slim, because the Japanese people are reluctant to resort to court actions.

One of the striking things that emerges from a study of this type, therefore, is that the processes and degree of implementation of the international agreements in the three different constitutional systems differs greatly. This could conceivably lead to some significant disparities in effective implementation of the international obligations. In a society where citizens have direct access to judicial institutions to enforce their rights, and have the right to rely directly on the international agreements or on statutory implementation that embraces the language of the agreements, it would seem plausible that the international agreements would be treated seriously. On the other hand, where such institutional mechanisms are not available to the ordinary citizen, or where whatever does exist contains considerable leeway for the play of governmental discretion, it is possible that at some point government officials involved will find themselves tempted to apply the international obligations less rigorously.

Implications for Future Negotiations

At least two important categories of implications for future negotiations on international economic matters stem from the analysis in this book. First: In which of the types of subject matter that are likely to be subjects of potential negotiations are constraints resulting from the three constitutional systems most serious? Second: How should negotiators be affected by the fact that the process of implementation in the three different constitutional systems vary so greatly?

In considering the first question, one can examine the potential constraints the national legal constitutional systems will impose on negotiations concerning a number of subjects, including trade in services, investment and capital flows, and subjects that have or have not been previously negotiated and relate to more traditional merchandise trade matters. For example, there is likely to be a major jurisdictional question within the EEC on the methodology of approving, and implementing international agreements on the subject of international trade in services. The same is likely to be the case for investment and capital flows. On the other hand, for negotiations that might continue on some of the matters left over from the Tokyo Round negotiations, it is more likely that the jurisdictional question will be considered clear, and that the central EEC institutions will be deemed to have greater control.

In the United States, it is likely that the Congress will either give the executive branch advance authority to enter into international negotiations and agreements on subjects such as services, or retain for itself the ultimate right to approve whatever emerges from the negotiations. This will have a profound effect on the structure and procedures of the negotiations.

In Japan, there will be little jurisdictional problem in negotiating and entering into international agreements on services and investment, since most of the powers in these areas are vested in some ministries whose ministers are members of the Cabinet. Problems may lie in the reluctance of ministries in charge of promoting and controlling these matters to adopt international agreements that may adversely affect the interests of industries under their jurisidiction.

The Structure of the International Economic System

The basic thesis of this book is that the international economic system is a complex structure that involves the intertwining of national constitutional systems and the international constitutional system. The international constitutional system is primarily that of the GATT and the other international economic organizations such as the Organization for Economic Organization and Development (OECD), the International Monetary Fund (IMF), and so on. Here we have focused on the GATT. Thus, we see the GATT (which has, as indicated in chapter 1, a very frail constitution, not designed for the role it has been forced to fill), as an international institution that strongly depends on certain national governmental structures. On the other hand, some of the national governmental structures concerned (particularly the United States) depend heavily on the existence of the GATT and its system in a number of ways. The Trade Act of 1974 and the Trade Agreements Act of 1979 would make little sense without it. Conversely, at the time the GATT was originally formulated, and at the time the Tokyo Round agreements were being negotiated, U.S. constitutional and other law relating to international trade had considerable influence on the shape of the GATT and on the various supplementary codes negotiated in its context.

This book has not been an examination of the GATT itself; that task has been taken up elsewhere.[3] It is not our purpose here, therefore, to review some of the statements of concern about whether the GATT can cope with contemporary international economic problems and trends, and whether the GATT needs some substantial revision for that purpose. Our purpose is to comment on the total GATT system in the context of its relationship to the national constitutional systems of GATT members, and in this context one can see strengths and weaknesses. The GATT has managed to survive despite the disparity of its members' constitutional systems, and indeed, despite the disparity of their economic systems. But it is also clear that the GATT applies in a way that is uneven as between economic systems, and may also be uneven as between constitutional systems. For example, direct citizen access—or the lack of it—to national judicial or administrative procedures designed to enforce international economic obligations has practical effects. Is an international agreement really fair, when it is in fact implemented in such different ways in different countries?

In addition, national constitutional structures may influence the ability of national representatives to negotiate effectively on behalf of their national interests. The United States, for example, with its constant power struggle between the executive branch and the Congress, may in some circumstances find its ability to conduct international negotiations constrained, either because Congress has not adequately delegated power to the executive branch, which conducts the negotiations, or because in delegating the Congress laid out the negotiators' scope or range of maneuver in too explicit detail thereby giving opposing negotiators some important intelligence about those positions.

A Proposal for the Future: Direct Citizen Access to the International System of Economic Obligations

Much has been written in recent decades about the tendency of international law to accept individuals as well as national states as its proper subjects. Without trying to get into the somewhat theoretical questions involved in those writings, we would like simply to point out that it has now become established that it is possible to design procedures under which private citizens or firms have some sort of direct access (usually limited) to international bodies for the purpose of asserting their rights.[4] The two prime examples that come to mind are the European Convention on Human Rights[5] and the International Convention for the Settlement of Investment Disputes (ICSID).[6] Under the former, an individual citizen can go to an international body with a complaint against his own government, on the grounds that it has violated its obligations under the international convention in a way that has directly affected him. The international procedures then call for a commission to look into the complaint and possibly to help mediate a solution between the citizen and his government. Where the commission feels it is justified, it may bring the complaint to a court—the European Court on Human Rights. That court then has the authority to rule on whether the state concerned has violated its obligations under the European Convention. Only states that have explicitly accepted this fairly far-reaching procedure under the appropriate convention can be brought into these procedures by their own citizens.

Likewise, the ICSID, set up under the auspices of the World Bank, provides a mechanism by which governments who have accepted the ICSID in advance can subsequently provide in any contract with a foreign private firm or citizen that disputes about the contract will be referred to an arbitration process set up by ICSID.

There are some interesting potentials in these precedents for the GATT and the international economic system, although they will probably not be readily accepted by the governments that participate in the GATT. But governments and business firms do desire greater predictability of national government economic actions in an increasingly interdependent world, and do desire greater balance and equality in actual implementation of negotiated international rules on economic matters. Those factors could lead governments to be willing to accept some sort of a mechanism by which individual citizens or firms could appeal directly to an international body like the GATT to determine whether a government obligated under the GATT or one of its codes has taken an action that is inconsistent with its international obligations.

Several particulars are likely to be necessary in any such procedure. First, a requirement that national internal administration and judicial remedies be exhausted before an international body is consulted seems appropriate. Second, some sort of a filter would probably be needed, much as is the case currently with the European procedure for human rights. Thus, some international body, such as a GATT unit, could be charged with initially receiving complaints from private citizens or firms and making a preliminary investigation to see whether they have any merit. This would prevent spurious complaints from getting very far. Third, it is likely that at the outset, any procedure of this type would have to accommodate itself to the lack of effective sanctions. It is doubtful that states would soon be willing to accept such a procedure if truly effective sanctions could be applied. However, that does not make such a procedure useless. The fact that there could be a reliable third-party determination on the facts and the application of the law (the international obligation) would itself be salutary.

To a certain extent, the mere fact of findings by an international pancl, when such findings are made public, is a sort of sanction that many governments try to avoid.

Clearly, the typical governmental reluctance to relinquish any power or to constrain its field of discretion would discourage a move in the direction of the procedures described. On the other hand, it should be recognized that there are some advantages for governments in such a procedure. For one thing, if it were carefully designed and became reliable, governments might well find that the procedure would tend to deemphasize and depoliticize many relatively minor trade or economic complaints that now exist between nations. For example, let us assume that Mr. A, a citizen in country A finds that his exports to country B are being restrained improperly by country B, inconsistent with country B's international obligations. Under the current procedure, Mr. A must go to his own national government and get it to take up his matter with the foreign government. Thus, his case has immediately been raised to a diplomatic level. That quite often means, by the nature of things, that it has been raised to a fairly high level of official attention and consequently of public perception. On the other hand, if an appropriate international procedure existed, when Mr. A came to his government to complain about country B, country A officials could refer Mr. A to that procedure and encourage him to use it, without taking any stand on the matter. It is quite possible that the issue could then be handled more expeditiously and routinely. The case would continue to be Mr. A's case, and not become country A's case. The issue would be Mr. A versus country B, instead of Mr. A and country A versus country B.

It is the view of at least one of the authors of this book that in all probability, early versions of such a procedure would have to allow the individual governments to exercise some kind of right of veto over their own citizens' attempts to invoke the process. However, this right could be accorded to national governments as a way to make them more comfortable with experimenting with the procedure, and could be designed to gradually die out (at least for all but the most exceptional cases).

Interdependence and Legal Systems: Some Concluding Remarks

The stresses currently imposed on the international economic system are formidable indeed. Phrases such as the "demise of GATT," or the "failure of the exchange rate mechanism" are being heard, as political leaders scramble for ideas and policies with which to alleviate the economic pain of their constituents. Many of the traditional assumptions of the Bretton Woods system are being questioned. People are asking if comparative advantage has the same meaning today as in previous years, and whether "industrial policy" as executed by some nations is a fair way to "play" in today's world. Political forces for protectionism loom large, and the traditional rules often seem to be bent more than they are applied. Arthur Dunkle, the current Director-General of GATT, has said:

> [I]nternational economic policy commitments, in the form of agreed rules, have far-reaching domestic effects,. . . . They are the element which secures the ultimate co-ordination and mutual compatibility of the purely domestic economic policies. They form the basis from which the government can arbitrate and secure an equitable and efficient balance between the diverse domestic interests: producers vs. consumers, export industries vs. import-competing industries. . . . [O]nly a firm commitment to international rules makes possible the all-important reconciliation, which I have already alluded to, of the necessary balance on the production side and on the financial side of the national economy . . . .
>
> In all these ways the commitment to international rules defines and fixes the permanent national interest in economic matters—which, I repeat, is an indispensable function in a democratic system providing for an orderly change of political governments at relatively frequent intervals.
>
> It is thus nothing but intellectual laziness to consider these international disciplines to be an undue constraint on governments, something of a concession from national interest to international comity. This amounts to saying that a government free from external constraints would be better or more completely able to secure all the interests of its nation. But this is about as deep and useful an insight as saying that in a world in which there was no scarcity of goods we would all be better off. Another way of explaining the current political and economic malaise is to say that it stems from an unwillingness to think carefully about the difficult but important concept of national interest.[7]

But if the rules are so important, they must be kept abreast of the fast changing conditions of the world. This implies an orderly and intelligent system by which the rules themselves can be changed. The complex mix of national legal institutions and constitutions, and the various international institutions are not now structured in a way that gives one confidence that the international economic system can evolve in an orderly fashion. What we have tried to do in this book is to shed some light on the legal aspects of this international economic system, and particularly on the little-studied interrelationship of the national legal systems to this international system. In doing so we hope we have contributed both to a modestly better understanding of that system and its strengths and weaknesses, and to stimulating further study of this perplexing subject.

NOTES

1. *See, e.g.,* GATT Press Release No. 1310 (1982); GATT Newsletter No. 14 (June 1982). A GATT ministerial meeting was held in Geneva in November 1982.
2. See chapter 1. We hope that other scholars will write about countries we have been unable to study, and will correspond with us about their work on this subject.
3. *See, e.g.,* J. JACKSON, WORLD TRADE AND THE LAW OF GATT (1969); K. DAM, THE GATT: LAW AND INTERNATIONAL ORGANIZATION (1970); R. HUDEC, THE GATT LEGAL SYSTEM AND WORLD TRADE DIPLOMACY (1975); E. MCGOVERN, INTERNATIONAL TRADE REGULATION: GATT, THE UNITED STATES AND THE EUROPEAN COMMUNITY (1982); items cited in notes to chapter 1.
4. W. FRIEDMAN, THE CHANGING STRUCTURE OF INTERNATIONAL LAW 225–49 (1964). See also an interesting short article, Sohn, *Proposals for the Establishment of a System of International Tribunals,* in INTERNATIONAL TRADE ARBITRATION—A ROAD TO WORLD-WIDE COOPERATION (M. Domke, ed. 1958).
5. European Convention for the Protection of Human Rights and Fundamental Freedoms, Nov. 4, 1950, 213 U.N.T.S. 222 (entered into force Sept. 3, 1953). *See generally* R. LILLICH & F. NEWMAN, INTERNATIONAL HUMAN RIGHTS: PROBLEMS OF LAW AND POLICY 560 (1979).
6. Convention for the Settlement of Investment Disputes Between States and Nationals of Other States, *opened for signature* March 18, 1965, 17 U.S.T. 1270, T.I.A.S. No. 6090, 575 U.N.T.S. 159. *See generally* Broches, *The Convention on the Settlement of Investment Disputes Between States,* 136 RECEUIL DES COURS 331 (1972).
7. GATT Press Release No. 1312 (1982).

APPENDIX

List and References for the Tokyo Round Agreements

[BISD is the acronym for GENERAL AGREEMENT ON TARIFFS AND TRADE: BASIC INSTRUMENTS AND SELECTED DOCUMENTS.]

1. Geneva (1979) Protocol to the General Agreement on Tariffs and Trade, GATT Doc. L./4875, BISD 3 (26th Supp. 1980), T.I.A.S. 9629, 23 O.J. EUR. COMM. (No. L 71) 3 (1980).
2. Agreement on Interpretation and Application of Articles VI, XVI, and XXIII of the General Agreement on Tariffs and Trade, BISD 56 (26th Supp. 1980), T.I.A.S. 9619, 31 U.S.T. 513, 23 O.J. EUR. COMM. (No. L 71) 72 (1980).
3. Agreement on Implementation of Article VI of the General Agreement on Tariffs and Trade, BISD 171 (26th Supp. 1980), 23 O.J. EUR. COMM. (No. L 71) 90 (1980).
4. Agreement on Government Procurement, BISD 33 (26th Supp. 1980), 23 O.J. EUR. COMM. (No. L 71) 44 (1980).
5. Agreement on Technical Barriers to Trade, BISD 8 (26th Supp. 1980), T.I.A.S. 9616, 31 U.S.T. 405, 23 O.J. EUR. COMM. (No. L 71) 29 (1980).
6. Agreement on Implementation of Article VII of the General Agreement on Tariffs and Trade, BISD 116 (26th Supp. 1980), 23 O.J. EUR. COMM. (No. L 71) 107 (1980).
7. Agreement on Import Licensing Procedures, BISD 154 (26th Supp. 1980), T.I.A.S. 9788, 23 O.J. EUR. COMM. (No. L 71) 102 (1980).
8. Agreement on Trade in Civil Aircraft, BISD 162 (26th Supp. 1980), T.I.A.S. 9620, 31 U.S.T. 619, 23 O.J. EUR. COMM. (No. L 71) 58 (1980).
9. International Dairy Arrangement, BISD 91 (26th Supp. 1980), T.I.A.S. 9623, 31 U.S.T. 679, 23 O.J. EUR. COMM. (No. L 71) 11 (1980).
10. Arrangement Regarding Bovine Meat, BISD 84 (26th Supp. 1980), T.I.A.S. 9701, 23 O.J. EUR. COMM. (No. L 71) 7 (1980).
11. Action by the Contracting Parties on the Multilateral Trade Negotiations, GATT Doc. L/4950, BISD 201 (26th Supp. 1980).

Index